S0-AIU-962

Bloom's Modern Critical Interpretations

The Adventures of Huckleberry Finn
All Quiet on the Western Front
Animal Farm
As You Like It
Beloved
Beowulf
Billy Budd, Benito Cereno, Bartleby the Scrivener, and Other Tales
The Bluest Eye
Brave New World
Cat on a Hot Tin Roof
The Catcher in the Rye
Catch-22
Cat's Cradle
The Color Purple
Crime and Punishment
The Crucible
Daisy Miller, The Turn of the Screw, and Other Tales
Darkness at Noon
David Copperfield
Death of a Salesman
The Divine Comedy
Don Quixote
Dracula
Dubliners
Emma
Fahrenheit 451
A Farewell to Arms
Frankenstein
The General Prologue to the Canterbury Tales
The Glass Menagerie
The Grapes of Wrath
Great Expectations
The Great Gatsby
Gulliver's Travels
Hamlet
The Handmaid's Tale
Heart of Darkness
I Know Why the Caged Bird Sings
The Iliad
The Interpretation of Dreams
Invisible Man
Jane Eyre
The Joy Luck Club
Julius Caesar
The Jungle
King Lear
Long Day's Journey Into Night
Lord of the Flies
The Lord of the Rings
Macbeth
The Merchant of Venice
The Metamorphosis
A Midsummer Night's Dream
Moby-Dick
My Ántonia
Native Son
Night
1984
The Odyssey
Oedipus Rex
The Old Man and the Sea
On the Road
One Flew Over the Cuckoo's Nest
One Hundred Years of Solitude
Othello
Paradise Lost
The Pardoner's Tale
A Passage to India
Persuasion
Portnoy's Complaint
A Portrait of the Artist as a Young Man
Pride and Prejudice
Ragtime
The Red Badge of Courage
The Rime of the Ancient Mariner
Romeo & Juliet
The Rubáiyát of Omar Khayyám
The Scarlet Letter
A Scholarly Look at The Diary of Anne Frank
A Separate Peace
Silas Marner
Slaughterhouse-Five
Song of Myself
Song of Solomon
The Sonnets of William Shakespeare
Sophie's Choice
The Sound and the Fury
The Stranger
A Streetcar Named Desire
Sula
The Sun Also Rises
A Tale of Two Cities
The Tale of Genji
The Tales of Poe
The Tempest
Tess of the D'Urbervilles
Their Eyes Were Watching God
Things Fall Apart
To Kill a Mockingbird
Ulysses
Waiting for Godot
Walden
The Waste Land
White Noise
Wuthering Heights

Bloom's Modern Critical Interpretations

Philip Roth's

PORTNOY'S COMPLAINT

Edited and with an introduction by
Harold Bloom
Sterling Professor of the Humanities
Yale University

Philadelphia

A Haights Cross Communications Company

Printed and bound in Malaysia.

10 9 8 7 6 5 4 3 2 1

Library of Congress Cataloging-in-Publication Data

Portnoy's Complaint / edited and with an introduction by Harold Bloom.
p. cm. — (Bloom's modern critical interpretations) Includes bibliographical references and index.
ISBN 0-7910-7582-6
1. Roth, Philip. Portnoy's Complaint. I. Bloom, Harold. II. Series.
PS3568.0855P67 2003
813'54—dc21

2003006757

Contributing editor: Gabriel Welsch

Cover design by Terry Mallon

Layout by EJB Publishing Services

Chelsea House Publishers
1974 Sproul Road, Suite 400
Broomall, PA 19008-0914

www.chelseahouse.com

Contents

Editor's Note

My Introduction celebrates the moral hilarity of *Portnoy's Complaint* (1969) as the ancestor of Philip Roth's Shakespearean masterwork, *Sabbath's Theater* (1995).

The genial George Plimpton interviews Roth on *Portnoy's Complaint* and elicits the superbly useful Rothian observation that Portnoy "is a man speaking out of an overwhelming obsession: he is obscene because he wants to be saved."

Jeffrey Berman admires Roth's fictive psychoanalysts, including Dr. Spielvogel of *Portnoy's Complaint*, after which Bernard F. Rodgers, Jr. accurately emphasizes the "profoundly American" nature of this novel.

To Sam B. Girgus, the achievement of Roth is the attempt "to make life more loving," while Helge Normann Nilsen rather severely stresses Alex Portnoy's "assimilationist stand." Judith Paterson Jones and Guinevera A. Nance see the *Complaint* as Roth's final playing out of what Freud had called "Family Romances," after which Steven Milowitz finds Portnoy's dilemma ultimately to be the Cartesian dualism of the ghostly soul trapped in the machine-like body.

Alan Warren Friedman reads the *Complaint* as an affirmation of Jewish exile, while Robert Forrey reduces Portnoy's lament to the Oedipal Complex.

Alan Cooper gives us instead the Alex Complex, which turns out to be Roth's reception of the negative reaction to him by the American Jewish establishment, after which Martha A. Ravits considers one of the most formidable of Jewish mothers, Sophie Portnoy.

In this volume's final essay, Joe Moran singles out Roth as the contemporary author who most searchingly explores the ironies of literary celebrity and its discontents.

HAROLD BLOOM

Introduction

After a full generation since it first appeared, *Portnoy's Complaint* superbly sustains rereading. Nothing of Roth's has dwindled to a Period Piece, even if *Letting Go* and *When She Was Good* now seem uncharacteristic for the author of *Sabbath's Theater*, *American Pastoral*, and *The Human Stain*. There are fictions by Roth that never found me: *Our Gang*, *The Breast*, *The Great American Novel*. From *My Life as a Man* (1974) to the present, Roth has been an Old Master, but *Portnoy's Complaint* remains the most vital of his earlier works.

Vitality, in the Shakespearean or Falstaffian sense, and its representation in personality and character, is Roth's greatest gift, which is why I would nominate *Sabbath's Theater* as his sublime achievement. It matters that we see how astonishing a creation *Sabbath's Theater* is. What are the authentic eminences of American fiction in the second half of the twentieth century? My experience as an obsessive reader would center first upon Thomas Pynchon's *The Crying of Lot 49*, *Gravity's Rainbow*, and *Mason & Dixon*, to which one adds Cormac McCarthy's *Blood Meridian* and Don DeLillo's *Underworld*. When I turn to Roth, I happily am deluged: the tetralogy *Zuckerman Bound*, *The Counterlife*, *Operation Shylock*, and then the American historical sequence that includes *Sabbath's Theater*, *American Pastoral*, *I Married a Communist*, and *The Human Stain*. The sheer drive and fecundity of this later Roth makes me think of Faulkner at his earlier splendor: *As I Lay Dying*, *The Sound and the Fury*, *Light in August*, *Absalom, Absalom!* Faulkner upon his heights is a frightening comparison to venture, but *Sabbath's Theater* and *American Pastoral* will sustain the contrast. Nothing even by Roth has the uncanny originality of *As I Lay Dying*, yet *Sabbath's Theater* and the terrible pathos of *American Pastoral* have their own uncanniness. The wildness and freedom of *Portnoy's Complaint* now seem very different when taken as a prelude to the advent of *Sabbath's Theater*, just over a quarter-century later.

Though the confrontation between the late Irving Howe and Roth over Roth's supposed self-hatred is pragmatically prehistoric (in 2003), it has left some scars upon what ought to be called the novelist's aesthetic consciousness. In Shakespearean terms, Roth writes comedy or tragi-comedy in the mode of the Problem Plays: *Troilus and Cressida*, *All's Well That Ends Well*, *Measure for Measure*. The exquisite rancidities of this Shakespearean mode do not appear to be Roth's object. He seems to prefer Falstaff and Lear among Shakespeare's characters, and both of them get into Mickey Sabbath, who necessarily lacks the Falstaffian wit and Learian grandeur. Sabbath is an heroic vitalist, but in retrospect what else is Alex Portnoy? The comedy, painful to start with, hurts unbearably when you reread *Sabbath's Theater*. How hurtful is the hilarity of *Portnoy's Complaint*?

My favorite Yiddish apothegm, since my childhood, I translate as: "Sleep faster, we need the pillows." Roth's inescapability is that he has usurped this mode, perhaps not forever, but certainly for the early twenty-first century. Sleeping faster is a cure for the anguish of contamination: by Jewish history; by Kafka; by one's audience after achieving celebrity with *Portnoy's Complaint*.

Alex Portnoy is not going to age into Mickey Sabbath: Roth's protagonists are neither Roth nor one another. But viewing Portnoy retrospectively, through Sabbath's outrageousness, allows readers to see what otherwise we may be too dazzled or too overcome by laughter to realize. Alex Portnoy, however mother-ridden, has an extraordinary potential for more life that he is unlikely to fulfill. Not that fulfillment would be glorious or redemptive; Sabbath's grinding vitalism carries him past the edge of madness. Portnoy, liberal and humane (except, of course, in regard to women he desires), calls himself "rich with rage," but his fiercest anger is light years away from Sabbath's erotic fury.

Aside from Roth's complex aesthetic maturation, the differences between Portnoy and Sabbath is the shadow of Shakespeare, of King Lear's madness and Falstaff's refusal of embitterment and estrangement. Sabbath is fighting for his life, within the limits of what he understands life to be: the erotic, in all its ramifications. So intense is Sabbath that the denunciations directed at him are at once accurate and totally irrelevant, as here from his friend, Norman:

> "The walking panegyric for obscenity," Norman said. "The inverted saint whose message is desecration. Isn't it tiresome in 1994, this role of rebel-hero? What an odd time to be thinking of sex as rebellion. Are we back to Lawrence's gamekeeper? At this late hour? To be out with that beard of yours, upholding the virtues of fetishism and voyeurism. To be out with that belly of yours, championing pornography and flying the flag of your prick. What a pathetic, out-moded old crank you are, Mickey Sabbbath. The discredited male polemic's last gasp. Even as the bloodiest of all centuries comes to an end, you're out working day and night to create an erotic scandal. You fucking relic, Mickey! You fifties antique! Linda Lovelace is already light-years behind us, but you persist in quarreling with society as though Eisenhower is president!" But then, almost apologetically, he added, "The immensity of your isolation is horrifying. That's all I really mean to say."
>
> "And there you'd be surprised," Sabbath replied. "I don't think you ever gave isolation a real shot. It's the best preparation I know of for death."

Roth has placed Sabbath near the outer limit of organized society: a beggar, vagrant, and courter of death. It does not matter: Sabbath is redeemed through sheer vitalism. Alex Portnoy now seems more a parody of that frenetic drive. *Portnoy's Complaint* is a marvelous comedy; *Sabbath's Theater* is a tragi-comedy, and its Shakespearean reverberations are legitimate and persuasive.

GEORGE PLIMPTON AND PHILIP ROTH

On Portnoy's Complaint

Would you say something about the genesis of Portnoy's Complaint? *How long has the idea of the book been in mind?*

Some of the ideas that went into the book have been in my mind ever since I began writing. I mean particularly ideas about style and narration. For instance, the book proceeds by means of what I began to think of while writing as "blocks of consciousness," chunks of material of varying shapes and sizes piled atop one another and held together by association rather than chronology. I tried something vaguely like this in *Letting Go*, and have wanted to come at a narrative in this way again—or break down a narrative this way—ever since.

Then there's the matter of language and tone. Beginning with *Goodbye, Columbus*, I've been attracted to prose that has the turns, vibrations, intonations, and cadences, the spontaneity and ease, of spoken language, at the same time that it is solidly grounded on the page, weighted with the irony, precision, and ambiguity associated with a more traditional literary rhetoric. I'm not the only one who wants to write like this, obviously, nor is it a particularly new aspiration on the planet; but that's the kind of literary idea, or ideal, I was pursuing in this book.

I was thinking more in terms of the character and his predicament when I asked how long you had in mind the "idea of the book."

I know you were. That's partly why I answered as I did.

But surely you don't intend us to believe that this volatile novel of sexual confession, among other things, had its conception in purely literary motives?

No, I don't. But the conception is really nothing, you know, beside the delivery. My point is that until my "ideas"—about sex, guilt, childhood, about Jewish men and their Gentile women—were absorbed by an overall fictional strategy and goal, they were ideas not unlike anybody else's. Everybody has "ideas" for novels; the subway is jammed with people hanging from the straps, their heads full of ideas for novels they cannot begin *to write*. I am often one of them.

Given the book's openness, however, about intimate sexual matters, as well as its frank use of obscenity, do you think you would have embarked upon such a book in a climate unlike today's? Or is the book appropriate to these times?

As long ago as 1958, in *The Paris Review*, I published a story called "Epstein" that some people found very disgusting in its intimate sexual revelations; and my conversation, I have been told, has never been as refined as it should be. I think that many people in the arts have been living in a "climate like today's" for some time now; the mass media have just caught up, that's all, and with them, the general public. Obscenity as a usable and valuable vocabulary, and sexuality as a subject, have been available to us since Joyce, Henry Miller, and Lawrence, and I don't think there's a serious American writer in his thirties who has felt restricted by the times particularly, or suddenly feels liberated because these have been advertised as the "swinging sixties." In my writing lifetime the use of obscenity has, by and large, been governed by literary taste and tact and not by the mores of the audience.

What about the audience? Don't you write for an audience? Don't you write to be read?

To write to be read and to write for an "audience" are two different matters. If you mean by an audience a particular readership which can be described in terms of its education, politics, religion, or even by its literary tone, the answer is no. When I'm at work I don't really have any group of people in mind whom I want to communicate with; what I want is for the work to communicate itself as fully as it can, in accordance with its own intentions. Precisely so that it *can* be read, *but on its own terms*. If one can be said to have an audience in mind, it is not any special-interest group whose beliefs and demands one either accedes to or challenges, but those ideal readers whose *sensibilities* have been totally given over to the writer, in exchange for his seriousness.

An example which will also get us back to the issue of obscenity. My new book, *Portnoy's Complaint*, is full of dirty words and dirty scenes; my last novel, *When She Was Good*, had none. Why is that? Because I've suddenly become a "swinger"? But then apparently I was "swinging" all the way back in the fifties, with "Epstein." And what about the dirty words in *Letting Go*? No, the reason there is no obscenity, or blatant sexuality either, in *When She Was Good* is that it would have been disastrously beside the point.

When She Was Good is, above all, a story about small-town Middle Westerners who more than willingly experience themselves as conventional and upright people; and it is their own conventional and upright style of speech that I chose as my means of narration—or, rather, a slightly heightened, somewhat more flexible version of their language, but one that drew freely upon their habitual clichés, locutions, and banalities. It was not, however, to satirize them, in the manner, say, of Ring Lardner's "Haircut," that I settled eventually on this modest style, but rather to communicate, by their way of saying things, their way of seeing things and judging them. As for obscenity, I was careful, even when I had Roy Bassart, the young ex-G.I. in the novel, *reflecting*—had him safely walled-up in his own head—to show that the furthest he could go in violating a taboo was to think "f. this and f. that." Roy's inability to utter more than the initial of that famous four-letter word, even to himself, was the point I was making.

Discussing the purposes of his art, Chekhov makes a distinction between "the solution of the problem and a correct presentation of the problem"—and adds, "only the latter is obligatory for the artist." Using "f. this and f. that," instead of The Word Itself, was part of the attempt to make a correct presentation of the problem.

> *Are you suggesting, then, that in* Portnoy's Complaint *a "correct presentation of the problem" requires a frank revelation of intimate sexual matters, as well as an extensive use of obscenity?*

Yes, I am. Obscenity is not only a kind of language that is used in *Portnoy's Complaint*, it is very nearly the issue itself. The book isn't full of dirty words because "that's the way people talk"; that's one of the *least* persuasive reasons for using the obscene in fiction. Besides, few people actually talk the way Portnoy does in this book—this is a man speaking out of an overwhelming obsession: he is obscene because he wants to be saved. An odd, maybe even mad, way to go about seeking personal salvation; but, nonetheless, the investigation of this passion, and of the combat that it precipitates with his conscience, is what's at the center of the novel. Portnoy's pains arise out of his refusal to be bound any longer by taboos which, rightly or wrongly, *he* experiences as diminishing and unmanning. The joke on Portnoy is that for him breaking the taboo turns out to be as unmanning in the end as honoring it. Some joke.

So, I wasn't simply after verisimilitude here; I wanted to raise obscenity to the level of a subject. You may remember that, at the conclusion of the novel, the Israeli girl (whose body Portnoy has been wrestling her for on the floor of his Haifa hotel room) says to him, with loathing, "Tell me, please, *why* must you use that word all the time?" I gave her this question to ask him—and to ask at the end of this novel—altogether deliberately: Why he must is what the book is all about.

Do you think there will be Jews who will be offended by this book?

I think there will even be Gentiles who will be offended by this book.

I was thinking of the charges that were made against you by certain rabbis after the appearance of Goodbye, Columbus. *They said you were "anti-Semitic" and "self-hating," did they not?*

In "Writing About Jews," an essay I published in *Commentary*, in December 1963, I replied at length to those charges. Some critics also said that my work furnished "fuel" for anti-Semitism. I'm sure these charges will be made again—though the fact is (and I think there's even a clue to this in my fiction) that I have always been far more pleased by my good fortune in being born a Jew than my critics may begin to imagine. It's a complicated, interesting, morally demanding, and very singular experience, and I like that. I find myself in the historic predicament of being Jewish, with all its implications. Who could ask for more? But as for those charges you mention—yes, they probably will be leveled at me. Because of the U.N. condemnation of Israeli "aggression," and anti-Semitic rage flaring up in the black community, many American Jews must surely be feeling more alienated than they have in a long time; consequently, I don't think it's a moment when I can expect a book as unrestrained as this one to be indulged or even tolerated, especially in those quarters where I was not exactly hailed as the Messiah to begin with. I'm afraid that the temptation to quote single lines out of the entire fictional context will be just about overwhelming on upcoming Saturday mornings. The rabbis have got their indignation to stoke, just as I do. And there are sentences in that book upon which a man could construct a pretty indignant sermon.

I have heard some, people suggest that your book was influenced by the nightclub act of Lenny Bruce. Would you consider Bruce, or other stand-up comics such as Shelley Berman or Mort Sahl, or even The Second City comics, an influence upon the comic methods you employ in Portnoy's Complaint?

Not really. I would say I was more strongly influenced by a sit-down comic named Franz Kafka and a very funny bit he does called "The Metamorphosis." Interestingly, the only time Lenny Bruce and I ever met and talked was in his lawyer's office, where it occurred to me that he was just about ripe for the role of Joseph K. He looked gaunt and driven, still determined but also on the wane, and he wasn't interested in being funny—all he could talk about and think about was his "case." I never saw Bruce perform, though I've heard tapes and records, and since his death I've watched a movie of one of his performances and read a collection of his routines. I recognize and admire in him what I used to like about The Second City company at its best, that joining of precise social observation with extravagant and dreamlike fantasy.

What about the influence of Kafka that you mention?

Well, of course, I don't mean I modeled my book after any work of his, or tried to write a Kafka-like novel. At the time I was beginning to play with the ideas for what turned out to be *Portnoy's Complaint*, I was teaching a lot of Kafka in a course I gave once a week at the University of Pennsylvania. When I look back now on the reading I assigned that year, I realize that the course might have been called "Studies in Guilt and Persecution"—"The Metamorphosis," *The Castle*, "In the Penal Colony," *Crime and Punishment*, "Notes from Underground," *Death in Venice*, *Anna Karenina* ... My own-previous two novels, *Letting Go* and *When She Was Good*, were about as gloomy as the gloomiest of these blockbusters, and fascinated, obviously, as I still was by these dark books, I was actually looking for a way to get in touch with another side of my talent. Particularly after several arduous years spent on *When She Was Good*, with its unfiery prose, its puritanical, haunted heroine, its unrelenting concern with banality, I was aching to write something freewheeling and funny. It had been a long time between laughs. My students may have thought I was being strategically blasphemous or simply entertaining them when I began to describe the movie that could be made of *The Castle*, with Groucho Marx as K. and Chico and Harpo as the two assistants." But I meant it. I thought of writing a story about Kafka writing a story. I had read somewhere that he used to giggle to himself while he worked. Of course! It was all so *funny*, this morbid preoccupation with punishment and guilt. Hideous, but funny. Hadn't I only recently sat smirking through a performance of *Othello*? And not just because it was badly done either, but because something in that bad performance revealed how *dumb* Othello is. Isn't there something ludicrous about Anna Karenina throwing herself under that train? For what? What after all had she done? I asked my students; I asked myself. I thought about Groucho walking into the village over which the Castle looms, announcing he was the Land Surveyor; of *course* no one would believe him. Of course they would drive him up the wall. They had to—because of that cigar.

Now—the road from these random and even silly ideas to *Portnoy's Complaint* was more winding and eventful than I can describe here; there is certainly a personal element in the book, but not until I had got hold of guilt, you see, as a comic idea, did I begin to feel myself lifting free and clear of my last book and my old concerns.

Note

The interviewer is George Plimpton; the interview appeared in *The New York Times Book Review* the Sunday *Portnoy's Complaint* was reviewed there. (1969)

JEFFREY BERMAN

Philip Roth's Psychoanalysts

When a Philip Roth character finds himself lying on a couch, more than likely he is engaged not in sex but in psychoanalysis. Therapy becomes the most intimate and imaginative event in life for the beleaguered hero, the one love affair he cannot live without. Of all novelists, Roth is the most familiar with the theory and practice of psychoanalysis, and from the beginning of his career he has demonstrated a keen interest in the therapeutic process. His characters are the most thoroughly psychoanalyzed in literature. Beginning with Libby Herz's dramatic encounter with Dr. Lumin in *Letting Go*, Roth has repeatedly returned to the psychoanalytic setting.[1] Through Alex Portnoy's stylized confession to the mute Dr. Otto Spielvogel in *Portnoy's Complaint*, Peter Tarnopol's troubled relationship to the greatly expanded Spielvogel in *My Life as a Man*, and David Kepesh's analysis with Dr. Klinger in *The Breast* and *The Professor of Desire*, Roth offers lively and fascinating accounts of the talking cure.

To his credit, Roth avoids stereotyping his analysts, and they remain conspicuously apart from and superior to other fictional therapists. Their uniqueness derives from their professional authenticity, sensitivity to language, and their refusal to subvert the therapeutic process. Indeed, Roth's analysts become more impressive when compared to other fictional healers who either misunderstand psychotherapy or exploit their patients' illnesses.

From *The Talking Cure: Literary Representations of Psychoanalysts*.

Roth's therapists do not marry their patients or have incestuous affairs with them, as do Dick Diver in *Tender Is the Night*, Palmer Anderson in Iris Murdoch's *A Severed Head*, and Erica Jong's lustful Adrian Goodlove in *Fear of Flying*. They do not perform lobotomies or administer drugs, as Kesey describes in his psychiatric horror story, *One Flew Over the Cuckoo's Nest*, nor do they use electroshock therapy, as in Plath's *The Bell Jar*. Dr. Lamb's "Explosion" therapy in Lessing's *The Four-Gated City* and the behavioral modification found in Anthony Burgess' *A Clockwork Orange* are both alien to Roth's world. His analysts are neither priests in disguise, as is Sir Harcourt-Reilly in Eliot's *The Cocktail Party*, nor therapeutic con artists, like Dr. Tamkin in Bellow's *Seize the Day*. And they are certainly unlike the sadistic caricatures posing as therapists in Nabokov's stories.

In short, Roth pays tribute to psychoanalysis by demystifying the patient–analyst relationship and by refusing to render therapists into caricatures or mythic figures. Even when Roth has been wildly inventive in his patients' confessions or symptoms, the novelist is scrupulously realistic in his portrayal of psychoanalysts. They are men of good will, expertise, and integrity. They maintain a proper distance from their patients, follow the rules of their profession, and avoid subverting their position into an instrument of evil power. They are orthodox Freudians in their theoretical orientation but pragmatic in their world view. They affirm the consolations of the reality principle, urging reconciliation and reintegration. They are scholarly, dignified, mildly ironic in speech, and even tempered. They are not charmed by their patients' praise, bullied by their threats, or horrified by their revelations. Above all, they are excellent listeners.

In *Reading Myself and Others* Roth has perceptively commented upon the importance of psychoanalysis in his fiction, but he has been characteristically reluctant to discuss the autobiographical sources of his artistic preoccupation with therapy or the exact parallels between his own life and those of his fictional creations. Referring to the varied therapeutic experiences of Libby, Portnoy, Tarnopol, and Kepesh, Roth notes that "All of these characters, in pain and in trouble, turn to doctors because they believe psychoanalysis may help them from going under completely. Why they believe this is a subject I haven't the space to go into here, nor is it what I've given most thought to in these books" (pp. 93–94). His main interest, he adds, is "in the extent to which unhappy people *do* define themselves as 'ill' or agree to view themselves as 'patients,' and in what each then makes of the treatment prescribed." Roth leaves unanswered, however, many important questions regarding the relationship between the creative and therapeutic process. Despite the profound similarities between the artist's and psychoanalyst's vision of reality, there are no less profound differences, chief of which is, perhaps, the assumptions of understanding reality.[2] Roth's patients, who are generally writers or professors of literature, maintain the belief that reality is intractable: Human passions are unruly, suffering cannot be explained or alleviated, and reality seems impervious to understanding. Roth's analysts, by contrast, believe that psychological illness derives from childhood experiences, that conflict can be understood psychodynamically, and that guilt and rage can be worked through.

Toward which paradigm of reality, the artist's or psychoanalyst's, is the reader more sympathetic? And what effect does psychoanalysis have on Roth's protagonists? It is clear that they continually brood over the subject of psychological illness, often becoming depressed or paralyzed. Yet why does "illness" liberate Portnoy's spirit while it only depresses Tarnopol's? In reading the analytic confessions of Roth's characters, where does one draw the line between healthy or humorous fantasies and pathological needs? And what is the relationship between art and aggression, creativity and psychopathology? In particular, can a novelist write about his own psychoanalysis and sharply disagree with his analyst's interpretation without engaging in "resistance" or "narcissistic melodramas"?

The 11-page segment of Libby Herz's stormy interview with Dr. Lumin in *Letting Go* represents one of the most brilliant fictional depictions of a patient's first analytic session. Although Libby summons all her strength to make the dreaded appointment, she still shows up 20 minutes late. To arrive on time, she fears, would be symptomatic of weakness. Upon seeing Lumin she is disheartened, for he fulfills none of the reassuring European stereotypes she has imagined. A short, wide man with oversized head and hands, he has the beefy appearance of a butcher, which intensifies Libby's terror. Roth invests the scene with a wonderful seriocomic tone, handling the problem of narrative distance with equal expertise. Everything is filtered through Libby's consciousness as the novelist records her small shocks, such as her indecision over whether to sit or lie down on the analytic couch and, if to lie down, whether to take off her shoes. Alarmed at having her preconceptions of therapy shattered, she fears she is boring or angering the analyst. She remains a prisoner of her nervousness, victimized by a frantic heart and perspiring body. "It was like living with an idiot whose behavior was unpredictable from one moment to the next: what would this body of hers do ten seconds from now?" (p. 344).

Like all of Roth's psychoanalysts, Lumin maintains a passive demeanor throughout the session, allowing Libby to direct the flow of talk. Midway through the hour, however, he grows impatient with her chatter and, during a bantering exchange, he almost springs out of the chair to demand: "Come on, Libby ... What's the trouble?" The unexpected question devastates her and for a full five minutes she breaks down and sobs, just as Tarnopol does when he begins his analysis with Spielvogel in *My Life as a Man*. When she finally looks up, Lumin is still there, "a thick, fleshy reality, nothing to be charmed, wheedled, begged, tempted, or flirted with" (p. 347). Neither a father surrogate nor an alter ego, Lumin remains Lumin. His name suggests his function in the novel: He helps Libby to illuminate her confused thoughts and to focus on her contradictory emotions. She reveals more to him in a few minutes than she has admitted to anyone in her life, including herself. She expresses anger toward her husband for not making love to her more than once a month. ("Well," says Lumin with authority, "everybody's entitled to get laid more than that.") She confesses to her self-preoccupation and self-pity, discovers that she does not love the rootless Gabe Wallach but only the freedom she imagines him to have, and admits to behaving badly. These are not great insights, but they do represent a beginning.

In a novel filled with endless small talk and self-absorption, Lumin's silence becomes paradoxically eloquent. His attentive listening jolts Libby into a more rigorous self-examination than she has ever undertaken. The analyst offers no psychological formulas or medical truisms. He simply listens to her and occasionally asks pointed questions. When Libby demands to know what is wrong with her, he restates the question; when she begins to play the role of the mental patient, claiming she is "cracked as the day is long," he abruptly stops her. In a gruff but compassionate voice, he reproaches her for exaggerating her problems. He is not exactly a mirroring or empathic analyst, but his no-nonsense approach works.

Letting Go has received harsh criticism for its sprawling structure, desultory plotting, and self-indulgence, yet the scene between Libby and Lumin demonstrates Roth's writing at its best. The compressed descriptions, dramatic pacing, expansion and contraction of Libby's point of view, and sparkling dialogue suggest that psychoanalysis has enlivened Roth's art. Lumin's speech has the desired effect on Libby, and she suddenly feels an awakening warmth for the analyst who has given her a new perspective to her problems. Interestingly, Libby brings to therapy an uncommon knowledge of the intricacies of the patient–analyst relationship. "She had, of course, heard of transference, and she wondered if it could be beginning so soon" (p. 350). It is questionable whether an inexperienced patient, in analysis for less than an hour, would be so aware of transference. Yet Roth's characters bring to psychoanalysis an extraordinary awareness of the mind, as if they had grown up on Dr. Freud instead of Dr. Spock. Libby's positive transference toward Lumin soon gives way to rage, however, upon learning at the end of the hour the expense of psychoanalysis. When Lumin informs her that the fee is 25 dollars an hour—a figure that surely dates the novel!—she nearly faints. The scene is both funny and sad and ends with Libby storming out of his office, convinced the analyst has betrayed her. Thus ends her only experience with therapy. It is significant that Roth reserves this psychoanalytic initiation for a woman, not a man: Gabe, not Libby, seems the more likely candidate for analysis, and in future stories psychoanalysis remains a distinctly male activity.

Portnoy's Complaint (1969) is not only Roth's most celebrated psychoanalytic monologue but the novel which brought the analytic couch into the living rooms of millions of American families. Alex's attitude toward the talking cure may be gleaned from his reading habits, both by what and how he reads. Describing the set of Freud's *Collected Papers* he has bought, he remarks: "since my return from Europe, [I] have been putting myself to sleep each night in the solitary confinement of my womanless bed with a volume of Freud in my hand. Sometimes Freud in hand, sometimes Alex in hand, frequently both" (p. 185). Freud as a soporific? Or as an aphrodisiac? Portnoy reads Freud's writings for the usual reasons—intellectual curiosity, historical awareness, personal self-discovery—yet, he embraces psychoanalytic theory primarily for self-justification. The analyst becomes for Portnoy an erotic plaything, a masturbatory sex object, a handy "how-to" book. As Spielvogel's name suggests in German, he is a "playbird" to be stroked, serenaded, seduced.

Portnoy thus transmutes Freudian ideas into imaginative self-play, the first of many instances in which Roth transforms clinical case studies into the stuff of art. Portnoy's preference for orthodox Freudian psychoanalysis, uncorrupted by revisionist doctrine, reveals the same purist impulse that allows him to quote freely from other great classical writers—Shakespeare, Dostoevsky, Kafka. Portnoy reads Freud's seminal essay, "The Most Prevalent Form of Degradation in Erotic Life," and then confides to us erotic fantasies and past exploits that would make the Viennese physician blush. In holding up the Freudian mirror to life, Roth's hero is bedazzled by what he sees and by the tantalizing possibilities of life imitating the psychiatric case study. Contemporary analysts speak of fusion with the lost object, but Portnoy's story is an example of a character in search of the author of the *Standard Edition* (or the less epical *Collected Papers*), from which he quotes with Mosaic authority. The promised land for Portnoy is not Israel, toward which he ambivalently moves, but the rich landscape of textbook Oedipal fantasies. Rendered impotent in his mother country, he suffers no loss of verbal potency or bravado when journeying through virgin psychoanalytic territory.

It is obvious from the manic comic tone of the novel that Portnoy hungers not for redemption, as he mistakenly asserts, but for applause and validation. Humor aside, Portnoy does not exist. To question his "illness" seems to be in bad taste, as if to perform an autopsy on a good joke or to translate a pun from another language. "*Traduttore–traditore,*" as Freud remarked in his own Joke Book.[3] Nevertheless, we may wonder whether Portnoy's reading of Freudian theory allows him to chart new imaginative territory or merely to restrict his vision. The question is not how much psychoanalytic theory Portnoy has studied but the uses and misuses of his knowledge. Accordingly, we may analyze one of the most intriguing aspects of the novel, Portnoy's transference relationship to Spielvogel. The inexperienced Libby knows enough about transference in *Letting Go* to call it by its proper name. Portnoy, however, seems indifferent to the transactional nature of psychoanalysis. Indeed, he refuses to allow Spielvogel to speak until the last line of the novel. The patient monopolizes the session in a dizzying display of Freudian virtuosity. He allows nothing to interrupt his monologue, neither doubts about psychoanalytic theory nor queries addressed to Spielvogel. All of Portnoy's questions are rhetorical.

Portnoy's transference relationship to Spielvogel suggests the desire to match his Freudian expertise against the analyst's, to compete with him, secure his approval, and ultimately to replace him as an authority. The intense identification with Spielvogel reveals the urge to incorporate him, as if Portnoy were digesting a book. Although he addresses him as "Your Honor" and "Your Holiness," the patient usually regards him as an intellectual equal. "Surely, Doctor, we can figure this thing out, two smart Jewish boys like ourselves." Portnoy never relinquishes his superiority. Identifying himself with Freud's famous case studies, he cites an illustrious artist whose fantasies coincide with his own. "I have read Freud on Leonardo, Doctor, and pardon the hubris, but my fantasies exactly: this big smothering bird beating frantic wings about my face and mouth *so that I cannot even get my breath*" (p. 121). Later Portnoy challenges Spielvogel (his own "playbird") to another competition, singing the songs of the service academies. "Go ahead, name your branch of service, Spielvogel, I'll sing you your song! Please, allow me—it's my money" (p. 235). *Portnoy's Complaint* is itself a raucous anthem to the psychoanalytic process, with the patient paying homage to His Majesty Spielvogel while at the same time making plans for his own succession to the throne.

What does all this mean? To the extent that Portnoy attempts to win his analyst's love and to usurp his magical potency, he recreates Spielvogel into an idealized father figure—a judge, lawgiver, king—the antithesis of his constipated and passive real father, Jack Portnoy. But insofar as Portnoy refuses to surrender verbal control to Spielvogel, thus enforcing silence and passivity upon the analyst, he attempts to manipulate him into his father's submissive position. The transference relationship is consequently an accurate reflection of his life. Portnoy's cocky attitude toward, Spielvogel is a disguised attempt to usurp the Oedipal father, to castrate him. Roth's hero never sees the irony. Nor does he comment upon the hidden meaning behind the exhibitionistic impulse to perform or spill forth to the analyst. In his nonstop verbal pyrotechnics, his quest for perfectionism and omnipotent self-control, his unceasing self-mythologizing, and his need to instruct Spielvogel with years of inherited wisdom, Portnoy becomes his own Jewish mother. The irony is crucial. Portnoy criticizes his seductive overprotective mother for overwhelming her docile son; but the son, now a grown man, has internalized his mother's values to the extent that even while rebelling against her, he cannot prevent himself from similarly overwhelming the analyst-father. The mother uses food to overnourish her son; Alex uses a more symbolic form of orality, language, to satiate his analyst. The words never cease. In its unrelenting intensity, Alex's language suggests love and hate, nourishment and suffocation.

And so despite his impressive reading of psychoanalytic theory, Portnoy misses the significance of his ejaculative performance to Spielvogel. "I lose touch instantaneously with that ass-licking little boy who runs home after school with his A's in his hand, the little over-earnest innocent endlessly in search of the key to that unfathomable mystery, his mother's approbation ..." (p. 49). Portnoy's colorful language offers the hope of rigorous self-examination and increased narrative perspective; yet, he still does not recognize that, instead of rejecting the mama's-boy values he professes to despise, he has unconsciously transferred these values to Spielvogel, whose approbation he is now demanding. Only now it is an "A" in psychoanalysis he is pursuing in his independent study.

How should Dr. Spielvogel react to Portnoy's artful monologue? In a satirical article entitled "Portnoy Psychoanalyzed," Bruno Bettelheim offers his interpretation of Spielvogel's responses. Portnoy's "diarrhea" of talk, observes Bettelheim's analyst, represents a reaction formation to his father's constipation of character. The patient's problem is reflected in his indiscriminate sexual and verbal discharge, a frantic defense against the threat of being unmanned. Accompanying Portnoy's castration fear is the contradictory wish to have a castrating father to restore his wounded image of male power. Portnoy's confession is self-indulgent, claims Bettelheim's Spielvogel, because he regards psychoanalysis as a quick and easy catharsis rather than as a difficult process of self-healing through self-discovery. The analyst suggests additionally that although Portnoy believes his psychic impotence arises from an Oedipal attachment, the oral attachments to the mother determine his wish to remain a child forever. Bettelheim's most provocative insight is that Portnoy's complaint of an overprotective mother disguises the disappointment that she was not more exclusively preoccupied with him. "While consciously he experienced everything she did as destructive, behind it is an incredible wish for more, more, more; an insatiable orality which is denied and turned into the opposite by his continuous scream of its being much too much."[4]

Ironically, Bettelheim's Spielvogel is as perceptive in analyzing Portnoy's transference relationship as he is imperceptive in admitting to his own negative countertransference. Unable to concede any sympathy for his "troublesome—aren't they all?—new patient," the analyst is filled with anger, contempt, and intolerance, as if the patient's narcissistic defenses have triggered off his own. He fails to acknowledge anything worthwhile about Portnoy's character. Reading "Portnoy Psychoanalyzed," one is unable to explain the vitality and wit of the Rothian hero, not to mention the novel's linguistic brilliance. Angered by his inability to break through Portnoy's monologue, and worried (rightly, as it turns out) that he will be unable to establish a minimal transference necessary for analysis to succeed, Bettelheim's Spielvogel never admits that countertransference is the key problem. Not even Eliot's Sir Harcourt-Reilly is as belligerent as Bettelheim's Spielvogel. He is offended by Portnoy's vulgar language, ingratitude toward his parents, inferiority complex, narcissistic rage, and failure in interpersonal relationships. Why, then, is the patient in analysis if he is not to work through these conflicts? In his narrow clinical judgments, threatening tactics, and European condescension, Bettelheim's Spielvogel becomes an unconscious parody of a self-righteous, withholding parent. Indeed, Roth could not have imagined a more unflattering portrait of an analyst. And the absence of authorial distance between the eminent psychoanalyst and his fictional creation makes "Portnoy Psychoanalyzed" more disturbing.

Bettelheim's hostility toward *Portnoy's Complaint* may derive in part from the psychoanalytic community's defensiveness of its image in literature. The angry denunciations of *Equus* suggest this, though certainly the play's flaws justify criticism. A more serious problem of "Portnoy Psychoanalyzed" is its unawareness of the satirical art of *Portnoy's Complaint* and Bettelheim's reduction of Roth's novel to a psychiatric case study. Only at the end of the essay does the author consider the possibility that *Portnoy's Complaint* is a literary production, not a clinical confession. He concedes that at best it is "not more than an effort to tell a good story." But he places no value on a good story. He also wishes to tell Portnoy—and his creator—that "it is time to stop being a man of letters so that, through analyzing himself, he might finally become a man" (p. 10). Behind Spielvogel's hostility toward Portnoy lies, of course, Bettelheim's rejection of Roth. Roth's own Spielvogel in *My Life as a Man* demonstrates greater compassion and understanding than the Spielvogel of "Portnoy Psychoanalyzed," which is to say that Roth is a better psychoanalyst than Bettelheim is a literary critic.[5]

Despite its appearance as a psychiatric case study, *Portnoy's Complaint* retains its allegiance to the interior monologue developed by Joyce, Faulkner, and Virginia Woolf. Beginning with *Portnoy's Complaint* and proceeding through *The Breast*, *My Life as a Man*, and *The Professor of Desire*, Roth has evolved his own narrative form in which the interior monologue is wedded to a contemporary psychoanalytic setting. The analyst, heard or unheard, becomes the recipient of the comic or anguished utterances of a patient searching for psychic relief and moral redemption. The free-association technique, the recurrent phallic-and-castration imagery, the Oedipal triangles, the idealization of the analyst, and the multilayered texture of Portnoy's consciousness help to create the psychoanalytic authenticity. "The style of *Portnoy's Complaint*," Sheldon Grebstein observes, "is the rhetoric of hysteria, or perhaps the rhetoric of neurosis."[6]

Roth's prose style also captures perfectly the nuances of psychoanalysis. His language is analytic, restlessly interrogative, self-mocking. The prose is always capable of anticipating the objections of an implied listener who usually turns out to be, of course, an analyst. The language is attuned to the nuances of spiritual imprisonment and, moral ambiguity, capable of distorting small humiliations into traumatic injustices, and straining for a release that never quite comes. The voice bespeaks a romantic disillusionment that rarely frees itself from the suspicion that, contrary to what an analyst might say, an unruly personal life is good for a novelist's art. There is a self-lacerating quality about Roth's prose that has remained constant over the years. David Kepesh's observation in *The Professor of Desire* holds true for all of Roth's heroes. "I am an absolutist—a *young* absolutist—and know no way to shed a skin other than by inserting the scalpel and lacerating myself from end to end" (p. 12). Roth's stories dramatize the struggle between the impulse for sensual abandon, on the one hand, and the capacity for pain-filled renunciation, on the other. And the novelist is always willing to incriminate himself in the service of art, preoccupied as he is in novel after novel with illicit and ungovernable passions at war with a rigid conscience.

Does Portnoy discover anything about himself in the course of the novel? The circular form of *Portnoy's Complaint* undercuts the illusion of self-discovery. Roth's comments in *Reading Myself and Others* indicate the contradiction between the realistic and satirical elements of the story. "It is a highly stylized confession that this imaginary Spielvogel gets to hear, and I would guess that it bears about as much resemblance to the drift and tone of what a real psychopathologist hears in his everyday life as a love sonnet does to the iambs and dactyls that lovers whisper into one another's ears in motel rooms and over the phone" (p. 94). The simile reveals Roth's own spirited love affair with psychoanalysis, at least during the creation of *Portnoy's Complaint*. In *My Life as a Man*, he will strive for and achieve stark realism in the treatment of the patient–analyst relationship, but, in *Portnoy's Complaint*, he uses a psychoanalytic setting mainly as the context for his protagonises lyrical confessions. Never has confession sounded as poetic as this, as free and spontaneous and inventive as these artful outpourings. Portnoy has acquired his psychoanalytic armor before the novel opens, and he seems disinclined to lay down his defenses as the story closes. Consequently, he reaches few if any real insights, nothing comparable to a Joycean epiphany.

Patricia Meyer Spacks has pointed out the affinities of *Portnoy's Complaint* to the picaresque novel, but Roth's story also recalls the dramatic monologue.[7] Robert Langbaum has called the dramatic monologue "the poetry of experience," the doctrine that the "imaginative apprehension gained through immediate experience is primary and certain, whereas the analytic reflection that follows is secondary and problematical."[8] Nearly all of Langbaum's observations in *The Poetry of Experience* apply to *Portnoy's Complaint*, including the tension between our sympathy and moral judgment for a speaker who is outrageous or reprehensible. They apply to the circular rather than linear direction of the narrative. ("The speaker of the dramatic monologue starts out with an established point of view, and is not concerned with its truth but with trying to impress it on the outside world.") Also, they apply to the gratuitous but lyrical nature of the speaker's utterance. "The result is that the dramatic situation, incomplete in itself, serves an ultimately self-expressive or lyrical purpose which gives it its resolution" (p. 182). And so it is with Portnoy's complaint. Interpreted as a Browningesque dramatic monologue, the novel ceases to be a psychiatric case study. The self-indulgent confession gives way to an internally structured monologue, the psychomoral complexity shifts away from Portnoy as character or object onto the reader's problematic relationship to him, the patient's self-analysis becomes linked to self-deception, and Portnoy's failure to achieve a therapeutic cure is offset by his refusal to have acknowledged any illness.

Nowhere is the reader's troubled relationship to Portnoy better demonstrated than by the enormous controversy the novel has generated. Portnoy shrewdly anticipates the accusations of his critics. "I hear myself indulging in the kind of ritualized bellyaching that is just what gives psychoanalytic patients such a bad name with the general public" (p. 94). Do we praise his candor or criticize his rationalization? Or both? How do we respond to his next set of questions? "Is this truth I'm delivering up, or is it just plain *kvetching*? Or is *kvetching* for people like me a *form* of truth?" The answer depends upon the reader's sympathy for Portnoy, but of course this evades the prior questions of how and why the reader's sympathy for Portnoy is or is not engaged. Irving Howe's influential indictment of *Portnoy's Complaint* in *Commentary* remains the most caustic evaluation. "There usually follows in such first-person narratives a spilling-out of the narrator which it becomes hard to suppose is not also the spilling-out of the author. Such literary narcissism is especially notable among minor satirists, with whom it frequently takes the form of self-exemptive attacks on the shamefulness of humanity."[9] This remains an extreme position, however, and amidst the claims and counterclaims of Roth's critics, a reader is likely to become confused. As Mark Shechner has noted in an admirable essay, one's enthusiasm for Roth's fiction is complicated though not necessarily diminished by the discovery that one's loyalty to *Portnoy's Complaint* as a version of the truth is not widely shared by other readers.[10]

Paradoxically, despite Portnoy's incessant complaints, it is hard to take seriously his demand for therapeutic relief. He may gripe that his parents have psychically crippled him, but they have also been responsible for shaping an imagination that never wavers in its comic inventiveness and vitality. The novel is less a complaint than a celebration. Why should Portnoy be cured of fantasies that are so entertaining? The exuberance of his language works against his claims for deliverance. The voice never assumes the flatness, fatigue, or disconnectedness that is symptomatic of depression. Narcissism notwithstanding, Portnoy realizes that he is not the center of the universe, and Roth's ability to conjure up a rogue's gallery of minor characters testifies to his escape from solipsism. Portnoy's voice never falters in its curiosity and delight in commentary. "The true center of Portnoy's heroism is his speech," Patricia Meyer Spacks has observed.[11] It is true that Portnoy has not figured out all the psychoanalytic dynamics of his situation. He prefers to discuss Oedipal fixations rather than pre-Oedipal narcissistic injuries. However, if he is consumed by guilt, he seems to be thriving on his imaginative disorders.

The delight in reading *Portnoy's Complaint* lies not in the analysis of a diseased mind but in the appreciation of one of the most fertile imaginations found in contemporary literature. Unlike *The Catcher in the Rye*, which ends with Holden Caulfield's psychotic breakdown, institutionalization, and uncertain return to society, *Portnoy's Complaint* concludes with the protagonist as an outpatient. Spielvogel's punch line, "So.... Now vee may perhaps to begin. Yes?", perfectly satirizes Portnoy's bookish self-analysis. Through Spielvogel's one-liner, Roth tells us that Portnoy's psychoanalytic (or pre-psychoanalytic) monologue is both inadequate and incomplete. The analyst has the last word and the last laugh. Yet, Portnoy has discovered one crucial truth that will prepare him for psychoanalysis or any other introspective activity. He has casually dropped upon us (in a parenthesis, no less) the moral of his story: "Nothing is never ironic, there's always a laugh lurking somewhere" (p. 93). *Portnoy's Complaint* appropriately ends with a Joycean "yes." And in the spirit of *Ulysses*, which also climaxes with Molly Bloom's final affirmation as she drifts off to sleep dreaming autoerotic visions of past and present lovers, so does Roth's self-reliant hero, far from being drained or limp from his imaginative foreplay, return to Freud, on the one hand, land himself, on the other, ready to play with his Spielvogelian truths.

* * *

Unfortunately, psychoanalysis proves less inspiring to Roth's next protagonist-patient. Portnoy's masturbatory fantasies pale in comparison to the endocrinopathic catastrophe befalling the unfortunate hero of *The Breast*. Worse still, David Kepesh's metamorphosis into a giant breast remains inexplicable to his psychoanalyst, Dr. Frederick Klinger, who insists upon, oddly enough, a physiological etiology. To accept Klinger's judgment is to reject all efforts to interpret Roth's story. Devoid of psychological interest, *The Breast* wanders in a no-man's land between *Portnoy's Complaint* and *My Life as a Man*, without the great comic exuberance of the former or the intriguing involutions of the latter.[12] Unlike Portnoy, Kepesh's complaints seem joyless and unimaginative; unlike Tarnopol, his life as a man seems unworthy of extended critical attention. *The Breast* strays between realism and fantasy, unable to commit itself to either outlook. For whatever reason, Roth restrains the farcical implications of the story. The problem with *The Breast* is that it is not fantastic enough. The premise of the story would seem to indicate an abandonment of the reality principle and a leap into pure fantasy; yet, Kepesh always sounds like Kepesh—before, during, and after the metamorphosis. The story remains exclusively preoccupied with the trivial facts of the transformation, thus neglecting the narrator's dislocation of consciousness. The metamorphosis into a breast fails to alter the dreary consistency of Kepesh's perceptions and speech, perhaps necessitating a more radical surgical procedure for Roth's curious novella.

In retrospect, *The Breast* occupies a transitional position in Roth's career. David Kepesh's life embodies most of the characteristics, external and internal, of the archetypal Roth protagonist. Kepesh and Tarnopol are similar in age, profession, parental and marital problems, and temperament. Both men have been in psychoanalysis for five years and teach English literature in colleges or universities where Roth himself has studied or taught. Interestingly, the age of the Roth narrator can be determined by subtracting the year of Roth's birth, 1933, from the publication date of the novel. The Roth hero ages from novel to novel at the same speed as the novelist himself. Gabe Wallach is 28, Roth's age when he finished writing *Letting Go*. Alex Portnoy is born in 1933. Kepesh says that he is 38 and that he turned into a breast in 1971 (the novella was published in 1972), thus placing his birth in 1933. Both Nathan Zuckerman and Tarnopol, in *My Life as a Man*, also were born in 1933. Similarly, the titles of Roth's stories reveal an allegorical pattern. They narrate the complaint of a professor of desire, whose struggle for manhood is undercut by the difficulty of letting go of a literal or metaphorical breast. Roth has always been striving to write *The Great American Novel*, though the title of *Goodbye, Columbus* may suggest the increasing remoteness of the quest. The titles *Goodbye, Columbus*, *Letting Go*, *When She Was Good*, and *The Ghost Writer* also hint at an element of nostalgia and perhaps elegy, as if the past is more romantic than the present. Yet there is a depressing fear that, to echo Roth's contemporary, Joseph Heller, something happened.

The Klinger–Kepesh relationship in *The Breast* dramatizes the tension between rationality and irrationality, restraint and hysteria, the reality principle and the pleasure principle. Like all of Roth's analysts, Klinger is concerned with normal rather than abnormal psychology. He never claims omniscience or omnipotence. Roth continues to demystify the analyst, making him eminently human and sensible. To his credit, Klinger avoids threatening clinical tactics, obscurantist theories, and professional jargon. "You are not mad," he tells Kepesh, "You are not in the grip of a delusion, or haven't been till now. You have not suffered what you call 'a schizophrenic collapse'" (p. 55). Klinger mercifully abstains from Laingian metaphors of "journeying through inner space" and other fashionable psychiatric theories.

Yet, if Kepesh's illness originates from a hormonal imbalance, what is Klinger doing in *The Breast*? The analyst insists that Kepesh's metamorphosis cannot be explained in psychoanalytic terms, such as wish fulfillment or regression to infancy. Does Roth need an analyst to tell us this? Better an endocrinologist. Klinger's vocabulary is not psychological but moralistic; he uses expressions like "strength of character" and "will to live" to help his patient adapt to the bizarre illness. Both the analyst and novelist take Kepesh's story too seriously. Perhaps one can excuse Kepesh's hypochondria and self-dramatizing; he is, after all, the patient and therefore entitled to his rightful suffering. "Alas, what has happened to me is like nothing anyone has ever known; beyond understanding, beyond compassion, beyond comedy ..." (p. 11). Klinger encourages Kepesh's self-inflation, and even the analyst's dialogue sounds wooden at times. "You have been heroic in your efforts to accommodate yourself to this mysterious misfortune" (p. 55). Roth's great gift for dialogue fails him here, suggesting that the novelist cannot believe in Kepesh's "heroic" plight. Nevertheless, Roth continues to insist upon his patient's heroic stature, arguing, in *Reading Myself and Others*, that Kepesh's predicament is far more poignant and harrowing than Lucy Nelson's, the heroine of *When She Was Good*, or Portnoy's. "Kepesh strikes me as far more heroic than either of these two: perhaps a man who turns into a breast is the first heroic character I've ever been able to portray" (p. 66). Despite Roth's intentions, his hero seems neither sick nor imaginative enough to justify his fantastic situation. Why the metamorphosis into a breast instead of a penis, mouth, anus, brain? Why Kepesh's five years of therapy prior to the opening of the story, only to be told that psychoanalytic reality does not apply to a biochemical disorder? Why attempt to remain a "citadel of sanity" when real madness seems more appropriate? Far from being the uplifting story Roth intended, *The Breast* remains pointless, a joke gone sour.

Notes

1. The following editions by Roth are cited in the text. All references are to these editions. *Letting Go* (New York: Random House, 1962); *Portnoy's Complaint* (New York: Random House, 1969); *The Breast* (New York: Holt, Rinehart and Winston, 1972); *My Life as a Man* (New York: Holt, Rinehart and Winston, 1974); *Reading Myself and Others* (New York: Farrar, Straus, 1975); *The Professor of Desire* (New York: Farrar, Straus, 1977); *The Ghost Writer* (New York: Farrar, Straus and Giroux, 1979).

2. For an extended discussion of the differences between the artist's endeavor and the psychoanalyst's, see Phoebe C. Ellsworth, "Regarding the Author as Patient," *New Literary History*, Vol. 12, No. 1 (Autumn 1980), pp. 187–197. The entire issue of *New Literary History* is devoted to contemporary trends in literature and psychology and contains several valuable essays, including Ernest S. Wolf's article, "Psychoanalytic Psychology of the Self and Literature," an examination of Kohut's contributions.

3. Sigmund Freud, *Jokes and Their Relation to the Unconscious, Standard Edition* (London: The Hogarth Press, 1960), Vol. VIII, p. 34.

4. Bruno Bettelheim, "Portnoy Psychoanalyzed," *Midstream*, Vol. 15, No. 6 (June/July, 1969), p. 4. All references are to this edition.

5. In *Surviving and Other Essays*, (New York: Vintage, 1980), Bettelheim prefaces the republication of "Portnoy Psychoanalyzed" with remarks intended to convey a more positive evaluation of the literary success of Roth's novel than he initially implied. "Asked to write a review of Philip Roth's *Portnoy's Complaint*, I attempted a satire instead. Only an interesting work of fiction permits and deserves to be made the substance of a satire—which suggests my evaluation of this book" (p. 387).

6. Sheldon Grebstein, "The Comic Anatomy of *Portnoy's Complaint*," in Sarah Blacher Cohen, ed., *Comic Relief: Humor in Contemporary American Literature* (Urbana: University of Illinois Press, 1978), p. 160.

7. Patricia Meyer Spacks, "About Portnoy," *The Yale Review*, Vol. 58 (Summer 1969), p. 623.

8. Robert Langbaum, *The Poetry of Experience* (New York: Norton, 1963), p. 35. All references are to this edition.

9. Irving Howe, "Philip Roth Reconsidered," *Commentary*, Vol. 54, No. 6 (December 1972), p. 72.

10. Mark Shechner, "Philip Roth," *Partisan Review*, Vol. 41, No. 3 (1974.), pp. 410–427. All references are to this edition. Shechner's essay, which remains the best psychological discussion of Roth's fiction, has been reprinted in Sanford Pinsker, ed., *Critical Essays on Philip Roth* (Boston: G. K. Hall, 1982), pp. 117–132.

11. Spacks, "About Portnoy," op. cit., p. 630.

12. For a psychoanalytic interpretation of *The Breast*, see Daniel Dervin, "Breast Fantasy in Barthelme, Swift, and Philip Roth: Creativity and Psychoanalytic Structure," *American Imago*, Vol. 33, No. 1 (Spring 1976), pp. 102–122.

BERNARD F. RODGERS, JR.

In the American Grain (Portnoy's Complaint)

Mention Philip Roth's name in conversation and nine times out of ten the response will be "*Isn't he the one who wrote that dirty book about....*?" For of all his novels *Portnoy's Complaint* is by far the best known—*Goodbye, Columbus* rivals it, but as a movie, not as a book—the one most firmly rooted in the popular consciousness. Almost half a million people bought the book in hardcover, millions more have read it in paperback. And those who have not bought or read the book seem at least to have heard of it by word of mouth, or through feature articles which appeared in mass-circulation magazines such as *New York*, *Time*, *Life*, and *Newsweek* when it first appeared in 1969. Eventually, the Portnoys may very well join Hawkeye, Huck Finn, and Holden Caulfield as permanent characters of American popular lore; discussion of the book's popular impact would seem to be mandatory in any popular history of the Sixties on the order of Frederick Lewis Allen's *Only Yesterday*; and when the literary history of the period is finally written it will certainly agree with Albert Guerard, Morris Dickstein, and many of the book's reviewers in their judgment that—for good or ill—it is one of the decade's cultural milestones as well.[1]

Although we may be willing to grant that *Portnoy's Complaint* is funny, true, even touching at times, the uneasy feeling persists, however, that any novel which revels in Jewish–Gentile stereotypes, overflows with obscenity, and treats masturbation, fellatio, cunnilingus, a *ménage à trois*, and assorted sexual deviations (with liver and other objects animate and inanimate) must be, *a priori*, pornographic and unworthy of extended critical examination. This feeling persists in spite of the fact that we know prurient *intention*, not sexual *matter*, defines a work as pornographic. Though we may recall Henry James's assertion that the reader should grant the writer his *donnée* and evaluate a literary work by the success or failure of the author's *treatment* of his chosen materials, when that *donnée* is explicitly sexual and patently obscene, we tend to balk. With Emerson (paleface extraordinaire), we may recognize that, in theory at least, "thought makes everything fit for use," that "the vocabulary of an omniscient man [i.e., a poet, an artist] would embrace words and images excluded from polite conversation. What would be base, or even obscene, to the obscene, becomes illustrious, spoken in a new connection of thought.... The meaner the type, the more pungent it is, and the lasting in the memories of men."[2] But like Emerson suddenly confronted with Walt Whitman's *Leaves of Grass*, when we find our theoretical liberality challenged by a novel like *Portnoy's Complaint*, which not only uses such words but incessantly shouts them at us in capital letters, our moral reservations frequently overshadow our critical receptivity—at least in public.

Yet our task as readers and critics is fundamentally the same as it is when we approach any other work of the imagination: we must try to judge whether the words and images employed by the author are those best-suited to the subject—whether, in the case of *Portnoy's Complaint*, words and images commonly designated obscene by polite society have been made "fit for use" by the quality and integrity of the author's thought, by the power of the overall conception of the work in which they play such a prominent part.

The history of the evolution of that conception is, like that of most works of art which arouse and hold critical interest, essentially a record of an artist's struggle to blend content and form in the service of a particular vision. A record, in this instance, of Roth's quest for a voice and a treatment which would allow him the imaginative freedom to combine realistic detail and comic fantasy—the impulses of the paleface and the redskin—in an effort to capture the tenor of contemporary American life in a way that his first two, strictly controlled, novels could not. "After such knowledge as the Grimes case offers to the creative imagination," one of Roth's correspondents had written after reading "Writing American Fiction," "it becomes clear that the writer who dares to handle this much American experience will have to have not only Ralph Ellison's wariness and distrust, but his capacity for high comedy—for the mode of comic insight (one finds it occasionally in Faulkner and Fitzgerald and Nathanial West as well) which allows for the appalling paradoxes of American life but does not forgive them or those who create them...."[3]

Roth apparently agreed, and as early as 1961 the basic outline of the central characters, themes, and situations of Portnoy's Complaint were already on his mind. In "The New Jewish Stereotypes," an essay published in that year, he summarized those materials as they had been repeatedly presented to him in the stories of his students at Iowa. His summary is lengthy but worthy of extended quotation. "There were several Jewish graduate students in the class I taught at the Writing Workshop of the State University of Iowa," he wrote,

> and during one semester three of them wrote stories about their childhood, or at least about a Jewish childhood.... Curiously enough, all of the stories had similar situations and similar characters. The hero in each of them was a young Jewish boy, somewhere between ten and fifteen, who gets excellent grades in school and is always combed and courteous. The stories are told in the first person and have to do with the friendship that grows up between the hero and a Gentile neighbor or schoolmate. The Gentile is from the lower class and he leads the Jewish boy, who is of the middle class, into the mysteries of the flesh. The Gentile boy has already had some kind of sexual experience himself. Not that he is much older than his Jewish companion—he has the chance for adventure because his parents pay hardly any attention to him at all.... This leaves their offspring with plenty of time to hunt girls. The Jewish boy, on the other hand, is watched—he is watched at bedtime, at study-time, and especially at mealtime. Who he is watched by is his mother; the father we rarely see .... what the hero *envies* the Gentile boy is his parental indifference—because ultimately he envies the Gentile his sexual adventure. Religion is not understood as a key to the mysteries of God, but to the mysteries of sex....
>
> I must hasten to point out that in these stories the girls to whom their Gentile comrades lead the heroes are never Jewish girls. The Jewish girls in the stories are mothers and sisters. The sexual dream—for whatever primal reason one cares to entertain—is for the Other. The dream of the *shiksa*.... Though there may be biographical fact at the bottom of these stories ... the satisfactions that are derived through the manipulation and interpretation of the real events are the satisfactions of one's dreams ... what the heroes of their stories learn at the end—as their Gentile comrades disappear into other neighborhoods and into maturity—is the burden of their reality. (SD, pp. 15–16)

In "Writing American Fiction" Roth asked why all of our fictional heroes didn't "wind up in institutions like Holden Caulfield, or suicides like Seymour Glass" (p. 226). And leaving the investigation of contemporary social life to the *amor-vincit-omnia* boys, he said in the same essay, "Would indeed be unfortunate, for it would be somewhat like leaving sex to the pornographers, where again there is more to what is happening than first meets the eye" (p. 231). *Portnoy's Complaint* finally grew out of four projects that Roth worked on between 1962 and 1967. Through these four projects the bare bones of the folkloric materials his students had presented to him, the psychiatric setting, and the sexual subject matter gradually coalesced to form the vision and voice of his novel. He traces this process in a 1974 essay appropriately entitled "In Response to Those Correspondents, Students and Interviewers Who Have Asked Me: 'How Did You Come to Write That Book, Anyway?' "

Each of the abandoned projects, as he now sees it, was "a building block for what was to come," but each "was abandoned in turn because it emphasized to the exclusion of all else what eventually would become a strong element in *Portnoy's Complaint*, but in itself was less than the whole story." The first of these projects, begun a few months after the publication of *Letting Go* at the same time that he was working on *When She Was Good*, was a "dreamy, humorous manuscript of about two hundred pages titled *The Jewboy*, which treated growing up in Newark as a species of folklore." He ultimately found it "unsatisfying" because it "tended to cover over with a patina of 'charming' inventiveness whatever was genuinely troublesome to me and ... intimated much more than I knew how to examine or confront in a fiction" at that time (RM, p. 33). "Yet there were things that I liked and, when I abandoned the book, hated to lose: the graphic starkness with which the characters were presented and which accorded with my sense of what childhood had felt like; the jokey comedy and dialogues that had the air of vaudeville turns; and a few scenes I was fond of, like the grand finale where the Dickensian orphan-hero (first found in a shoebox by an aged *mohel* and circumcised, hair-raisingly, on the spot) runs away from his loving stepparents at age twelve and on ice skates sets off across a Newark lake after a little blond shiksa whose name, he thinks, is Thereal McCoy" (RM, p. 34).

The second project was a play called *The Nice Jewish Boy*, written between 1962 and 1964 with the help of a Ford Foundation grant in playwrighting and read as a workshop exercise at the American Place Theatre in 1964 with Dustin Hoffman in the title role. Like *Letting Go* and *When She Was Good*, *The Nice Jewish Boy* used realistic conventions which, to a certain extent, inhibited Roth's ability to explore the more fantastic elements of his character's "secret life." Though the play also had dialogue and comic touches he liked, he finally felt that "the whole enterprise lacked precisely the kind of inventive flair and emotional exuberance that had given *The Jewboy* whatever quality it had ... So: the struggle that was to be at the source of Alexander Portnoy's difficulties, and motivate his complaint, was in those early years of work so out of focus that all I could do was recapitulate his problem technically, telling first the dreamy and fantastic side of the story, then the story in more conventional terms and by relatively measured means" (p. 35).

Roth goes on to describe this dichotomy as "symptomatic" of Portnoy's dilemma. But, as "Reading Myself" makes clear, it is also symptomatic of the contending influences, allegiances, and aspirations that were at the heart of Roth's own *artistic* dilemma during this transitional period. How to join the fantastic and the real, the amoral and the moral, the language and humor of Jake the Snake and the moral thrust of James's art—these were the unresolved questions which Roth had to answer technically before *Portnoy's Complaint* could finally become a coherent artistic whole.

Writing *When She Was Good*—"with its unfiery prose, its puritanical, haunted heroine, its unrelenting concern with banality"—oppressed Roth's spirit, frustrated his imagination, and, according to Albert Goldman, even led him to talk of giving up his writing career entirely.[4] When he finally managed to complete it midway through 1967, he was "aching to write something extravagant and funny," to "get in touch with another side of" his talent (RM, p. 21). And the sense of freedom and relief he felt expressed itself in a third project, an uncensored monologue, "very foul indeed, beside which the fetid indiscretions of *Portnoy's Complaint* would appear to be the work of Louisa May Alcott" (RM, p. 36). Conceived as a lecture accompanied by a slideshow, it "consisted of full-color enlargements of the private parts, fore and aft, of the famous," accompanied by a running commentary. "It was blasphemous, mean, bizarre, scatological, tasteless, spirited, and largely out of timidity, I think, remained unfinished ... except that buried somewhere in the sixty or seventy pages were several thousand words on the subject of adolescent masturbation, a personal interlude by the lecturer, that seemed to me on rereading to be funny and true, and worth saving ..." (p. 36).

"Not that at that time," Roth continues, "I could have set out directly and consciously to write about masturbating and come up with anything so pointedly intimate as this. Rather it had required all the wildness and roughhousing—the *merriment*, which is how I experienced it—for me even to *get* to the subject. Knowing what I was writing about ... was simply unpublishable—a writer's hijinks that might just as well not see the light of day—is precisely what allowed me to relax my guard and go on at some length about the solitary activity that is so difficult to talk about and yet so near at hand. For me writing about the act had, at the outset at least, to be as secret as the act itself!" (RM, pp. 36–37).

At the same time that the redskin in Roth was so merrily at work trying to outdo Mark Twain's *1601* and his lecture on onanism—in the style of the literary comedians and comic lecturers of the nineteenth-century's lyceums and chautauquas—the paleface began a fourth project.

Simply titled *Portrait of the Artist*, this manuscript of several hundred pages was a strongly autobiographical piece based on the experiences of his own Newark boyhood which was eventually transformed into parts of both *Portnoy's Complaint* and *My Life as a Man*. "By sticking closely to the facts," Roth writes, "and narrowing the gap between the actual and the invented, I thought I could somehow come up with a story that would go to the heart of the particular Jewish ethos I'd come out of. But the more I stuck to the actual and the strictly autobiographical, the less resonant and revealing the narrative became" (p. 37).

However, in *Portrait of the Artist* he invented as upstairs neighbors to the central character a family named Portnoy—a composite portrait, Roth tells us, loosely based on the families in his neighborhood—who had a son named Jack, Jr. Gradually the Portnoys began to take over his story, and as they did Roth realized that the family they were coming to resemble most was not any of the particular ones he had known as a boy, but the folkloric one his students had described in their fiction at Iowa. As he "played" with this material, he chose not to treat the folklore *as* folklore—as he had done in *The Jewboy* by "emphasizing the fantastical, the charming, the quaint, the magical and the 'poetic'"—but instead, "under the sway of the autobiographical impulse that had launched *Portrait of the Artist*, I began to ground the mythological in the recognizable, the verifiable, the historical. Though they might *de rive* from Mt. Olympus (by way of Mt. Sinai) these Portnoys were going to live in a Newark and at a time and in a way I could vouch for from observation and experience" (pp. 39–40).

Roth finally abandoned *Portrait of the Artist*, as he had earlier abandoned *The Jewboy*, *The Nice Jewish Boy*, and the slideshow—but dialogue, scenes, and characters from all four of these projects became a part of *Portnoy's Complaint*. And the approach to his materials which he had decided upon while writing *Portrait of the Artist*—grounding the mythological and fantastic in the recognizable, verifiable, and historical—was one that he would use in *Our Gang*, *The Great American Novel*, *The Breast*, and *My Life as a Man*, as well as in *Portnoy's Complaint*.

He recast parts of *Portrait of the Artist* into a story he published at about this time, "A Jewish Patient Begins His Analysis" (the indefinite article suggests the material's folkloric roots), which eventually became the first part of *Portnoy's Complaint*. A relatively restrained and realistic first-person narrative, the story was presented as the childhood reminiscence of one Alexander Portnoy delivered as a prepsychoanalytic monologue. There was nothing spectacular or radical about either the content or the style: Roth had used the psychoanalytic situation before—notably in *Letting Go*, where Libby Herz visited a Dr. *Lumin* in the hope that he would shed some light on her problems, in some of the early drafts of *When She Was Good*, and in the 1963 story "Psychoanalytic Special"—and, as Theodore Solotaroff has pointed out, the story's revelations about the tensions in Jewish family life were "hardly news" either. "Nor did a psychoanalytic setting seem necessary to elicit the facts of Jack Portnoy's constipation or Sophie's use of a breadknife to make little Alex eat."[5]

But the story was a crucial breakthrough, nevertheless, a beginning because "strictly speaking, the writing of *Portnoy's Complaint* began with discovering Portnoy's voice—or more accurately his mouth—and discovering along with it, the listening ear: the silent Dr. Spielvogel. The psychoanalytic monologue ... was to furnish the means by which I thought I might convincingly draw together the fantastic elements of *The Jewboy*, and the realistic documentation of *Portrait of the Artist* and *The Nice Jewish Boy*. And a means too of legitimizing the obscene preoccupations of the untitled slideshow on the subject of the sexual parts" (RM, p. 41). Shortly after "A Jewish Patient Begins His Analysis" was published in *Esquire* (April 1967), "Whacking Off" and "The Jewish Blues" appeared. And from the very first sentence of "Whacking Off"—"Then came adolescence—half my waking life spent locked behind the bathroom door, firing my wad down the toilet bowl, or into the soiled clothes in the laundry hamper, or *splat*, up against the medicine-chest mirror ..."—the need for the psychoanalytic setting became clear.

In each of his earlier fictions Roth had attempted to find the most effective means to convey the feel of our cockeyed world, the quality of the social being's private life, the forces at work in those public and private worlds as a particular, representative individual perceived them. In *Portnoy's Complaint* he found a new, perhaps ideal, way of telling that tale. His desire to find the "aesthetically appropriate vessel" to express that feel fully and originally—and to express the interrelationship of fantasy and reality which he saw as central to it—was a central factor in his decisions to scrap each of the projects which paved the way for *Portnoy's Complaint*. *The Jewboy* and the slideshow were too fantastic; *The Nice Jewish Boy* and *Portrait of the Artist* were too realistic. The fantastic nature of the former two undermined their credibility as felt life; the realistic conventions of the latter two militated against their adequately capturing that feel and its confusion of the realms of fantasy and reality. Through the device of the psychoanalytic monologue Roth managed to combine the best features of both approaches.

The advantages of this stylistic choice are numerous. The psychoanalytic setting provides a realistic justification for Portnoy's vehement soul-baring and finger-pointing, for his use of words and images which would be unacceptable in a more public context, and also for his emphasis on sexual memories. It also provides him with an audience, essential since Portnoy is both analysand and performer, character and author in his own seriocomic tale. The dramatic monologue which this setting provokes has the effect of locking us into Portnoy's vision of the world; and his viewpoint is unqualified by any other (until the punch line), reveals as no other could *his* interpretation of the burden of his reality. Through the monologue we learn what reality feels like to him and, in the process, we are forced (as he is) constantly to question where the line between objective reality and his pathological fantasies lies. We are, in other words, forced to consider the interpenetration of reality and fantasy in *a* life, and are, by extension, made conscious of the same interpenetration in *our* lives. The monologue form also permits digressions, exaggerations, repetitions, descriptions, and oversimplifications which, while vital to our understanding of Portnoy's character and psychology, would be less acceptable in another narrative context.

Critical discussion of *Portnoy's Complaint* has focused almost exclusively on its ethnic dimensions, but it is also important to recognize that Roth's novel is very much in the American grain in spite of its Jewish specifics. Its essential conflicts, its themes, its characters, its language and comic technique all link it to classic works of the American imagination, works to which it is finally related like a foul-mouthed nephew with a Yiddish accent. Perhaps nowhere is the novel's distinctly American character more marked than in its style—the concrete result of those four abandoned projects—and in its use of that style to achieve freedom of consciousness and expression for both its author and its hero.

"The classic American writers," Richard Poirier argued in *A World Elsewhere: The Place of Style in American Literature*, "try through their style to temporarily free the hero (and the reader) from systems, to free them from the pressures of time, biology, economics, and from the social forces which are ultimately the undoing of American heroes and quite often their creators. What distinguishes American heroes of this kind ... is that there is nothing within the real world, or in the systems which dominate it, that can possibly satisfy their aspirations ... they tend to substitute themselves for the world."[6]

The heroes of *Goodbye, Columbus*, *Letting Go*, and *When She Was Good*, as we have already seen, were plagued by just such unsatisfiable aspirations to freedom, just such inclinations toward solipsism—and so is Portnoy: "Nothing but self. Locked up in me!" he moans. But in *Portnoy's Complaint* the style and form of the narrative itself work to achieve such freedoms as well, in a way that they do not in the earlier books. Although Poirier does not discuss Roth's work, his comments can illuminate the connection between Roth's use of style in *Portnoy's Complaint* and the novel's profoundly American character. There is a parallel, Poirier observed, between "the writer, struggling to express himself in language," as Roth had in his abandoned projects, "and the defiant hero, contending with the recalcitrant materials of reality,"[7] as Portnoy does in his life and monologue. In *Portnoy's Complaint* and the major works which succeed it, that parallel—implicit from the beginning in Roth's preference for first-person narrators who shape their own retrospective stories—becomes increasingly more explicit as the identities of "artist" and hero merge. That process culminates in *My Life as a Man*.

The artistic defiance which Poirier saw as the source of the styles of the classic American writers manifests itself in characteristics which also mark *Portnoy's Complaint*. Our writers, Poirier says, try in the face of overpowering social realities to create environments in their fiction that "might allow some longer existence to the hero's momentary expansion of consciousness";[8] in the face of similarly overpowering realities, Roth uses the psychoanalytic session to provide the occasion for a similar expansion. To Poirier, American fictions are characterized by "extravagances of language" which are "an exultation in the exercise of consciousness momentarily set free";[9] Roth told George Plimpton that Portnoy is "obscene because he wants to be saved" (RM, p. 19), and Portnoy's use of obscenity is an attempt to break free from the hold of the conditioning which he is struggling to overcome. The monologue rather than the dialogue, according to Poirier, has been the most congenial form for our classic writers, as it has been for Roth. American writers are dedicated to the effort to liberate consciousness—an effort with which Roth allied himself early in his career—and their concerns have produced a long line of heroes who are, Poirier observed, cast as liberators in their fictional worlds; as Assistant Commissioner for the City of New York Commission on Human Opportunity, Portnoy, like Hawkeye and Huck, is assigned such a liberator's role. Portnoy, like Holden Caulfield or Isabel Archer, is a "stock character" who enacts what Poirier calls "the American hero's effort ... to express the natural self rather than merely to represent, in speech and manner, some preordained social type."[10] The environment American writers have characteristically struggled to create through their language is, again according to Poirier, one in which "the inner consciousness of the hero can freely express itself, an environment in which he can sound publicly what he privately is"—or thinks he is;[11] and that is exactly the kind of verbal space which Roth struggled to create in *The Jewboy*, *The Nice Jewish Boy*, and *Portrait of the Artist*—a linguistic environment he finally achieved in *Portnoy's Complaint*.

This perennial effort to free the hero and his consciousness from social strictures of heredity and environment is, of course, inevitably an unsuccessful one. Since the "world elsewhere," the "city of words" which our authors seek to create, is one which must be wholly built of language, the complete freedom which the author and his defiant hero seek constantly eludes them both. To communicate verbally is to use conventions and, to a certain extent, to be bound by them. In recognition of that ultimate failure of freedom, Poirier pointed out, "American writers are at some point always forced to return their characters to prison. They return them to 'reality' from environments where they have been allowed most 'nakedly' to exist, environments created by various kinds of stylistic ingenuity";[12] and so in *Portnoy's Complaint* Dr. Spielvogel must have the last word—a punch line promising that writers' failures to achieve the freedom they seek are never complete if they can create that expansion of consciousness even fleetingly. And in that effort, writers as different as Melville, James, and Roth are "quite willing, for themselves and for their heroes, to accept the appearance of failure in the interests of this free exercise of consciousness"[13]—an assertion which helps to explain the artistic pressures which produced *Our Gang*, *The Great American Novel*, and *The Breast* as well as *Portnoy's Complaint*.

Roth's exercise of style as a means to freedom of consciousness and expression, then, is in the American grain; and so is the subject which that style is meant to expose and explore—Portnoy's *complaint*. For like his American forebears, Alexander Portnoy wants most of all to be free—of his past and its burdens, of the weight of a culturally formed conscience and consciousness. Like Ahab, Huck, and Holden, like the heroes and heroines of *Goodbye, Columbus*, *Letting Go*, and *When She Was Good*, he seeks impossibly total satisfactions, impossibly complete freedoms from his environment, and lashes out at the world where he cannot find them. And reaction to his particular experience of the traditional American conflicts—of self vs. society, freedom vs. responsibility, pleasure vs. duty, self-definition vs. societal definition—is to pursue equally traditional American dreams of escape.

Part of him, for example, longs for the comforts of the "old agrarian dream" of escaping back to nature and the "good and simple life" he sees in Iowa and Vermont (PC, p. 186); but instead of capturing that idyllic world beyond social pressures—as Huck did (for a while) on his raft, and John Hawkes's Skipper does on his floating Caribbean isle—Portnoy feels compelled to reject it, manages only to soil the virgin land with his misspent semen. He longs nostalgically for the simplicity and male camaraderie of the softball diamond ("Oh, to be a center fielder, a center fielder—nothing more") and the Turkish bath (a habitat where he could be natural, "A place without *goyim* and women"); but he is inexorably drawn to the forbidden *shiksa*. Where Hawkeye, Rip, and Huck—heroes of another century—could "light out for the territory" and thereby temporarily elude civilization's grasp, for contemporary heroes like Holden and Alex there is no longer any unspoiled frontier to light out *for*—except, perhaps, the internal frontier of madness. So Holden wanders frustrated through a grimy and debased urban wilderness and longs to be a catcher in a field of rye where innocence, not hypocrisy, will rule. And Alex reverses the nineteenth-century vectors, flees to Europe (as Paul Herz had thought of doing and Gabe Wallach had done) in his desperate search for an escape route. But the Old World decadence of Rome and Greece only produces further degradation and guilt; and exile to Israel—the modern American Jew's romantic vision of the last frontier—renders him guilty and impotent. Like Holden, Alex cannot escape his civilization's discontents through physical flight because he has already internalized them. He is a victim of what Tony Tanner has characterized as the American hero's worst nightmare—conditioning. And he can find no escape from it except obscenity and the psychiatrist's couch—and even there he is not really free.

As sociologist Alan Segal observed in the *British Journal of Sociology* in 1971, the central irony of Portnoy's plight is that the very nature of his rebellion against his parents and his past—the primary element in his character, the source of his most extreme behavior—is clear evidence of the extent to which his character and actions are determined by exactly the values he is trying to escape. His mode of rebellion against social conditioning, in other words, is totally conditioned. Segal explains it this way: "Portnoy's dilemma is that he faces two alternatives almost equally unsatisfying and untenable: one, that he comply with his parents' wishes, thus getting them off his back but incurring his own permanent displeasure; two, that he pursue short-lived and specific satisfactions which involve the constant complaints of his parents and which, he fears, will lead to his public unmasking as some kind of sexual pervert. He has determinedly turned his back on the former possibility, is compelled to pursue the latter, yet yearns for a third alternative which is not forthcoming."

More importantly, Segal perceives that "Portnoy is trapped because he can only express his desires for independence from the Jewish world against [the WASP world] and in terms of the Jewish scheme of things.... Portnoy's complaint is this: in order to overcome his condition he must shed the Jewish identity with which he has been imbued. But this would involve the undermining of the channel of his independence—sex with the *goyim* on a compulsive scale—which is ironically both his present emancipation from the Jewish world and his imprisonment in its scheme of things."[14] Like Gabe Wallach and Paul Herz, he is more his parents' son than even he realizes. Considering his antipathies, the ultimate irony of his monologue is how often he sounds and acts exactly like the mother he attacks with such verbal gusto.

Portnoy mocks his mother for complaining that she was always "too good," yet he honestly believes that "I am too good too, Mother, I too am moral to the bursting point—just like you!" (p. 124). The books in his parents' home, he says, were chiefly books "written by Sophie Portnoy, each an addition to the famous series of hers entitled, *You Know Me, I'll Try Anything Once*" (p. 93). He is also the hero of his own melodramatic series, *Portnoy's Complaint* or "*My Modern Museum of Gripes and Grievances.*" Sophie's tales all show a flair for self-dramatization, and in her epic she casts herself as "a woman on the very frontiers of experience, some doomed dazzling combination of Marie Curie, Anna Karenina, and Amelia Earhart" (p. 93). He sees *himself* as Oedipus, Cordelia, Raskolnikov, and Daedalus—and as Alexander the Great, Alex in Wonderland, Joseph K., John Lindsay's Profumo, and Duke Snider (as well as Al Port, Al Parsons, Alexander Porte-Noir, Alton Peterson, Anthony Peruta, "Big Boy," "The Knight on the White Steed," and the son in a Jewish joke). In his story as in hers, "nothing is ever said once-nothing!" (p. 99).

She overdramatizes, speaks in capital letters, exaggerates *ad absurdum*: "Alex ... *tateleh*, it [the effect of eating French fries] begins with diarrhea, but do you know how it ends? With a sensitive stomach like yours, do you know how it finally ends? *Wearing a plastic bag to* do your business in!" (p. 32). But he has refined the family tradition of verbal overkill to an art.

Sophie and Jack blame all their troubles on the *goyim*; Portnoy blames all his trouble on *them*. He ridicules his mother for feeling superior to her neighbors because she gives the black housekeeper a whole can of tuna for lunch—"and I'm not talking *dreck*, either. I'm talking Chicken of the Sea, Alex ... even if it is 2 for 49"—and then runs scalding water "over the dish from which the cleaning lady has just eaten lunch, alone like a leper" (p. 13). But he is guilty of far greater hypocrisies. Though he prides himself on his position as Assistant Commissioner for Human Opportunity—a post which charges him to "encourage equality of treatment, to prevent discrimination, to foster mutual understanding and respect"—he denies all of these ideals in every one of his personal relationships. He treats the women in his life like objects, goes so far as to deprive them of their names and refer to them as

The Pilgrim, The Pumpkin, The Monkey, and the Jewish Pumpkin. He rages at his parents, "*I will not treat any human being* (outside my family) *as inferior*!" Though he describes his affair with The Pilgrim as "something nice a son once did for his dad," from the evidence in his monologue there is little to suggest that the adult Alex *ever* did *anything* nice for his dad—or for anyone else close to him. His mother would have a "conniption" if he were to marry a *shiksa*; and in spite of his protestations that his religion means nothing to him, when The Pumpkin, whom he is planning to marry at the time, says that she sees no reason to convert to Judaism, the vestiges of religious pride cause him to reject her just as his mother would.

In spite of his bitter resentment of his mother's disciplinary measures against him when he was a child, their views of just reward and punishment hardly turn out to be very far apart. Her sense of values is so deeply ingrained in him that the behavior of his two sexually knowledgeable adolescent friends, Mandel and Smolka, was adequately explained for him—as it would have been for his mother and Roth's students at Iowa—by the fact that one was "*a boy without a father*" and the other had "*a Mother who works*." When he learns that Mandel is now a salesman and Smolka is now a professor at Princeton—Princeton!—Alex is flabbergasted. "Why they're supposed to be in jail—or the gutter. They didn't do their homework, damn it!" (p. 176).

Though the irony which these parallels point up is not totally apparent to Portnoy, he does sense the futility of his attempts at rebellion. His obscenity is both a product and a symptom of his awareness of his condition. Raised in Sophie and Jack Portnoy's home, he is fully aware of the overwhelming power of *words*. He knows, for instance, that in the right context the word "cider" can cause tears, and that the word "CANCER" can cause hearts to stop and prayers to rise from the throats of adolescent atheists. He knows that the words "Jew" and "*goyim*" can define and circumscribe a world, that "love" can smother and "fear" can debilitate and warp. He knows that some words ("conniption," "aggravation," "spatula") seem to be Jewish words, and that using the *wrong* words can ruin his chances with the *shiksas* at Irvington Park (or Mary Jane Reed's chances with him).

So Alex is anything but a "hip" young Sixties man who uses obscenity almost unconsciously as an indication of his liberation from the older mores and taboos. *To Portnoy obscenity is an achievement*—and a weapon. He uses it *because*, like his parents and the society whose sexual conventions he is struggling so hard to violate, *he* thinks it is "dirty" too. He knows that the words he uses offend; they are meant to. He is obscene because he believes that through language he can break down the battlements of his own moral defenses—defenses which have been imposed on him by his society. But since he *has* internalized his Jewish and American societies' values, by talking and acting "dirty" all he really manages to do is increase the guilt which binds and tortures him. The guiltier he feels, the more frustrated he becomes; the more frustrated he becomes, the more vehement is his obscenity and his sexual promiscuity. Until finally he is literally speechless, caught in the whirlpool of this vicious circle, only able to express himself through an anguished howl of pain at his condition.

"Why must you use that word all the time?" Portnoy's Jewish Pumpkin asks two pages before that closing howl (p. 270); and "Why he must," Roth told Plimpton, "is what the book is all about" (RM, p. 19). It is finally fair to say of the "bad" language in *Portnoy's Complaint* what James M. Cox has said of the "bad" language in *Huckleberry Finn*: it is a perfect expression of the conflict in the book.[15] That language places *Portnoy's Complaint* in the tradition of native American humor, and that central conflict indicates his relationship to the characters of Roth's earlier and later fiction.

The interpenetration of reality and fantasy has been one of native American humor's most persistent subjects; obscenity has always been one of the staples of its techniques. Although the discussion of *The Great American Novel* which appears below has been designed to detail the techniques of the nineteenth-century humorists which Roth has drawn on in *all* his comic fictions, since the obscenity of *Portnoy's Complaint* is so pronounced and so often lamented its literary precedents warrant brief comment here as well. Aristophanes, Chaucer, Rabelais, Swift, James Joyce, and D. H. Lawrence aside, Roth's language is clearly part of an American tradition represented by George Washington Harris's *Sut Lovingood's Yarns*—published in 1867, exactly one hundred years before "Whacking Off"—and the other major works of the humor of the Old Southwest. As Walter Blair has pointed out, these humorists were all "consciously or unconsciously, local colorists, eager to impart the flavor of their particular locality,"[16] just as Roth's novel imparts the flavor of his boyhood Newark. If Portnoy is a foul-mouthed nephew with a Yiddish accent, Sut is one of his uncles, and Simon Suggs, Mike Fink, Davy Crockett, Jim Doggett, and Pap Finn are all members of the same raucous, rough-and-tumble family.

Native American humor has *always* been in bad taste. Like the oral tales which are such a decisive factor in that humor's form and content—whether the tales are exchanged in Jake the Snake's Newark candy store or Pat Nash's Tennessee grocery—*Portnoy's Complaint* is marked by its homespun diction, its word coinage, its informal but rhythmical sentences, by onomatopoeia and assorted similes, metaphors, hyperboles, synecdoches, and other ludicrous imagery. As Blair has noted, these oral tales "typically mingle the circumstantial and the precise with the outrageous and the imprecise. Though meticulous about dates, dimensions, and techniques, the storyteller unashamedly introduces men and animals that are impossible monsters."[17] Blair's comments are echoed in Roth's description of the approach to his materials which he discovered while writing *Portrait of the Artist.* And this combination of realism and fantasy explains why Sophie Portnoy is no more a wholly realistic description of a Jewish mother than the Big Bear of Arkansas was of a real bear. Roth makes Portnoy the quintessential son of a quintessential Jewish family, gives that mythological son mythological parents, and then squarely locates them behind the venetian blinds and bathroom doors of a recognizably historical Jewish community.

As mythological personages, exaggerations of common characters, the Portnoys are a composite of many of Roth's other, more realistic, characters. Jack Portnoy, who pounds the Harlem pavement trying to sell insurance, is much like Leo Patimkin, Paul Herz's father, and the fathers of Nathan Zuckerman and Peter Tarnopol; his more successful brother, Hymie, is like Leo's older brother Ben. Mordecai Wallach is ruled by a wife who is "Very Nice to People"; Jack is dominated by a wife who is "too good." Like Mordecai, Jack suffers from chronic constipation, but both men's problems—like both their sons' verbal diarrhea—are a product of their "sympathies," not their sympathetic nervous systems.

Sophie Portnoy and Mary Jane Reed are also familiar. Like *Letting Go* and *My Life as a Man*, *Portnoy's Complaint* focuses on the women who are central to the hero's dilemma. Like Neil's Aunt Gladys and Roy Bassart's mother, Alice, Sophie is a contemporary Mrs. Partington or Aunt Polly, dedicated to overprotecting and controlling her boy in the name of religion and civilization. Mary Jane, like Libby and Lucy, Martha Reganhart, Lydia Jorgenson Ketterer, Maureen Johnson Tarnopol, and Helen Baird, is an all-American *shiksa* who is both predator and prey of the Jewish lover she is drawn to. Like *When She Was Good*'s, *Portnoy's Complaint*'s subject is "a grown child's fury against long-standing authorities believed" by its hero to have misused their power (RM, p. 9).

Like all of Roth's hero's, Portnoy is torn between the redemptive impulses of the moralist and the less-worthy impulses of the self-indulgent libidinous slob. Paul and Gabe's conflicting imperatives are his, and so are Kepesh, Zuckerman and Tarnopol's tendencies to self-dramatization. Like them Portnoy feels called upon to redeem the neurotic woman he is involved with; like them, he both shuns and covets that role. He is, like all of Roth's heroes, "locked up in self," struggling to come to terms with the burden of his past, to submerge the pleasure principle to the reality principle and emerge from the process whole.

Albert Goldman summed up the book's significance when he said that Roth has "explored the Jewish family myth more profoundly than any of his predecessors, shining his light into all its corners and realizing its ultimate potentiality as an archetype of contemporary life." For, in spite of its Jewish specifics, "*Portnoy's Complaint* boldly transcends ethnic categories. Focusing its image of man through the purest and craziest of stereotypes, the book achieves a vision that is, paradoxically, sane, whole and profound."[18] And profoundly American.

NOTES

1. See Guerard, "Notes on the rhetoric of anti-realist fiction," *Tri-Quarterly* 30 (Spring 1974): 12, and Dickstein, "Black Humor and History: Fiction in the Sixties," *Partisan Review* 43 (Spring 1976): 191–94 (reprinted in his *Gates of Eden: American Culture in the Sixties*). The book's impact on the cultural scene is suggested by the fact that, in a survey of prominent intellectuals who were asked to name those who had influenced their opinions on cultural matters—a survey conducted in 1970, one year after *Portnoy's Complaint* appeared—Roth and Saul Bellow were the only fictionists listed among the "top" choices. See Charles Kadushin, *The American Intellectual Elite* (Boston, 1974), pp. 28–32.

2. "The Poet," in Brooks Atkinson, ed., *The Complete Essays of Ralph Waldo Emerson* (New York, 1940), p. 397.

3. "American Fiction," p. 248.

4. For a discussion of Roth's frustrations with *When She Was Good*, see Albert Goldman, "Wild Blue Shocker: *Portnoy's Complaint*," *Life*, February 7, 1969, pp. 62–63.

5. "The Journey of Philip Roth," p. 70.

6. Richard Poirier, *A World Elsewhere* (New York, 1966), p. 5.

7. Ibid., p. 6.

8. Ibid., p. 15.

9. Ibid., p. 7.

10. Ibid., p. 27.

11. Ibid., p. 35.

12. Ibid., p. 29.

13. Ibid., p. 7.

14. "*Portnoy's Complaint* and the Sociology of Literature," *British Journal of Sociology* (September 1971): 260, 267.

15. "Mark Twain: The Height of Humor," in Rubin, ed., *The Comic Imagination in American Literature*, p. 144.

16. Walter Blair, *Native American Humor*, rev. ed. (San Francisco, 1960), p. 64.

17. "A Man's Voice, Speaking," in Harry Levin, ed., *Veins of Humor*, Harvard English Studies 3 (Cambridge, 1972), p. 197.

18. "Wild Blue Shocker," p. 58F.

SAM B. GIRGUS

Portnoy's Prayer: Philip Roth and the American Unconscious

In his extraordinary essay on 'The Unconscious' (1915), Freud writes:

> An instinct can never become an object of consciousness—only the idea that represents the instinct can. Even in the unconscious, moreover, an instinct cannot be represented otherwise than by an idea. If the instinct did not attach itself to an idea or manifest itself as an effective state, we could know nothing about it. When we nevertheless speak of an unconscious instinctual impulse or of a repressed instinctual impulse, the looseness of phraseology is a harmless one. We can only mean an instinctual impulse the ideational representative of which is unconscious, for nothing else comes into consideration.[1]

Freud's simple description of the difference between the conscious and the unconscious in terms of the distinction between ideas, which relate to consciousness, and instincts, which are outside of this psychic realm, represents Freud's genius for theoretical construction. His concept of an 'ideational representative' of instinctual impulses constitutes the key, as Paul Ricoeur indicates, to understanding 'how the unconscious can be reintegrated into the realm of meaning by a new interrelation—"within" the unconscious

From *Reading Philip Roth*, edited by Asher Z. Milbauer and Donald G. Watson.

itself—between instinct (*Trieb*) and idea (*Vorstellung*): an instinct can be represented (*repräsentiert*) in the unconscious only by an idea (*Vorstellung*).'[2]

In addition, this association of ideas and the unconscious also helps to explain how the unconscious partakes in the transmission of cultural ideas and values. Accordingly, for Juliet Mitchell, the unconscious comprises the centre of the process of the individual's integration into and adaptation to culture. For Mitchell one of the great contributions of Freudian psychoanalysis concerns its elucidation of the involvement of the unconscious in the interaction between the individual and culture. She writes, 'In each man's unconscious lies all mankind's "ideas" of his history; a history that cannot start afresh with each individual but must be acquired and contributed to over time. Understanding the laws of the unconscious thus amounts to a start in understanding how ideology functions, how we acquire and live the ideas and laws within which we must exist.'[3] The concept of 'ideational representatives' that enlightens the darkness of the unconscious also provides a format for incorporating and relating to the ideas that form culture. The unconscious relates to ideology and the ideas of culture in part because it knows itself through ideas. This drama of the unconscious in culture that Freud scripted and Mitchell discusses constitutes a crucial aspect of the significance of Philip Roth's *Portnoy's Complaint*. When poor Alexander Portnoy sent forth his extended whine in 1969 from the couch of his silent psychoanalyst, Dr Spielvogel, most readers and critics heard it as a grumbling and *kvetching* from the interior of the Jewish-American soul, a psychic ghetto of unconscious fears and insecurities. In retrospect, however, it can be argued that in writing *Portnoy*, Roth was mining more than a seemingly bottomless pit of Jewish angst. He was, in fact, dealing in a new way with questions of sexuality and the unconscious that have been central to American literature and culture. While his work maintains a long tradition of seeing love and ideology in the context of the making of American culture, Roth also adds a new chapter to the history of the American unconscious. He seeks to counter the forces of repression and guilt and to answer fears of dependence and weakness with an alternative ideology of understanding and enlightenment. Never proffering psychological placebos that dissimulate the guilt, fear, and anxiety of the human psyche, refusing to sentimentalise or minimise the inherent difficulty of achieving love and happiness, Roth, nevertheless, advances the contemporary battle for liberation by dramatising the conflict of hidden and manifest psychological forces.

Portnoy's Complaint constituted a breakthrough on many different levels and directions. Roth was propelled by Portnoy to a new plateau of international recognition and fame. Whether you liked the novel or not, its instant popularity established Roth as a literary celebrity. It gave him the success of a John Updike or William Styron. In addition, the novel also seemed to break new ground for the genre of the Jewish-American novel. Already under attack for his critical perspective of Jewish subjects and characters, Roth's treatment in *Portnoy* of the domineering mother and the self-effacing father and the galaxy of Jewish fears, prejudices, and insecurities pushes his penchant for social parody and black humour to a new extreme. What to Roth was the exposure of self-assimilation, appeared to others to be the blatant distortion and exaggeration of self-hating anti-Semitism and the vulgarisation of a deep tradition of authentic liberalism and social commitment. Also, the novel's uninhibited burlesque of such sexual subjects as masturbation and oral sex and its explicit descriptions of bathroom scenes and bodily functions certainly entailed a dramatic extension of the boundaries of acceptable taste.

At the same time, Roth's body of work, including *Portnoy's Complaint*, occupies an important place in a vital tradition of Jewish-American writers and thinkers who are deeply intrigued and concerned about the meaning of the American idea and experience. Ranging from Abraham Cahan and Louis Brandeis through Anzia Yezierska and Henry Roth to Saul Bellow, Johanna Kaplan, E. L. Doctorow, and Norman Mailer, this group of writers and intellectuals revivifies the rhetorical and narrative structures of the myth and ideology of America. Often considering the symbol and ideal of America in terms of redemption, renewal, and revolution, they write as New Jeremiahs to awaken individual and national conscience and to modernise the symbols and metaphors of the American idea. As writers of fiction and literature, they transformed the modern novel. *Portnoy's Complaint* exemplifies this new novelistic form. At its core in the figure of Portnoy is the new 'hero of thought' who embodies the consciousness of his times. Other aspects of the novel include the setting of the urban wilderness, the quest for upward mobility and success as well as moral affirmation, the psychological theme of anxiety, and the sociological motif of alienation.[4]

However, one other major element or theme in his new narrative structure is especially important in demonstrating how *Portnoy's Complaint* relates to the development of the American unconscious. This is the theme of the *shikse*, or Gentile love-goddess. In *Portnoy* the psychological and social role of the *shikse* establishes a vital thread from the unconscious desires of the hero to a crucial aspect of American culture as perceiving America in sexual and feminine terms. From its beginnings America was seen, as Annette Kolodny says, as a feminine pastoral image. While the land was female, men were hunters or yeoman farmers. For Kolodny these universal symbols achieve a special significance in America because here such symbols actually entered history and personal experience. In *The Lay of the Land* she writes,

> If the initial impulse to experience the New World landscape, not merely as an object of domination and exploitation, but as a maternal 'garden' receiving and nurturing human children, was a reactivation of what we now recognize as universal mythic wishes, it had one radically different facet: *this* paradise really existed.... Only in America has the entire process remained within historical memory, giving Americans the unique ability to see themselves as the willful exploiters of the very land that had once promised an escape from necessities.

Following Henry Nash Smith's *The Virgin Land*, Kolodny argues that from our earliest history such figures as William Byrd of Virginia and Robert Beverley of North Carolina devised 'a uniquely American pastoral vocabulary' the heart of which dramatised 'a yearning to know and to respond to the landscape as feminine'.[5]

Kolodny provides many examples of early thinking of the New World, and of America in particular, as a woman to be possessed. William Byrd saw in the landscape 'a Single Mountain [in the Blue Ridge range], very much resembling a Woman's breast' and a 'Ledge that stretch't away to the N. E. ... rising in the Shape of a Maiden's Breast'; Walter Raleigh portrayed Guiana as 'a country that hath yet her maydenhead, never sackt, burned, nor wrought'; for John Smith the New England coast aroused intimations of a New Eden because of 'her treasures having neuer beene opened, nor her originalls wasted, consumed, nor abused'; the rebellious and profligate Thomas Morton believed America to be a '*Paradise* with all her Virgin Beauties', while John Hammond expressed a more chivalrous attitude in his desire to protect the innocence of 'The Two Fruitful Sisters Virginia and Maryland'. Since one may consider these statements as sixteenth- and seventeenth-century rhetorical exaggerations that do not represent modern attitudes, it should be noted that expansion into the West was explained throughout our history in similar metaphors. Thus, those who went to the unsettled territory of Wisconsin were promised to see that 'the land foams with creamy milk, and the hollow trees trickle with wild honey'.[6]

Portnoy's treatment of the *shikses* in his life develops this motif in American literature and culture. The Gentile women in the novel are not merely Americans; they embody America. As such they become vessels for the expression of Portnoy's deepest desires and insecurities. He recalls that his first encounter with such girls occurs during the winter ice-skating on the lake in Irvington Park, a town that neighbours Portnoy's 'safe and friendly Jewish quarter'.[7] He writes,

> But *shikses*, ah, the *shikse's* are something else again. Between the smell of damp sawdust and wet wool in the overheated boathouse, and the sight of their fresh cold blond hair spilling out of their kerchiefs and caps, I am ecstatic.... How do they get so gorgeous, so healthy, so *blond*? My contempt for what they believe in is more than neutralized by my adoration of the way they look, the way they move and laugh and speak—the lives they must lead behind those *goyische* curtains. (pp. 144–5).

For Portnoy the beauty of these wonderful creatures is enhanced by their surface representation of a whole culture. He says,

> These people are the *Americans*, Doctor.... O America! America! It may have been gold in the streets to my grandparents, it may have been a chicken in every pot to my father and mother, but to me, a child whose earliest movie memories are of Ann Rutherford and Alice Faye, America is a *shikse* nestling under your arms whispering love love love love! (pp. 145–6)

Portnoy's prayer for love from an American *shikse* is not so far removed from the mixture of love and belief that mystified the vision of earlier admirers and explorers of the wonder of America. Roth's blend of humour, exaggeration, parody, and pathos renders a Jewish version of this American phenomenon. Through the *shikse* motif, Roth relates sexuality to culture. He particularises the process of how the unconscious works in placing the individual within culture. The sexual basis of Portnoy's fascination for America demonstrates how the unconscious factors of guilt, ambivalence, and fear that are usually associated with sexuality also play an important part in the acquisition of culture itself. Thus, Portnoy combines his most extreme sexual fantasy with his desire to be a real American by conjuring up the name of 'the real McCoy' (p. 127) for any imaginary *shikse* who unites pure lust with pure American features. She is the real thing in terms of both her sexual abandonment and her cultural identity. As he schemes to pick up *shikse* skaters, he also contrives new names for himself, thus seeking an identity that will reciprocate hers. He thinks to himself, "'Portnoy, yes, it's an old French name, a corruption of *porte noir*, meaning black door or gate. Apparently in the Middle Ages in France the door to our family manor house was painted ..." et cetera and so forth. No, no, they will hear the *oy* at the end, and the jig will be up' (p. 149). When he finally manages the pick-up he thinks he will need to 'speak absolutely perfect English. Not a word of Jew in it' (p. 164).

He introduces himself to the girl as Alton C. Peterson but is so obsessed with 'what I'll say when she asks about the middle of my face and what happened to it (old hockey injury? Fell off my horse while playing polo after church one Sunday morning—too many sausages for breakfast, ha ha ha!)' that he loses his footing and goes 'hurtling forward onto the frost bitten ground, chipping one front tooth and smashing the bony protrusion at the top of my tibia' (p. 164). The wounds, clearly, are psychic, guilt over the denial of his father, a form of death wish. Also his Gatsby-like fantasy indicates a fear that his love will not be strong enough to allow for his transformation by 'this perfect, perfect-stranger, who is as smooth and shiny and cool as custard, will kiss me—raising up one shapely calf behind her—and my nose and my name will have become as nothing' (p. 151).

Portnoy's pattern of relating sexuality, the unconscious, and America persists in his subsequent relationships with women. There is Kay Campbell, the All-American 'Pumpkin'—so named because of 'her pigmentation and the size of her can' (p. 216)—who brings Portnoy home from Antioch for a Thanksgiving dinner that anticipates the wonderful 'Grammy Hall' scene in Woody Allen's *Annie Hall*. Later, there is Sarah Abbot Maulsby, labelled 'The Pilgrim' because of her Yankee appearance, prestigious pedigree and élite social background. The inherent connection between the forces of the unconscious and sexuality and the incorporation of the ideas and forms of culture is especially clear in Portnoy's attitude toward Maulsby. Moreover, Portnoy's personality provides further demonstration of a Jewish version of the historic connection between sexuality and the making of American culture. Thus, for Portnoy sex with *shikses* constitutes a rediscovery of America. Through sex the metaphor of the penetration of the virgin land and the symbolism of the cultivation of the land become Portnoy's personal reality. Such penetration equates psychologically to possession and domination. 'What I'm saying, Doctor, is that I don't seem to stick my dick up these girls, as much as I stick it up their background—as though through fucking I will discover America. *Conquer* America—maybe that's more like it. Columbus, Captain Smith, Governor Winthrop, General Washington—now Portnoy. As though my manifest destiny is to seduce a girl from each of the forty-eight states' (p. 235). Ultimately, Portnoy's most important and emotionally significant relationship with a Gentile goddess involves Mary Jane Reed or 'The Monkey'.

The intensity of the sexuality between Mary Jane Reed and Portnoy compels him to confront the quagmire of unconscious forces that help make him so miserable. The relationship with Mary Jane suggests a crisis of love itself. Driven by inner doubts and fears into humiliating and abandoning her in Rome and into subsequent impotence with an Israeli woman, Portnoy must examine the psychic pain beneath his living joke about *shikses*. He realises that the desire for assimilation through sex indicates a deep association of sexuality, the unconscious, and cultural adaptation. However, at the core of this psychosocial phenomenon are questions about the nature of love and growth that Portnoy obstinately avoids until crippling guilt demands confrontation. Roth's use of Freudian analysis to explain this psychological situation is not terribly subtle. As Steven David Lavine says, 'Roth's first step is to offer a psychological reading of Portnoy's behavior even more complete than Portnoy's self-analysis.... The application of Freud's ideas to *Portnoy's Complaint* is straightforward.'[8] In his excellent essay, Lavine expands upon Roth's own discussion of Freud to describe the sources for Portnoy's illness. The key to this discussion comes from Freud's 1912 essay on 'The Most Prevalent Form of Degradation in Erotic Life' which is part of his 'Contributions to the Psychology of Love'. Roth even titles one of the chapters in *Portnoy* after this essay. However, the brilliant insights of this essay actually originate in Freud's masterpiece of 1905: *Three Essays on the Theory of Sexuality*. In the latter, Freud structures human sexuality in terms of sexual impulse or aim and the love object of that aim. He argues that the connection between object and aim are far more tenuous than most people assume. In fact, the instability of the bridge between object and aim accounts for the pervasiveness of deviations in the form of perversions and homosexuality. Furthermore, the tendency in western culture to idealise or overvaluate the sexual object greatly complicates the object–aim relationship. In a footnote added in 1910 Freud indicates the implications of such overvaluation.

> The most striking distinction between the erotic life of antiquity and our own no doubt lies in the fact that the ancients laid the stress upon the instinct itself, whereas we emphasize its object. The ancients glorified the instinct and were prepared on its account to honour even an inferior object, while we despise the instinctual activity in itself, and find excuses for it only in the merits of the object.[9]

This tendency to idealise the object at the expense of the power of the sexual impulse encourages, according to Freud, a separation of sexuality from love. Accordingly, in the 1912 essay that occupies so much of Portnoy's attention, we learn that this separation of love and sexuality results in such forms of degradation as impotence and frigidity. Of course, Portnoy's fixation with his knife-wielding mother, who still thinks of him as lover, demonstrates Freud's theory that in neurosis unresolved Oedipal drives provide the edifice for the idealised sexual object. The resounding silence of Dr Spielvogel, the object of Portnoy's monologue, indicates that this patient repeats Freud's own experience of self-analysis. However, such self-awareness and insight do not serve to mitigate the pain involved in his dilemma.

Mary Jane Reed, or 'The Monkey', creates the crisis that forces Portnoy to engage the ghosts of lust and guilt that haunt him. Epitomising Portnoy's penchant for degrading women by renaming them, Mary Jane's pleasure in sexuality satisfies his greatest fantasies and finally elicits a degree of feeling and affection that astounds him. 'What a night! I don't mean there was more than the usual body-thrashing and hair-tossing and empassioned vocalizing from The Monkey—no, the drama was at the same Wagnerian pitch I was beginning to become accustomed to: it was the flow of feeling that was new and terrific' (p. 190). The moment of love and excitement occurs during a car trip to New England and several factors help make it happen. Out of discretion for his position as Assistant Commissioner for the New York City Commission on Human Opportunity, he signs them into cosy inns and hotels as a married couple by using the name of an old friend from Newark, a delinquent of sorts who never faced the prohibitions of Portnoy's parents. Mary Jane enjoys the pretence of being a newlywed on the trip and calls him by his alias, Arnie. The new name encourages the illusion of a reckless identity. Also, the beauty of the New England scenery nourishes their mood.

> Saturday we drove up to Lake Champlain, stopping along the way for The Monkey to take pictures with her Minex; late in the day we cut across and down to Woodstock, gaping, exclaiming, sighing, The Monkey snuggling. Once in the morning (in an overgrown field near the lake shore) we had sexual congress, and then that afternoon, on a dirt road, somewhere in the mountains of central Vermont, she said, 'Oh, Alex, pull over, now—I want you to come in my mouth,' and so she blew me, and with the top down! (p. 191)

Probably given public acceptance of previously taboo sexual practices, Roth today would be hard pressed to invent a sexual act or situation shocking enough to current audiences to dramatise Portnoy's conversion to a new way of thinking—perhaps celibacy or chastity would work. Nevertheless, to his amazement Portnoy finds himself undergoing a temporary metamorphosis into a man who both loves and feels. 'What am I trying to communicate? Just that we began to feel something. Feel *feeling*! And without any diminishing of sexual appetite!' (p. 191). The new harmony of sex and love, body and mind achieves a special degree of intimacy when Portnoy gambles on both her character and intelligence and teaches her about William Butler Yeats's 'Leda and the Swan'. She justifies his faith in her by having an orgasm. He touches her and says, 'Sweetheart! You understood the poem!' (p. 194). They celebrate with 'idyllic' love making 'under the red and yellow leaves' of New England and with 'glorious acrobatics' in their Woodstock room, all of which leads to a crucial discovery: 'What a deal! And yet it turns out that she is also a human being—yes, she gives every indication that this may be so! A human being! Who can be loved!' (p. 194).

Unfortunately, Portnoy's revelation of her humanity leads him to the horrible question of his own feelings and values. Yes, he realises, she can be loved, 'But by *me*?' (p. 194). Of course, through Portnoy's pornographic imagination and consciousness, Mary Jane Reed remains a joke. However, as usual, the joke is on Portnoy because she also is presented with enough credibility as to dramatise Portnoy's own sickness. Ironically, it turns out to be she who wishes to grow and change, while Portnoy seems incapable of escaping the confinement of his own ego and guilty conscience. Thus, she does not provide Portnoy with an answer to his sexuality and life but only a question about his ability to learn to love, while Naomi, the Jewish Pumpkin from Israel, punishes him by engendering impotence.

In the way he confronts the question of love, Portnoy, it is important to remember, is not alone as a character in either Jewish novels or in American literature. The themes of the overvaluation of the sex object, the transference of this form of idealisation on to the image and symbol of America and the related problems of love, sexuality, and moral development are all intrinsic to American literature and culture. In our century both Fitzgerald and Hemingway established basic patterns for discussing these themes that reflect the modern environment. It can be argued, therefore, that Roth's work actually maintains and modernises this tradition. What more compatible company could Portnoy request than Jay Gatsby who worships Daisy Buchanan by confusing her with the green light of American success and renewal. Both Gatsby and Tom Buchanan are archetypal American males who idealise their women as mother figures while also holding them in contempt for their carnality, thereby placing all women in the impossible position of being responsible for men's illusions and disappointments. For Gatsby the real woman is of no consequence in comparison with the dream and mission she represents for him. To survive in this situation the American woman must become a Jordan Baker of sexual ambiguity and hardness. Of course, Gatsby pays for his illusions with his life. Because of their mutual idealisation of the American woman, it is not too hard to imagine Gatsby and Portnoy engaged in conversation about The

Real McCoy during a luncheon with their friend Meyer Wolfsheim. In the same vein, Portnoy certainly would understand the devastation desire demands in the world of Jake Barnes and Brett Ashley. Although he would be leery of the way she and her friends regard Jews, Portnoy would see Brett as the flip side to Daisy, a competing pagan goddess of insatiable sensuality who ultimately leaves men as lifeless and dead as Gatsby. The classic Hemingway response to this situation of lovelessness and death involves the creation of the famous Hemingway hero who adopts a style of indifference and toughness that Humphrey Bogart popularised into a new manner of speaking and acting. Thus Jake Barnes in *The Sun Also Rises* says, 'Then I thought of her walking up the street and stepping into the car, as I had last seen her, and of course in a little while I felt like hell again. It is awfully easy to be hard-boiled about everything in the daytime, but at night it is another thing.'[10] Supposedly Frederick Henry in *A Farewell to Arms* also will adopt a hard-boiled posture of existential detachment after his beloved Catherine Barkley dies. Catherine, we recall, also was an English goddess who devoted herself to creating a world safe from death and loneliness for the boyish Frederick. This results, of course, in his utter dependence upon her. Thus, from the perspective of the Hemingway hero, the failure of Frederick's and Catherine's 'separate peace' and of the wall they build around themselves suggests the need for an even greater constriction and withdrawal of self. The vulnerability love induces in these Hemingway novels teaches the need to protect the self against dependence on anyone or anything. The psychology of these heroes dramatises Freud's statement in 'Analysis Terminable and Interminable' (1937) about attitudes toward dependence:

> At no other point in analytic work does one suffer more from an oppressive feeling that all one's repeated efforts have been in vain, and from a suspicion that one has been 'preaching to the winds', than when one is trying to persuade a woman to abandon her wish for a penis on the ground of its being unrealizable or when one is seeking to convince a man that a passive attitude to men does not always signify castration and that it is indispensable in many relationships in life. The rebellious overcompensation of the male produces one of the strongest transferences—resistances.[11]

Of course, to simply state that Portnoy radically differs from the Hemingway hero constitutes a serious venture in understatement. Although facing similar sexual forces of overvaluation, dependence and impotence, Portnoy in contrast to the Hemingway hero comes from a culture where 'they wear the old unconscious on their *sleeves*!' (p. 97). While Hemingway assiduously strives to merely suggest the life of the unconscious, Roth obviously trumpets it forth. Moreover, Hemingway's famous style of omission, his dedication to writing so as to give greater potency to what remains hidden also relates to his treatment of the unconscious. For example, at the end of chapter 12 of *The Sun Also Rises*, Jake describes fishing and life at Burguete with a friend. Not until the very last line of the paragraph do we realise that the fine details actually dissemble Jake's inner thoughts of love and jealousy concerning Brett.

> We stayed five days at Burguete and had good fishing. The nights were cold and the days were hot, and there was always a breeze even in the heat of the day. It was not enough so that it felt good to wade in a cold stream, and the sun dried you when you came out and sat on the bank. We found a stream with a pool deep enough to swim in. In the evenings we played three-handed bridge with an Englishman named Harris, who had walked over from Saint Jean Pied de Port and was stopping at the inn for the fishing. He was very pleasant and went with us twice to the Irati River. There was no word from Robert Cohn nor from Brett and Mike.[12]

This is a style that seems to replicate the very processes of repression that it dramatises. It suggests an ideology of hardfaced aversion to emotional expression. It challenges the hint of dependence with detachment and counters feelings and emotions by concentrating on surface detail. As Saul Bellow so pointedly wrote years ago:

> For this is an era of hardboiled-dom. Today, the code of the athlete, of the tough boy—an American inheritance, I believe, from the English gentleman—that curious mixture of striving, asceticism, and rigor, the origins of which some trace back to Alexander the Great—is stronger than ever. Do you have feelings? There are correct and incorrect ways of indicating them. Do you have an inner life? It is nobody's business but your own. Do you have emotions? Strangle them. To a degree, everyone obeys this code.[13]

Roth, of course, proffers a serious alternative to this code that represents more than a mere difference of style between a Jewish voice and All-American stoicism. In spite of his neurosis and weakness, Portnoy works toward an ideology of love and growth as opposed to mere resistance and distance. That ideology could be described primarily in Freud's phrase from 'The Most Prevalent Form of Degradation in Erotic Life' that serves as something of a centerpiece for Roth's novel: 'To ensure a fully normal attitude in love, two currents of feeling have to unite—we may describe them as the tender, affectionate feelings and the sensual feelings.'[14] Accordingly, Portnoy discovers that the source of his greatest weakness also constitutes his greatest strength. He realises that these beautiful *shikse* love objects are yearning for someone like him who can deal with emotion and think of love with something more than resigned independence.

> Only what I don't know yet in these feverish years is that for every Eddie yearning for a Debbie, there is a Debbie yearning for an Eddie—a Marilyn Monroe yearning for her Arthur Miller—even an Alice Faye yearning for her Phil Harris. Even Jayne Mansfield was about to marry one, remember, when she was suddenly killed in a car crash. Who knew, you see, who knew back when we were watching *National Velvet*, that this stupendous purple-eyed girl who had the supreme *goyische* gift of all, the courage and knowhow to get up and ride around on a horse (as opposed to having one pull your wagon, like the rag-seller for whom I am named)—who would have believed that this girl on the horse with the riding breeches and the perfect enunciation was lusting for our kind no less than we for hers? (p. 152)

It occurs to Portnoy that the inner confluence of sensuality and tenderness that proves necessary for love and happiness applies to both men and women. Portnoy learns that because women also need to associate feelings with sexuality, they will be attracted to individuals who are not afraid of emotions and the so-called inner life. Thus, Portnoy's inner turmoil, which he perceives as signs of embarrassing weakness and immaturity, can appear to others as visible evidence of a vital emotional life.

> Who knew that the secret to a *shikse*'s heart (and box) was not to pretend to be some hook-nosed variety of *goy*, as boring and vacuous as her own brother, but to be what one's uncle was, to be what one's father was, to be whatever one was oneself, instead of doing some pathetic little Jewish imitation of one of those half-dead, ice-cold *shaygets* pricks, Jimmy or Johnny or Tod, who look, who think, who feel, to talk like fighter-bomber pilots! (p. 152)

Ironically, Portnoy's new insight into the importance of being oneself and loving oneself is difficult to put into action. For Portnoy the most obvious objective of growth and maturity becomes the most elusive. Roth summarises this aspect of the book in the theme of becoming a man, of achieving a mature selfhood and identity. In effect the book opens and closes with Portnoy's pleas to become a man. Early in the novel he says, 'Bless me with manhood! Make me brave! Make me strong! Make me whole!' (p. 37). Similarly, the book closes with Portnoy flying into Israel but weeping over the memory of the men he used to watch play ball when he was a kid. 'And that's the phrase that does me in as we touch down upon *Eretz Yisroel*: to watch the men. Because I love these men! I want to grow up to *be* one of these men!' (p. 245). This hope of growing into manhood and the difficulties attendant upon that task persist in Roth's fiction. David Kepesh in *The Professor of Desire* confronts the same challenge and realises in Prague, Czechoslovakia, that Kafka suffered the same experience of fighting for his manhood. 'Of all things, marking Kafka's remains—and unlike anything else in sight—a stout, elongated, whitish rock, tapering upward to its painted glans, a tombstone phallus.' Upon further examination of the grave, Kepesh realises the Oedipal overtones of the fact that 'the family-haunted son is buried forever—still!—between the mother and the father who outlived him'.[15] Similarly, Peter Tarnopol in *My Life as a Man* is reduced to putting on his wife's clothes during a fight and proclaiming that he wears the 'panties in this family'. He later asks, 'How do I ever get to be what is described in the literature as *a man*? I had so wanted to be one, too—why then is it always beyond me?'[16]

In *Portnoy's Complaint* Roth places the subject of being a man in the context of what many consider to be Freud's most profound study, *Civilization and Its Discontents*. As Portnoy says, 'Oy, civilization and its discontents!' (p. 183). Obviously, neither Freud in this masterpiece of psychoanalysis nor Roth in his dramatisation of some of its major ideas believes they have devised a final answer to mankind's unhappiness in society and culture. In fact, Freud's disavowal of an ultimate cure for unhappiness has inspired generations of psychologists into espousing programmes and practices that promise easier resolution of pervasive problems. Relatively early in his career, Freud countered such hopes for absolute answers with the statement that in the battle against mental sickness 'we succeed in transforming your hysterical misery into common unhappiness'.[17] Accordingly, in *Civilization and Its Discontents* Freud does not render a final solution but an analysis of man's continuing unhappiness and self-inflicted misery even in the face of enormous technological progress. He argues the immutability of primitivism in human nature. Unsatisfied love desire, and violence are ineradicable, and the attempt to cleanse these forces from the human psyche only causes them to grow stronger under the repression of the unconscious. Freud maintains therefore, that we need to accept this aspect of human character and psychology. We need to leave room for this inherent primitivism. As Portnoy says, ‘Because to be bad, Mother, that is the real struggle: to be bad—and to enjoy it! That is what makes men of us boys, Mother’ (p. 124). Out of appreciation for the power of instinctual energy, Portnoy cherishes Mary Jane’s ability to put ‘the id back in Yid’ while he only puts the ‘oy back in goy’ (p. 209). Portnoy accepts Freud’s argument that the failure to account for this libidinal aspect of human nature not only results in inevitable depression and disillusionment over man’s moral imperfection, as occurred during the First World War, but also can produce neurosis. Fuelled by instinctual energy that turns upon the self, the super-ego or moral conscience becomes another form of sickness. As Freud says, ‘Since civilization obeys an internal erotic impulsion which causes human beings to unite in a closely-knit group, it can only achieve this aim through an ever-increasing reinforcement of the sense of guilt.’ He goes on to declare that ‘the price we pay for our advance in civilization is a loss of happiness through the heightening of the sense of guilt’.[18] Portnoy, of course, demonstrates Freud’s claim that such frustration results in individual and cultural neurosis. Thus, Portnoy complains about ‘That tyrant, my super-ego, he should be strung up, that son of a bitch, hung by his fucking storm-trooper’s boots till he’s dead!’ (pp. 160–1).

All of Roth’s work, but especially *Portnoy’s Complaint*, argues Freud’s life long principle that the first step toward moral responsibility, freedom, and maturity demands an honest confrontation with the brutal and searing conflict between love and guilt. Driven on one side by boundless desire and haunted on the other by crippling guilt, existence still thrusts upon man the needs to love and to be moral. Portnoy cries,

> The things that other men do—and get away with! And with never a second thought! To inflict a wound upon a defenseless person makes them smile, for Christ’s sake, gives a little lift to their day! The lying, the scheming, the bribing, the thieving—the larceny, Doctor, conducted without batting an eye. The indifference! The total moral indifference! They don’t come down from the crimes they commit with so much as a case of indigestion! But me, I dare to steal a slightly unusual kind of a hump, and while away on my *vacation*—and now I can’t get it up! (p. 273)

For Freud the proclivity to invent illusions of false freedom and happiness compounds the difficulty of this human condition. For Portnoy, however, the luxury and indulgence of such illusions seem long past. There is instead the idea of a new beginning, of a new life with the moral, emotional, and intellectual obligation to seek the dim light of analysis. Moreover, this vision of enlightenment through the painful process of analysis carries with it certain political and cultural assumptions about the psychological and philosophical basis of individual freedom. In Freud the potential for human freedom exists but only within the context of the individual and cultural structures to sustain it. As Lavine says,

> All the turning and twisting in search of an escape from the past, all the desperate energy of Portnoy's monologue, all the desire to leave nothing unsaid, indeed, even all the hate directed at his family, grew from Portnoy's desire for the dignity that comes with independent moral choice. For Roth, this very energy and persistence of the desire for freedom and dignity are the evidence—or, better, the sign—that man may indeed have some freedom and dignity.[19]

Regardless of what some critics feel about Roth's work, he certainly sees himself as a leader in the effort to gain both freedom and dignity. He imagines freeing those who imprison themselves in their own illusions, beliefs, and fears. Thinking of Kafka and *The Trial* he asks: 'If only one, *could* quit one's pulpit, one might well obtain decisive and acceptable counsel. How to devise a mode of living completely outside the jurisdiction of the Court when the Court is of one's own devising?' He seriously considers *Portnoy's Complaint* to be an important weapon in the battle for such freedom.

> I sometimes think of my generation of men as the first wave of determined D-Day invaders, over whose bloody, wounded carcasses the flower children subsequently stepped ashore to advance triumphantly toward that libidinous Paris we had dreamed of liberating as we inched inland on our bellies, firing into the dark. 'Daddy,' the youngsters ask, 'what did you do in the war?' I humbly submit they could do worse than read *Portnoy's Complaint* to find out.[20]

No doubt others, including Hemingway and Fitzgerald, preceded Roth on that beachhead of liberation that leads to Paris. However, he can claim leadership of a Special Forces brigade. In the extended war for liberation and freedom, Roth devised brilliant strategies in some significant battles. These battles are now part of a long war that has been fought in the American unconscious since our founding. He helped to sabotage and demolish for at least a while the foundation and edifice for the American goddess. He saw the dangers of dependence and admitted he was a victim. He looked into the hard-boiled American face of detached indifference. Instead of blinking, he complained. He served in the underground as a double agent working on behalf of both sexual instinct and the force of conscience to help unify them in the greater cause of bridging sexuality and feeling. Equally important, he saw that any gains in the battle could be lost in a peace based upon the illusions of the permanent pacification of the intractable forces of hatred and guilt. Thus, in spite of the controversy surrounding his career and work, Roth stands as a leader in the modern movement to make life more loving, more meaningful, more peaceful.

Notes

1. Sigmund Freud, 'The Unconscious', in *The Standard Edition of the Complete Psychological Works* (London: Hogarth Press, 1957) vol. 14, p. 177.
2. Paul Ricoeur, *Freud and Philosophy: An Essay on Interpretation*, trs. Denis Savage (New York: Yale University Press, 1970) pp. 115–16.
3. Juliet Mitchell, *Psychoanalysis and Feminism* (New York: Vintage, 1975) p. 403.
4. For a more extensive study of this tradition as well as Philip Roth's place within it see Sam B. Girgus, *The New Covenant: Jewish Writers and the American Idea* (Chapel Hill, N. Carolina: University of North Carolina Press, 1984).
5. Annette Kolodny, *The Lay of the Land: Metaphor as Experience and History in American Life and Letters* (Chapel Hill, N. Carolina: University of North Carolina Press, 1975) pp. 5, 8.
6. Ibid., pp. 9, 11–12, 67.
7. Philip Roth, *Portnoy's Complaint* (New York: Random House, 1969) p. 143. All subsequent references to this book will be to this edition and will be included parenthetically in the text.
8. Steven David Lavine, 'The Degradation of Erotic Life: *Portnoy's Complaint* Reconsidered', *Michigan Academician*, 11 (1979) pp. 358, 359. See also Judith Paterson Jones and Guinevera A. Nance, *Philip Roth* (New York: Frederick Ungar, 1981), and Maurice Charney, *Sexual Fiction* (London and New York: Methuen, 1981) pp. 113–31.
9. Sigmund Freud, *Three Essays on the Theory of Sexuality*, trs. James Strachey, introd. Steven Marcus (1905; rpt. New York: Harper Colophon Basic Books, 1975) p. 15, n. 1.
10. Ernest Hemingway, *The Sun Also Rises* (1926; rpt. New York: Scribner, 1954) p. 34.
11. Sigmund Freud, 'Analysis Terminable and Interminable', in *The Standard Edition of the Complete Psychological Works* (London: Hogarth Press, 1964) vol. 23, p. 252.
12. Hemingway, *The Sun Also Rises*, p. 125.
13. Saul Bellow, *Dangling Man* (1944; rpt. New York: Bard, 1975) p. 7.
14. Sigmund Freud, 'The Most Prevalent Form of Degradation in Erotic Life', in 'Contributions to the Psychology of Love', in *Freud: Sexuality and the Psychology of Love*, ed. Philip Rieff (New York: Collier, 1963) p. 59.

15. Philip Roth, *The Professor of Desire* (New York: Farrar, Straus & Giroux, 1977) p. 175.

16. Philip Roth, *My Life as a Man* (New York: Holt, Rinehart and Winston, 1974) pp. 246, 299.

17. Josef Breuer and Sigmund Freud, *Studies on Hysteria*, in *The Standard Edition of the Complete Psychological Works* (London: Hogarth Press, 1955) vol. 2, p. 305.

18. Sigmund Freud, *Civilization and Its Discontents*, trs. James Strachey (1930; rpt. New York: Norton, 1962) pp. 80, 81.

19. Lavine, 'The Degradation of Erotic Life', p. 363.

20. Philip Roth, *Reading Myself and Others* (New York: Farrar, Straus & Giroux, 1975) pp. 8, 108.

HELGE NORMANN NILSEN

Rebellion Against Jewishness: Portnoy's Complaint

The Jewish-American fiction written after World War II naturally reflects the changes that occurred in American society and in the lives of the Jews as an ethnic group. Living conditions improved dramatically, and many Jews entered the middle class. The writers, like so many others, were better educated and began to merge into the mainstream of American life. At the same time they retained their commitment to humanistic values and their ancestral awareness of the tragedy of human existence. Thus the stage was set for the exploration of important conflicts between the Jewish sensibility and the agnostic consumer mentality of the larger society. J. D. Salinger's *The Catcher in the Rye* is a striking example of this clash, and there are also traces of it in Bellow's *Dangling Man* and Malamud's *The Assistant*. At the same time Jewish writers did not advocate any return to ethnic orthodoxy, being products of the modern age and regarding themselves as Americans, or humanists first and Jews second. Nevertheless, the basic conflict between their ethnic heritage and the wholly secularized environment emerges in various ways in much of the fiction that was produced. The early immigrants had embraced America, but for the writer of the fifties and sixties the situation had become more complex. No simple response or solution was possible any longer.

From *English Studies* 65 (December 1984).

There had been uncertainties before the war, but there had also been valid alternatives. Jew or American, radical or moderate, these were some of the possibilities. But in the work of Nathanael West there is a tendency to discard all alternatives and embrace nihilism, and it is his voice that speaks most clearly for those who came after him. Philip Roth and Bellow may not be quite so bleak in their despair, but their work shows a rootlessness and scepticism which can be seen as the hallmark of contemporary Jewish-American prose fiction. For the first time, the effects of assimilation and Americanization are fully felt by writers of Jewish descent, and their Jewish heritage is perceived either as an impediment or a type of sensibility rather than any set of beliefs. *The Assistant* may be said to affirm Jewishness, but only in the vaguest of terms.

Portnoy's Complaint is thought of as a novel that is typical of the sixties, of a generation in rebellion against established values, but it has a curious resemblance to the immigrant school of Jewish-American fiction. Its hero rejects all things Jewish and struggles to become integrated into what he regards as a desirable, secular and liberal way of life. 'His is a late version of the old story of the newcomer struggling to become an American, bent on full assimilation, away from ghetto identity and towards American identity with its much wider horizons of possibility'.[1] However, the focus is different. The protagonists in immigrant fiction were caught up in a historical process of upward mobility that prevented them from concentrating too much on their individual psyches. In the case of Alexander Portnoy, Jewishness is above all a psychological burden that he labors to rid himself of. The intensity of his struggle is evidence of the power both of the tradition and the larger culture that is opposed to many of its mores and attitudes. Generally speaking there is much to be said for the view that Portnoy's battle against his heritage ends in a draw. It is a modern paradox that the hero cannot quite escape from a tradition that he no longer believes in and thus is doubly victimized.

Roth's novel has a great deal of psychological awareness built into it. The hero is prodigiously intelligent and well versed in his Freud and Marx, but his knowledge is of no help to him. Instead, he employs it as the instrument of an endless self-analysis that becomes an exercise in masochism. But on the theoretical level, at least, Portnoy's insight into his own predicament is remarkable: 'A disorder in which strongly-felt ethical and altruistic impulses are perpetually warring with extreme sexual longings, often of a perverse nature'.[2] This diagnosis can be applied to the entire Judeao-Christian tradition, not just the specific Jewish context. But because of their embattled situation the Jews have enforced the dictates of their religion and morality with greater severity than most of the surrounding world in order not to capitulate to it. The nearest parallel to their orthodoxy is found in Christian fundamentalist groups, among whose adherents the psychological dilemma of Portnoy may be as widespread as among the Jews themselves.

The novel consists of an uninterrupted monologue by the protagonist, with the psychoanalyst Dr. Spielvogel as silent audience. However, the principle of free association is discarded in favor of a coherent presentation by Portnoy of his conviction that his problems have been mainly caused by his background and his parents, especially his mother. Psychoanalysis becomes a vehicle for his attack on Jewish customs and values. The aim of analysis, to obtain emotional insight and experience catharsis, is largely subverted by a Portnoy who is bent on polemic and revenge rather than therapeutic breakthroughs. His portrait of his parents and the Jewish neighborhood is onesided, to put it mildly, and even if he is right in his criticism, his relentless attacks serve as an escape from himself and his own share in the continued existence of his problems.

One might question Alex's reliability as a narrator who is also a patient undergoing analysis, and it is clear that he is not wholly perceptive with regard to the nature of his condition. Also, he sees others largely in terms of his own needs and reactions. One cannot take everything he says at face value, but at the same time there is a persistent pattern of rejection in his reaction to the Jewish milieu. On the intellectual level, at least, he leaves no doubt as to his complete lack of enthusiasm for all the basic tenets of Judaism and the attitudes that go with them. There is a quality of sincerity in his abandonment of Jewish beliefs which seems to belong to a norm which is stronger, as it were, than the troubled hero himself, or remains unaffected by his problems. It may be here that Roth, as implied author, is perceived most clearly in the novel, whereas Alex, the narrator, generally suffers from a lack of distance between himself and much of his experience. This trait may weaken *Portnoy's Complaint* as a protest novel, but it makes the hero very convincing as a psychological portrait. Another indication of the author's distance from the narrator is Dr. Spielvogel's remark at the end of the book, where he suggests that Alex's treatment is yet to begin.

Alex's parents are close enough to the immigrant experience to cling to certain old world viewpoints, but they are also in a stage of transition, having moved into the suburbs and apparently also withdrawn themselves from Jewish religious activities. Portnoy senior has no higher education and seems to have only vague notions about the culture of his own race, yet he looks upon 'the saga' of the Jewish people with great reverence. But the atmosphere in the household is far from orthodox, and the Portnoys have been more strongly influenced by American values than they seem to be aware of. In fact, the greatest achievement they can think of is material success, and they persecute their son with demands that he fulfill their expectations and establish himself as a respectable citizen with a wife and family. They protest against his atheism, but they are not in any position to teach him Jewish cultural and religious values. The only active remnant of these are certain dietary bans on shellfish and hamburger meat which are ferociously upheld by Mrs. Portnoy. According to Harold Fisch, Alex's mother wants her son to marry and subject his children to 'the rituals of bar-mitzvah and marriage in an atmosphere of observance evacuated of any transcendent meaning'.[3]

Given such a background, the striving of Alex toward integration and secularization is a natural one, notwithstanding the horrified reactions of his parents. Seen in the larger context of the historical development from oppression in Europe to freedom in America, the entire Portnoy family have been moulded by the greater forces that have shaped the destiny of Jews in the United States. In Europe there was the misery of poverty, but the land of opportunity also exacts its price. It takes hard work to get ahead, and the family breadwinner has labored, 'in that ferocious and self-annihilating way in which so many Jewish men of his generation served their families' (7). This is the trap that Alex wants to escape from, but he finds that he carries a burden of remorse and loneliness that may be the price that he will have to pay for his freedom.

Jake Portnoy is proud of his success as an insurance salesman and speaks with great respect of the Anglo-Saxon gentlemen who run the corporation that he works for. But he also feels their prejudice very keenly and is occasionally overcome with fury at these supercilious snobs. Similarly, Alex dreams of non-Jewish girls and wants to obliterate his ethnic background in order to become acceptable to them, although his sister Hanna warns him, arguing that he cannot escape his background. Being a Jew is an historical fact which the surrounding world will never allow to be forgotten. The argument is a time-honored one, but Alex refuses to accept it. He continues to protest and rebel, and it is hard to refute his indictment of the possessive and domineering ways of his mother. They were a source of torment for him when a child and have no doubt contributed to the formation of his present problems and anxieties.

Alex's main charge against his father is that he is weak and submissive and allows himself to be dominated both by his non-Jewish employers and his overpowering wife. He is a man who gives up any attempt at discovering and asserting his individuality and therefore becomes a negative example to his son. The elder Portnoy wants his son's love and to give him the same, but the latter cannot accept the premises: 'But what he had to offer I did not want—and what I wanted he did not have to offer' (28). The father has gone too far in his acceptance of the rules laid down by the mother for Alex to be able to communicate with him. He is too much a man of his generation, for whose members conventional success was of overwhelming importance, to be able to allow his son to develop in his own way. Moreover, he has a strong sense of his tradition as a Jew, although he cannot formulate his commitment very well, and thus feels impelled to see his son as one who will fulfill the father's ambitions and be a Jew of the kind that he himself would have wanted to be.

But the son turns against what he regards as the tyranny of the entire older generation of Jewish middle class citizens and singles out two prominent cases of parental oppression among them. His cousin Heschie had decided to marry a girl of Polish descent, but his father compelled him to relinquish her because she did not belong to the tribe. Soon after Heschie was killed in the Great War. This tragedy is eloquent testimony to the dark underside of the Jewish family feeling and sense of togetherness, that is, an intolerance and prejudice that are just as deplorable as anti-Semitism. The story of Ronald Nimkin, the obedient Jewish boy who commits suicide because of his parents' 'selfishness and stupidity', is a pathetic one, though the question of who is responsible for the tragedy is not as clear here as in the case of Heschie. The causes of Ronald's death may be more complicated than Alex is ready to allow for, but then his whole approach to the Jewish milieu is that of the prosecutor rather than the impartial observer. But he no doubt has a valid point when he draws attention to the self-righteousness of the Jews and their imaginary moral superiority.

However, when looking back on his past, Alex is aware that there is another and more positive dimension that was also part of his childhood. There is never any doubt that the Portnoys loved their children, though Alex finds is easier to focuson certain happy moments with his father than recollecting similar ones with his mother. He does remember such episodes with his mother, too, and the pleasure associated with them is more poignant than anything else, but he had also been all too familiar with her threats of withdrawal of motherly love. But the story of how his father had taken Alex swimming one day in summer at the seashore is so full of tenderness that it seems almost incongruous amidst the welter of angry accusations that make up the major portion of the novel. Alex also asserts that he has many more such happy memories of his parents, and in that case the question inevitably arises why he concentrates so intensely on the negative influences of his early life. It seems unsatisfactory to argue that he does this because he is a social critic whose purpose it is to expose the shortcomings of a certain environment. The enormous self-concern of Roth's protagonist is not easy to reconcile with the intentions of the literature of social protest because it diverts the attention from the problems in question to the person who is complaining about them. Even if his personality is considered relevant as evidence of what a narrowminded upbringing can lead to, a certain detachment is required when dealing with the narrator's own condition in order to convey successfully the idea that social criticism is the main concern of the novel.

Alex's relationships with women follow a pattern that is established in his battles with his mother. She uses a technique of alternately smothering him in love and threatening to cast him out of her life altogether, all in the name of giving him a good upbringing. In any case, this is how Alex remembers her behavior. He is extraordinarily sensitive and dependent on women's favors, but at the same time he is afraid of being trapped by them, thus loosing his independence and even identity. His need for love is as strong as his desire for freedom from commitment, and the only 'solution' that seems possible for him as an adult is to lead a life of promiscuity. During his adolescence he indulges in frequent masturbation both as a means of satisfying his sex drive and of asserting his rebellious individuality in the face of the many taboos that the home and the entire environment impose upon him. At the deepest level, his sexual excesses may be regarded as part of his struggle to free himself of his identity as a Jew.

Alex is ambivalent in his feelings towards his parents, but not towards everything they stand for. He cannot forget the moments of love and bliss, but he is unequivocal in his rejection of their use of emotional blackmail and their sentimental and primitive attachment to Jewish customs and beliefs. Above all, Alex abandons the religion of his tribe, indeed, all religions, in favor of an atheism that is combined with a radical political commitment. He is also politically naive, with his belief that 'the rights of man' are realized in the Soviet Union, but he is sincere in his rationalism and atheism, and there is no sign that he ever recants from this position. His own experience supports his views, in that the Jews he has observed have accepted many of the secular standards of the surrounding society and uphold them with a zeal that is second to no other group. Alex is merciless, but also to the point, in his analysis of the function of religion. It is an 'opiate' for the ignorant masses, and the clergy, of any denomination, has an economic interest in maintaining the status quo. It is generally difficult to find any flaws in Alex's arguments against the intolerance, superstition and backwardness of the people of his parents' generation, and he is lucid and consistent in his criticism. His scepticism and rationalism are convincing and based on a keen understanding of human realities and motivations. But his maturity in this field is offset by his inability to utilize his insights in the area of his own emotional problems. Here he seems to be the victim of forces beyond his control, a helpless spectator to a conflict within him that he can analyze but not resolve.

No one can be more eloquent in his diagnosis of his condition than Alex himself. His is the conflict of Western culture, between duty and pleasure, conscience and transgression. But his goal, however difficult, is to rid himself of his own taboos and lead a life according to his own convictions. He wants to follow his own desire and enjoy it, but he has to admit that he is oppressed by 'shame and inhibition and fear'. Eileen Z. Cohen suggests that Alex is 'literal' and 'priggish in his expectations of perfection in himself'.[4] Every rebellious act is followed by guilt and remorse, no matter how much Alex hates his own inhibitions and knows that they have no rational foundation.

With regard to religion, dietary laws, tribal prejudices and materialistic obsessions, Alex has quite a good case against all of them, but this is not so clear in questions of sexual morality. His promiscuity may be an attempt to establish sexual freedom for himself, and even for others, but the project is utopian. People seem to need emotional security and stability also, even Alex, and besides, his many affairs cannot even provide him with a lasting sense of self-esteem. As far as sex is concerned, he is up against a deep-seated division within himself which is a major cause of his sufferings. He wants to be a swinger, a carefree hedonist, but his sexual and emotional egotism leads to disappointments and disillusion both for himself and his partners.

The women feel exploited by Portnoy, and with reason. He is an attractive man and quite successful in the social sense, but he has very little regard for the women's feelings if they fall in love with him and want to marry. He blames himself for having an overdeveloped superego in sexual matters, but he does not actually experience much remorse in connection with his various colorful sexual experiences, whether with his mistress, the Monkey, or prostitutes and other girls. Alex gives himself too much credit here, perhaps to cover up for an insensitivity and sheer coarseness in him which do not fit the image of himself that he wants to preserve. He experiences a fantasy of ending up in Hell for his sins and of being castigated for his lack of regard for others. He is told here in no uncertain terms that 'suffering mankind' means nothing to him and that the only feelings he has ever experienced have been located in his sexual organs. These charges have an unmistakable ring of truth about them. However, they are not expressed directly by Portnoy to himself, but by the Devil in the shape of Rabbi Warshaw, a character whom Alex regards as a pompous fraud. Thus he manages to take some of the edge off this self-criticism. Moreover, he skilfully draws the attention away from his own flaws by constantly finding fault with his partners, the Monkey in particular. He attacks Naomi, the Israeli girl, for criticizing him, but his own attitude to everyone he meets, including the women once he starts reacting to their personalities, is hypercritical, if not downright misanthropic.

The Monkey is unbalanced and sometimes even hysterical, but this must be seen in relation to her frustrated love for Alex. He is unable to respond to this feeling in her, and his behavior is almost entirely mechanical and sex-oriented. She justly accuses him of lack of feeling and involvement and stands out, in contrast to him, as a person who is alive and human in a broader sense than he is. According to Jesse Bier, 'He is even worse off, since some benighted *shiksas*, like the Monkey, try to fight back into human love or devotion, while the Portnoys of the modern world heartlessly run out on them'.[5] Alex is right in condemning the idiocies of his Jewish background, but in the process of liberating himself from it he has largely lost the warmth and ability to care for each other that the people of the tribe possessed.

Alex pursues non-Jewish girls as status symbols out of a sense of inferiority that derives partly from his minority origins. When he becomes acquainted with families and institutions different from his own, his reaction is highly ambivalent. He accepts an invitation to visit the family of his girlfriend Kay Campbell in Iowa, and he is impressed by their politeness and cool self-confidence. But his description of them is satirical, if anything, and during the Thanksgiving celebrations he has to admit to a feeling of homesickness. In spite of himself, Alex reacts like a Jew among Gentiles. He plans to marry Kay and jestingly suggests that she must then convert to Judaism, but when she refuses he becomes furious, much to his own surprise. But in fact he reacts in a fashion shared by many of his brethren to what he perceives as the haughty dismissal of the *goy*, or non-Jew, of his Jewish heritage, although these 'inherited reflexes of a pogrom-threatened enclave are inappropriate and self-defeating'.[6] He is fully aware of this and asks himself wonderingly: 'How could I be feeling a wound in a place where I was not even vulnerable?' (260–1).

Clearly, the liberation from Jewishness is a more complex process than Alex has reckoned with. His relationship with Kay also deteriorates when he begins to find her boring and predictable. Her placid demeanour is foreign to him, as he is used to the more tempestuous relations between people that he has witnessed in his own family. The Monkey does provide him with the sort of drama in question, but his own fear of commitment ultimately proves stronger than anything any woman can offer. Moreover, when he leaves a woman behind, he cannot help feeling gratified by the hurt that he inflicts on her. Beginning with his mother, he has developed an attitude of excessive dependence on female attentions and a consequent vulnerability towards women which is bound to stir resentment against them within him. Another complicating factor is that he mixes romance with social climbing in Gatsby-fashion; in his flight from Jewishness he falls in love with the background of the Sarah Maulsbys and Kay Campbells. The Monkey's main attraction is sexual, and she has a lower-class background, but her case parallels the others in that Alex establishes an object relationship to both categories of women. When Sarah refuses to perform fellation on him, he feels doubly wounded because he thinks her refusal is an expression of anti-Semitism. But when he looks back on their affair, he demonstrates a keen insight into the reasons why he failed to love her: 'Intolerant of her frailties. Jealous of her accomplishments. Resentful of her family' (271). However, when she finally gives in to his sexual demands, he does not really appreciate that this is her way of expressing her love for him. He registers and portrays vividly female suffering, but he does not take it quite seriously and detaches himself from it. He tries to excuse himself by regarding his behavior as a revenge upon the Wasps for their treatment of his father, but it seems obvious that he does this for motives of his own.

Alex complains to Dr. Spielvogel about the fatal flaws of the Jewish race: 'Please, who crippled us like this? Who made us so morbid and hysterical and weak?' (40). His identification of the problem here verges on a deterministic acceptance of the very stereotypes that he otherwise passionately rejects. In other words, he comes to surrendering not only to his Jewish weakness as a phase that can be overcome but as an ineradicable historical fact. It is at the point of this recognition that Arthur Levy in Ludwig Lewisohn's *The Island Within* goes the other way and embraces his heritage, whereas Portnoy balances on the sharp edge that divides his sense of hopelessness from his determination to transcend the limits that his background threatens to impose upon him. But he also reveals the influence of his birth in the contradiction between the self-contempt that he expresses and the pride he also feels as a Jew in his culture, and its accomplishments, being secretly convinced that he is mentally superior to most non-Jews.

These and other examples suggest that Alex is endowed with a set of attitudes that define him as Jewish though he is wholly sincere in his rejection of the ancestral heritage. Quoting from Roth's novel, Seymour Siegel invokes Mordecai M. Kaplan's philosophy of Judaism as a 'civilization' and states that 'one may be identifiably Jewish even though denying the basic tenets of the faith'.[7] Alex himself is very much aware of this, but sees it as a curse rather than a potential for a positive development and sense of identity.

The firmness of Alex's assimilationist stand may be a reason for the vehement reactions against the novel demonstrated by a number of Jewish-American readers of the novel. Irving Howe recognizes the basic thrust of

Roth's book when he argues that it is not anti-Semitic or an expression of a 'traditional Jewish self-hatred'. Howe argues that 'What the book speaks for is a yearning to undo the fate of birth', and this may be what Alex wants. But Howe proceeds from analysis of content to direct polemic when he goes on to say that this wish is a mere fantasy that any Jew worth his salt can only 'dally with' for a moment before rejecting it.[8] Such a dogmatic assertion that ethnicity equals fate is hardly in keeping with reality and is as much an admission of defeat as a recognition of the value of Jewish identity. Ruth Wisse aptly argues that *Portnoy's Complaint* 'presents the schlemiel condition as unbearable', rejecting a traditional Jewish way of turning pain into laughter and concentrating on revealing the pain to the fullest possible extent. But Wisse still shares the view expressed by Howe that assimilation is impossible and speaks of Alex's 'rather self-loving notion that we could be better if only we tried, the tired but persistent thesis of the little engine that could'.[9] It is no wonder that Alex is tired, given the magnitude of the task, but the novel does not support the idea that the objective is impossible. For all his outpourings about guilt and feeling hampered by his background, Alex's daily life seems to have virtually no 'Jewish' content at all. During his visit to Israel he dutifully sees all the sights and immerses himself in the atmosphere of the homeland of the Jews, but he has no sense of contact or identification with the land and its people. His trip rather seems to be his final and successful test of his own seriousness as an apostate. For him, Israel turns out to be a disappointment in the most vital sense when he discovers that he is impotent with one of its women.

Portnoy's position at the end is quite clear. He intends to leave Jewishness behind, although this does not mean that he wants to replace it with any new ideology or set of beliefs. Rather, he seeks to lead a life based on certain rational insights and values that he regards as having a much broader basis than any kind of tribal grouping. One may disagree with his generally liberal and left-oriented outlook, but there is no reason to deny that an individual, whether Jewish or not, can adhere to such views, even if someone like Portnoy will probably never be able to rid himself of his irrational reactions and sentiments. But he is ready to pay the price of assimilation more in full than the earlier generation who felt so greatly rewarded in the new homeland that the loss of ethnic traditions was softened in its impact. Moreover, at that stage in history those values were more intact, taken for granted and perhaps carried along in an unconscious or unthinking manner even as a wholly new life was taking shape for the Jews in America.

Notes

1. Tony Tanner, *City of Words: American Fiction 1950–1970* (New York, 1971), p. 315.
2. *Portnoy's Complaint* (New York, 1969), p. vii. Subsequent citations are given page references in brackets.
3. 'Fathers, Mothers, Sons and Lovers: Jewish and Gentile Patterns in Literature', *Midstream* (March, 1972), 41.
4. 'Alex in Wonderland, or Portnoy's Complaint', *Twentieth Century Literature*, 17 (1971), 162.
5. 'In Defense of Roth', *Etudes Anglaises*, 26 (1973), 53.
6. Ruth Wisse, *The Schlemiel as Modern Hero* (Chicago, 1971), p. 119.
7. 'Mordecai M. Kaplan in Retrospect', *Commentary*, 74 (1982), 59.
8. *Jewish-American Literature: An Anthology of Fiction, Poetry, Autobiography, and Criticism*, ed. Abraham Chapman (New York, 1974), p. 66.
9. Op cit., p. 121.

JUDITH PATERSON JONES AND GUINEVERA A. NANCE

Good Girls and Boys Gone Bad

Portnoy's Complaint

The issue in *Portnoy's Complaint* is how Alexander Portnoy, the good little Jewish son of Jake and Sophie Portnoy, can be as "bad" as he wants to be and also be free of guilt. The point of the novel is that Portnoy can be neither. For all his defiance of parental and cultural taboos, which he tries to express through sexual excess and verbal obscenity, he can never be bad enough to be liberated from the proscriptions of his upbringing. His masturbation, lasciviousness, and dirty language are just so much graffiti written on the bathroom wall for all the effect they have in exorcising the code of respectability his Jewish parents have instilled within him. Consequently, at the age of thirty-three, Portnoy is not only imprisoned by a superego that sounds like the voice of his mother, he is also debilitated by an overwhelming sense of guilt. Describing himself as a Freudian case study, he offers up his repressions, inhibitions, and complexes to the scrutiny of Dr. Spielvogel, his psychoanalyst, in a diatribe that is sheer exhibitionism.

This diatribe, couched as a confession, constitutes the novel. *Portnoy's Complaint* is told in narrative blocks arranged around the protagonist's confessions and only loosely linear in chronology. Student of Freud that he is, Portnoy takes himself back to his earliest childhood memories to begin his

---

From *Philip Roth*. © 1981 by Frederick Ungar Publishing.

account of the forces that turned him into a tormented fugitive from family and culture. Consequently, the book and his recollections begin with a description of his mother: "the most unforgettable character I've met." Sophie Portnoy is portrayed as sexual, intriguing, and powerful in an almost magical way. She is the object of Alex's first sexual impulses, a fact that he readily acknowledges and that is obviously intended to summon up the conditions of Freud's Oedipus complex.[14] Alex describes her as being so "deeply embedded" in his consciousness that he mistakes his teachers for her when he begins school and later attempts to rape an Israeli woman who, he realizes in analysis, closely resembles his mother. She is not only the central figure in his infantile fantasies and adult sexual aggressions, she is also the arbiter of goodness and morality in the household—the commanding Jewish mother under whose tutelage Portnoy learns the lessons of "self-control, sobriety, and sanctions." Thus, Portnoy presents Sophie as the object of his oedipal fixation and the stereotypic Jewish mother combined to explain the irrevocable influence she has over his life.

The father in this Freudian allegory with overtones of a Jewish folktale also fits two roles. As the third component in an oedipal situation, he is the object of Alex's jealousy and rage. Portnoy remembers a scene when, as a young child, he basked in his mother's undivided attention and wished that the man they called his father would never return from work. He also recalls a period of rage when he wanted to commit violence upon his father's "ignorant, barbaric carcass." Yet as the father in this Jewish family, Jake (or Jack) Portnoy is actually rather ineffectual and poses no real threat to Alex's love–hate relationship with Sophie. He is the typical hardworking family man who dreams of his son's having opportunities that were denied to him. Portnoy admits that "in that ferocious and self-annihilating way to which so many Jewish men of his generation served their families, my father served my mother, my sister Hannah, but particularly me. Where he had been imprisoned, I would fly: that was his dream." Portnoy, however, experiences Jake's love and sacrifice for him as a burden that contributes to his guilt and keeps him ambivalent about his father. Unable to separate and simplify his emotions for the man whose inadequacies can move him both to tears and to rage, Portnoy asks Dr. Spielvogel a most provocative question about human relationships: "Doctor, what should I rid myself of, tell me, the hatred ... or the love?"

This ambivalence about his parents, the conditions which produced it, and the consequences of it constitute the subject of the novel. After establishing the centrality of his mother to his earliest childhood memories, Alex moves back and forth in his monologue between reminiscences of his childhood and family life and recollections of his sexual urges and frustrations from adolescence to "manhood." From first to last chapter, however, the unifying element among all these disparate memories is Portnoy's consciousness of himself in conflict—with his parents, with his Jewishness, and with his desire to live autonomously and guilt-free. He is caught in what is perhaps the most complex and effective double bind to be depicted in literature.

Portnoy describes his predicament quite simply as one of being "torn by desires that are repugnant to my conscience, and a conscience repugnant to my desires." His conscience requires that he respond to his parents' guidance and love by being a "nice little Jewish boy"—dutiful, respectable, and continent. His desire to be a "Man," the self-determining investigator of his passions and appetites, urges him to break whatever parental and cultural taboos restrict his individuality. To be "good" with conviction is to remain a boy; to be "bad" with abandon is to become a man. The double bind for Portnoy is that he can neither be good without feeling diminished nor be bad without feeling guilty. He attempts to resolve the dilemma by asserting his autonomy in secret, through expressions of sexuality, while maintaining the appearance of conformity to his parents' notion of goodness; but that only intensifies his guilt and shame. His desire, as he tells his mother in one of his imaginary retorts, is "to be bad—and enjoy it!" But since he finds that impossible to achieve by his own will, he pleads with Dr. Spielvogel: "Bless me with manhood! Make me brave! Make me strong! Make me *whole*! Enough being a nice Jewish boy, publicly pleasing my parents while privately pulling my putz! Enough!"

Against the suffocating ubiquity of his mother, Portnoy pits his penis, which he describes symbolically as his "battering ram to freedom." As an adolescent, masturbation becomes his primary method of self-assertion, and the voice of the imaginary being who rouses his appetites and calls him "Big Boy" momentarily drowns out the monitory tones of his mother. Finally, when he is thirty-two, this fantasy woman who had urged him to solitary sexual excess materializes as a flesh-and-blood sexual enthusiast whom he calls "The Monkey." She becomes Portnoy's partner in erotic experimentation, fulfilling his adolescent dreams; but the more he enjoys her, the more he lives in fear of public exposure and of jeopardizing his position as Assistant Commissioner of Human Opportunity for the City of New York.

Portnoy feels guilty about the disparity between his public role as a humanitarian and his private pleasure in what he views as degradation, just as in his adolescence he had felt guilty about the disjunction between his public image as a nice Jewish boy and his private profligacy. Consequently, he discovers that sex with women, like masturbation, leaves him confused. He thumbs his nose at the sanctions in order to assert his independence of them, only to find that he is overcome with guilt and fear—the sanctions undo him every time. Far from helping Portnoy batter his way to freedom, his penis, as the symbol of his defiance and his obsession with self, alienates him from the sustaining aspects of family and culture and imprisons him within his own conscience. The poignancy of this condition emerges in his question: "How have I come to be such an enemy and flayer of myself? And so alone! Oh, so alone! Nothing but *self*! Locked up in *me*!" Rather than liberating him, Portnoy's sexual exploits condemn him to solitary confinement within a guilt-ridden self. As Roth adroitly puts it in one of his interviews, "the joke on Portnoy is that for him breaking the taboo turns out to be as unmanning in the end as honoring it."

It is one of the primary ironies of this novel, so renowned for its unrestrained treatment of sex, that it actually undercuts the efficacy of sexuality as a sacred rite of passage to manhood and freedom. For all his maneuvering to satisfy his lusts and exorcise his mother in the process, Portnoy is still locked up in his childish fear of retribution. For all his bravado, he continues to imagine himself as a little boy threatened by his mother with a knife because he will not eat. The sophisticated analysand, he translates this scene of Sophie wielding the bread knife into a "threat of castration" that restrains his sexual freedom and coerces him into a semblance of conformity. Consequently, no amount of sexual activity convinces him that he is truly a man, independent of his mother's direction.

Portnoy does, however, remember two nonsexual experiences that produced a sense of wholeness and freedom. One occurs when he plays center field for a softball team, and the other when he goes with his father to the Turkish baths. Both center field and the baths offer sanctuary from his mother. Portnoy describes being in center field in terms of glorious aloneness in space and of perspective—as a position in which "you are able to see everything and everyone, to understand what's happening the instant it happens." The clarity of vision he achieves here is in sharp contrast to the confusing view of things he has at home, where his mother alternately smothers him with love and disregards his vulnerability. And he feels at ease playing baseball, having mastered all the moves to the point where he responds instinctively with the right motion, the right gesture. Reflecting on this feeling of assurance that for him was limited to the baseball field, Portnoy realizes that "there are people who feel in life the ease, the self-assurance, the simple and essential affiliation with what is going on, that I used to feel as the center fielder for the Seabees."

Similarly, Portnoy experiences this "simple and essential affiliation" on his monthly visits with his father to the baths. In fact, in recalling this regular retreat from everyday aggravations, Portnoy describes being in the company only of men as the most basic and primitive kind of affiliation. The masculine world of the steam room reminds him of prehistoric times, of "some sloppy watery time, before there were families such as we know them." The implication is that men without the civilizing influence of women can profitably revert to primitivism. Certainly Portnoy indicates that in association with these Jewish men he changes for the better, ceasing for a while to be the nice little boy in quest of his mother's approbation. He feels safe here, and, most significantly, he thinks of this habitat that is the exclusive domain of men as "natural" because it is a place "without *goyim* and women.

Such an antipathy for, and fear of, Gentiles and women seems, on the surface, peculiar in a man who generally rejects his parents' attitudes about Jewishness and is obsessed with sleeping with *shikses*. Portnoy consistently asserts his humanity over his Jewishness in response to the distinction he sees his family making between things that are Jewish and things that are "goyische." But asserting that he "*happen*[s] *also to be a human being*" does not prevent Portnoy from feeling disenfranchised in a country where a Jew does not fit the media image of an American.

Nurtured on movies and radio programs in which Gentiles typify Americans, Portnoy finds himself caught between his own Jewish culture and the picture of the pervasive American culture he has imbibed from, the media. He has learned from the movies that "America is a *shikse* nestling under your arm," and so he yearns for this mysterious "Other" as the fulfillment of the American dream; but his Jewish teachings forbid his having her, and his Jewishness ostracizes him from her. This conflict manifests itself as a defiant obsession with possessing "Thereal McCoy," an idealized version of the all-American girl that arises from both envy and hatred. He envies these gentile girls their "grammatical fathers" and "composed mothers" and their harmonious family life. At the same time, he hates them for being the "real" Americans and for what this authenticity implies about his own cultural legitimacy. As a result of these conflicts and ambivalences, Portnoy's sexual experiences with several gentile girls represent more than the simple gratification of his lust. His sexual acts with the blond, blue-eyed daughters of the dominant culture are a kind of vengeance against the image of the American Dream whose reality is inaccessible to him; they are, as he finally admits, attempts to "*conquer* America."

In recounting his sexual aggression against gentile girls (and their American backgrounds), Portnoy reveals the extent to which women are primarily representational to him. He identifies most of his conquests, for example, by names that describe what they represent to him rather than by their proper names. There is first Kay Campbell, his "girl friend" at Antioch College, who is sensible, midwestern, and Protestant; he calls her "The

Pumpkin." Then there is Sarah Abbott Maulsby, an aristocratic New Englander, whom he calls "The Pilgrim." Finally, there is Mary Jane Reed, a semiliterate hillbilly from West Virginia, who seems to love Portnoy and whom he calls "The Monkey." These women are primarily types to Portnoy, characterized first by being non-Jewish and next by being representative of a particular segment of Americana. Their individuality is of no real significance to Portnoy because he seems to be constitutionally incapable of loving women with whom he has a sexual relationship. It is only in fleeting moments with "The Monkey" that he can manage to unite desire and feelings of affection. Most of the time his desire is mixed with feelings of contempt for the women whose gentile "differentness" is both their primary attraction and the thing he despises.

Whatever success he has in subjugating the shikses, Portnoy is never able to assuage his sense of separateness as a Jewish-American. As the book ends, he takes a trip to Israel, partly to escape the intensity of his personal conflicts and partly to try to reach some conclusions about his Jewish-American identity. Ironically, he discovers that in the Jewish homeland he is as much an isolate as he ever was in Newark and that there even his sexuality cannot be relied upon to provide him with a semblance of control over his destiny. All the strands of Portnoy's several conflicts—his guilt over sexuality, his oedipal fixation, his sense of alienation from American culture because of his Jewishness and from the Jewish culture because of his violation of its sanctions—come together here in Portnoy's brief encounter with an Israeli woman named Naomi.

He envisions this freckled, redheaded Jewish girl, who at first reminds him of his midwestern "Pumpkin" and later of his mother, as his salvation. He thinks that she will make him whole, bring together the warring elements of Jewishness and sexuality, mother and shikse. She turns out to be, however, his "final downfall and humiliation." When she rebuffs his advances, he attempts to rape her, only to discover that he is impotent—"Im-po-tent in Israel," as Portnoy sings to himself in realizing the symbolic irony of his condition. After his defeat, Portnoy is left whimpering on the floor like a child and still fearful of retribution for not being "good." His obscenity and sexual aggression have not freed him; they have left him full of rage and self-hatred and, ultimately, impotent—powerless. The novel ends with Portnoy's howl of frustration and the enigmatic words of Dr. Spielvogel: "Now vee may perhaps to begin. Yes?" This is the punch line of the extended joke about guilt and the desire for autonomy that constitutes the novel.

In coming to realize what he calls "guilt ... as a comic idea" and allowing that realization to dictate the concerns and methods of *Portnoy's Complaint*, Roth acknowledges a new literary influence. *Letting Go* had been full of Jamesian references and, at times, had been suggestive of the Jamesian style. *When She Was Good* had been evocative of Flaubert in its authorial detachment and had recalled specifically *Madame Bovary*[15] in its rendering of bourgeois conventionality and its presentation of a woman who chafes at the restrictions of life and the weaknesses of men. In each of these earlier novels, Roth's tone had been serious and somber. Like Peter Tarnopol, the writer in *My Life as a Man*, Roth had shown himself to be a devotee of "complicated fictions of moral anguish." But in turning to the comic mode for *Portnoy's Complaint*, Roth did not abandon the fiction of moral anguish. He merely shifted his perspective enough to discover that an obsession with moral anguish is potentially comic; and this discovery, Roth suggests, came through the German writer Franz Kafka, one of the most serious of fictionalists.[16] Picturing Kafka "giggling" while he composed his grim stories of conflict and remorse, Roth realized, he says, that "it was all so funny, this morbid preoccupation with punishment and guilt. Hideous, but funny."

In translating this perspective into *Portnoy's Complaint*, Roth was obviously not concerned with writing a "Kafkaesque" novel in the usual sense of that term; but he does take the Kafkaesque preoccupation with victimization and guilt to its limits in an exaggeration that resembles burlesque. He structures a situation that has the optimum possibilities for producing guilt: the "nice Jewish boy," mothered, adored, and protected, in conflict with family and culture as he attempts to exercise the libidinous side of his nature. He endows his protagonist with an acute sense of himself as the guilt-ridden victim of parental conditioning, and he places him on the analyst's couch, where he is free to indulge in excoriating his parents and exploring his psyche. He then turns the narrative over to this protagonist, who regards himself not only as the casualty of an oedipal conflict but also as the "smothered son in the Jewish joke." The result is a novel of excess, where the language is hyperbolic and the style exclamatory, and where guilt, recrimination, and rage are inflated to Gargantuan proportions.

While Roth may have found in Kafka a perspective for the comic mode of *Portnoy's Complaint*, a substantial portion of the material for the novel was embedded in Roth's previous work. This is not meant to suggest that the novel is merely a reworking of previous themes but to emphasize the point that, despite departures in tone and style, Roth's work is consistent in the concerns it addresses. Perhaps more than any other of Roth's novels, *Portnoy's Complaint* is the culmination of a series of fictional efforts—a compendium of themes that, in combination, reach their Zenith in this book constructed on exaggeration.

For example, the question that Neil Klugman in *Goodbye, Columbus* asks himself, "But how carnal can I get?" becomes Portnoys challenge as he attempts through his various sexual exploits to "PUT THE ID BACK IN YID!" Similarly, other questions, conditions, and themes from the earlier fiction emerge in this novel. Neil Klugman's inability to commit himself fully to a love relationship is reflected and expanded in Portnoy's incapacity for commitment to any one of a series of women. The question of what it means to be a Jew in America that dominates "Eli, the Fanatic" also absorbs Portnoy, who would willingly trade his "suffering heritage" for "Thereal McCoy." The association of sexuality with guilt that is played out in the story of adultery in "Epstein," as well as the equation of sexual assertiveness with freedom, becomes central in Portnoy. Ozzie Freedman's defiance of the restrictiveness of his religion in "The Conversion of the Jews" anticipates Portnoy's "refusal to be bound any longer by taboos which ... *he* experiences as diminishing and unmanning"; in fact, Roth acknowledges that Alexander Portnoy is an "older incarnation of claustrophobic little Freedman." However, Roth suggests, Portnoy is less oppressed by external forces than Ozzie and more the victim of his own rage than anything else, and in this he is an appropriate counterpart to Lucy Nelson, the defiant heroine of *When She Was Good*. Finally, the potential for the characterization of the ubiquitous mother and the long-suffering father whose influence is pervasive in *Portnoy* can be found in *Letting Go*. Portnoy's constipated and passive father is, in many ways, a blend of Gabe Wallach's and Paul Herz's fathers; and Sophie Portnoy, the most vivid of Jewish mothers, dominant and omnipresent in her son's consciousness, appears to be a fleshed-out version of Gabe Wallach's mother. Each of them exerts a powerful influence on her son's behavior; each thinks of herself as being, perhaps, a little "too good." Yet if Anna Wallach prefigures Sophie Portnoy in many ways, it is still Sophie one thinks of as the archetypal Jewish mother; and this fuller realization of her character reflects largely the extent of Alex's obsession with her. She is presented exclusively through his perspective, yet so indelibly etched is she in his memory that she comes to life in a way that Anna Wallach was never intended to do.

Although *Portnoy's Complaint* is a climactic novel for Roth in the sense that several of his previous themes reach their greatest intensity of expression here, the originality of the mode of the novel attracted new and unprecedented attention to Roth's work. The confessional aspect of the book coincided with a current in the 1960s that was tolerant of candor, and Portnoy's impious baring of the psyche to reveal his obsessions and secret degradations made his creator famous—and also notorious. For not all the reactions to *Portnoy's Complaint* were favorable. Many readers found the indecorous language offensive, and segments of the Jewish community were incensed at what they determined to be its anti-Semitic overtones. The extent to which the novel was regarded at once as a success and a scandal is indicated by the dual reviews the *Saturday Review* carried when *Portnoy* first appeared. One review called it "something very much like a masterpiece"[17]; the other called it a "mixture of bile, sperm, and self-indulgence."[18] Long after *Portnoy* had become a bestseller, this duality of response continued. Some readers questioned the novel's artistic merit, and others maintained that it was a masterful demonstration of the confusion that afflicts not only Portnoy but many of us in one way or another.

Roth himself has been quite prolific in attempting to explain why the obscenity that many regarded as gratuitous is actually integral to the novel. He has also acknowledged the irony that it was his most controversial book which brought him fame. In a particularly poignant essay, he indicates that his training had instilled within him a sense of the "moral seriousness" of art and of the priestly vocation of the artist. He assumed, then, that if fame ever came to him, it would come as it had to Aschenbach, the artist in Thomas Mann's *Death in Venice*, as "Honor." Aschenbach, of course, had wrought his art out of Apollonian restraint and gave vent only in his personal fantasies to the Dionysian side of his nature.[19] Ironically, Roth, the author of several restrained and morally serious works, achieved fame through the artistic expression of the Dionysian side of Portnoy's nature and found himself personally identified with "everything that Aschenbach had suppressed and kept a shameful secret right down to his morally resolute end."

In addition to being the novel that catapulted Roth into the public view, *Portnoy's Complaint* represents something of a turning point in Roth's work. Beginning with *Goodbye, Columbus*, the issue of personal sovereignty versus external authority had been presented in various ways, but its most pervasive expression up through *Portnoy* had been in terms of the individual in conflict with the family. This family conflict becomes more central with each succeeding novel and gains in intensity from one novel to another until it reaches a peak in *Portnoy's Complaint*. Roth's exploration, for example, of the individual's experience of the family as a conditioning and controlling force figures significantly but somewhat indirectly in *Letting Go*, dominates *When She Was Good*, and becomes the *raison d'être* for *Portnoy's Complaint*. Alexander Portnoy is Roth's most vocal exemplar of resistance to the authority of the family and the most self-conscious and intentional "bad boy" among his characters.

After *Portnoy's Complaint*, however, Roth seems less engrossed with the family as the central force in his characters' lives. Although the family conflict still has a place in *The Professor of Desire*, *My Life as a Man*, and *The Ghost Writer*, in these later works the family as determinant is subordinate to characterological determinism—those aspects of the protagonist's nature which he struggles to reconcile or overcome. Subsequent to Portnoy, Roth's characters are divested of the adolescent rage against their parents that distinguishes Alex and his female counterpart, Lucy Nelson. Seemingly, while Portnoy's attempts to dispossess himself of his family's dominance failed, Roth's exorcism of his own preoccupation with the family worked, and the writing of the novel allowed him to turn toward investigating other manifestations of the problem of self-determination.

NOTES

14. "Oedipus complex" is a psychoanalytic term deriving from the Greek myth of Oedipus and implying the libidinal feelings of a child, usually male; for the parent of the opposite sex.

15. The French writer Gustave Flaubert (1821–1880), like Henry James, is one of Roth's models of the "novel of restraint." In *Madame Bovary*, Flaubert recounts the tragic story of a dissatisfied woman unable to adjust to the mediocrity of bourgeois life.

16. Franz Kafka (1883–1924) used comedic and absurd techniques to depict the serious and tragic in fiction.

17. Granville Hicks, "Literary Horizons," *Saturday Review*, 22 February 1969, pp. 38–39.

18. Marya Mannes, "A Dissent from Marya Mannes," *Saturday Review*, 22 February 1969, p. 39.

19. Thomas Mann (1875–1955), the Nobel Prize-winning German novelist, published *Death in Venice* in 1911. It portrays the moral collapse of a successful writer, brought about by an uncontrollable and humiliating passion for a boy.

STEVEN MILOWITZ

Portnovian Dilemmas

> Ven der putz shtcht, ligt der sechel
> in drerd.
>
> — Philip Roth
>
> — *Portnoy's Complaint*

Descartes formulated a world torn in two, a world where the individual feels a chasm within, a clear separation between the thinking mind and the extending body. "This 'I' by which I am what I am," Descartes writes, "is entirely distinct from the body and could exist without it" (10). The body is a machine which belongs to the world of matter, while the mind resides in a higher dimension, defiled by the body's urgings. Descartes's arguments are designed ultimately to prove the incorporeality of the soul, its nonreliance on the body's existence.

Roth, too, writes of a world newly dissected, but Roth begins not in Descartes's metaphysical realm but within the quotidian world. He begins by positing the question of the mind/body dualism as it fashions itself on earth, in life, within the day to day dalliances and conflicts of man's existence. For the metaphysical world is now responsive to the world of atrocity. The individual who makes the decision to believe himself either a corporeal machine, a servant to Dionysus, or a rational mind, a slave of Apollo, makes

---

From *Philip Roth Considered: The Concentrationary Universe of the American Writer.*

a choice not unlike that of the Nazi puppet. And so Roth inherits Cartesian dualism and repositions it in his fiction, making Descartes's abstractions real, and moving gradually towards a consideration of Descartes's questions of soul and body, matter and mind, rethinking and re-enlivening Descartes's metaphysics for the concentrationary universe.

The historic dualism Descartes first uncovers is transformed in Roth into two versions of letting go: one which finds solace in the moral and intellectual sphere of the brain, letting go of the Dionysian body, and the other in the guiltless hedonism of the corpus, letting go of the Apollonian mind. But, as David Hirsch writes, "both the 'Apollonian' and the 'Dionysian' present a troubled reality in the context of the Holocaust" (12). Both are suspect. For, as Hirsch continues, "We know that Hitler exploited Dionysian tendencies in the German Volk" (12). To exist as only a body is to allow all excess. "At the same time," Hirsch argues, "Reason was put to use in organizing a brilliant bureaucratic structure designed to exterminate human beings. The death camp itself is the ultimate example of Rationalism gone mad" (12). Man, in Roth, must choose whether to isolate one side of his self and conform to one version of letting go—to relapse into a Nazi-like emptiness—or allow the two sides to exist simultaneously within, to allow the traumas and the pain of their confrontation to continue unabated in order to hold fast to an integrated self, to exist—without letting go—as a divided being, never at rest.

The Portnovian dilemma replaces Cartesian dualism: The body and the conscience war with one another, two disparate entities fighting over the same personage. "Portnoy's Complaint" (port'-noiz kem-plant') is defined as "A disorder in which strongly-felt ethical and altruistic impulses are perpetually warring with extreme sexual longing, often of a perverse nature" (7). The ethical and altruistic impulses are societally generated and responsive to the mind, while the extreme sexual longings are a product of the body's organic pulsations.

The body exerts its influence: Portnoy admits, "Ven der putz shtcht, ligt der sechel in drerd" ("When the prick stands up, the brains get buried in the ground") (128). It complains of repression and promises extraordinary delights. It searches for instances of release without fear of punishment. The mind promises its own rewards, rewards of honor, pride, respect, but it can diminish one, fill one so surfeit with prohibitions that the body becomes impotent, unable to even act on the most harmless of instincts. "But," yells Portnoy, "What my conscience, so-called, has done to my sexuality, my spontaneity, my courage" (124). The mind protects but protection taken too far is imprisonment. "I am marked like a road map from head to toe with my repressions," Portnoy exclaims (124). Both mind and body practice a form of totalitarianism, and it is that totalitarian strength that both tempts one and pushes one away.

Both the mind and body provide pleasures and aches and in their interaction they seem to make pain a prerequisite of life, or so imagines Portnoy. Portnoy's session is an attempt to subdue the id or the super-ego. But the solution he imagines stands not as a victorious end but as a final defeat, a severing. By seeking a certain letting go, a closing down of either mind or body, characters fall into a preset trap Roth mentions in an interview with Joyce Carol Oates. Speaking specifically of *My Life as a Man* Roth says,

> "I have always been drawn to a passage that comes near the end of *The Trial*, the chapter where K., in the chapel looks up toward the priest with a sudden infusion of hope.... 'if the man would only quit his pulpit, it was not impossible that K. could obtain decisive and acceptable council from him which might, for instance, point the way, not toward some influential manipulation of the case, but toward a circumvention of it, a breaking away from it altogether, a mode of living completely outside the jurisdiction of the Court. This possibility must exist, K. had of late given much thought to it'" "Enter Irony when the man In the pulpit turns out to be oneself" (RMAO 108).

One's pulpit is not so much what Rodgers calls one's "useless fictions" (49). Rodgers places too much emphasis on the one fiction discarded or retained. What permeates the novels, and what animates the characters, is not so much a fiction from youth but rather the idea of fictions, of structured patterns and codes of behavior and thought. When Roth speaks about one's pulpit he means both the individual fictions a person grasps to and a mindset adaptable to any unalterable system. To be trapped is to be made a subject of a system, to conform to it without question, as the victims were forced to do, and as the victimizers chose for themselves.

Securing themselves to a pulpit, to a half-life of the mind or of the body, the men and women flay a layer of their selves. The pulpit is the means of repressing the Portnovian dilemma, but ultimately it becomes a means for repressing individuality. To watch as this repression is enacted is to witness the ways in which man has been tempted to a self-severing, how he, even now, is drawn to a Nazification of self.

In *Letting Go* Roth provides sketches of many characters who willfully subscribe to a pulpit, who slay their duality with a fascistic faith in either rationality or in corporeality. Only Gabe refuses this easy fixity. As Donald Kartiganer argues, "Gabe yet remains at the centre of the novel's transformational power" (93). He is ever transforming himself, letting need and purpose battle on still.

Gabe Wallach's complexity allows for a frequent misreading of his character. Gabe is often read as the antihero of the text, the failed man, the villain whose coldness displaces all human characteristics. Rodgers claims that every action Gabe takes "can be viewed as the result of ulterior or selfish motives" (51). Everything about Gabe, according to this perspective, is calculated, the result of a solipsistic plan to keep others from interfering or colliding with his minutely constructed personal world. Gabe's story is less clear. It is more revealing to see him as a man wanting only to be good, and torn apart by his disparate drives.

Gabe is burdened by a particular guilt. His is a post-Holocaust sensibility which makes him feel responsible for the world, as if his every action had the potential for causing disaster, as if his ostensibly easeful life inversely creates another's hard life. When he sees an ambulance on the road, he pulls his car over and rushes toward the stretcher. He looks down at the victim and admits, "What I saw surprised me. The face sticking up above the blanket belonged to nobody I knew" (54). His conscience tells him to remain uninvolved, for involvement leads to damage. Both Gabe and Paul subdue their hearts, trying to "do no violence to human life" (3). Gabe's adeptness surpasses his double's and thus his heart seems absent to those around him, but it is most assuredly there, "pulsing" with life (350). Alone with Martha that pulsing beats fervidly as Gabe grasps Martha's breast. His conscience never reigns supreme, the hands as though willful spring into action.

Gabe and Paul share a basic dilemma, the dilemma of dualism. Though they come from different backgrounds, have different relationships with their families, and are, in essence, vastly different men, they both are decimated by the interplay of heart and head within, and by their desire to enact a vivisection of themselves. Dualism for the children of the Holocaust generation is a frightening prospect, more evidence of an uncontrollable, precarious civilization, while for the victim generation, for those like Charlotte Delbo, duality must be forced into being.

Towards the middle of the novel Paul and Gabe shake hands. Gabe comments, "I don't think it would have shocked either of us then if we had embraced" (227). And later, grasping each other's hand again, they finish speaking and yet "continued to grip each other's hand" (441). In those moments they express an inexpressible, wordless, bond between them, a bond of both heart and mind. The hands, the embodiment of both mind's rationality and the heart's chaos, join together finding comfort in one another, comfort in the emotional connection, a connection of skin, and in the connection that seemingly suspends action for a moment, a grip that keeps the hands under control, surrounded, encased. The difficulty they find in releasing one another is the difficulty of re-entering their conditions. For a moment they have equanimity.

But that moment, which might act as a opening, an elucidation, instead is a parting for Gabe and Paul. As they release each other it is as though they have touched for the last time. Paul anesthetizes his divisions, performing surgery upon himself, while Gabe finds no panacea for his own. After his dissolution—brought on by a brief but compelling complete surrender to the heart he had battled for so long—Gabe ends unafraid, receptive even, of his own dualism. Kartiganer recognizes that Gabe is about to enter into "a full engagement of the opposing sides of self" by refusing to accept "accommodation" (93).

Only Gabe survives, like Ishmael. Gabe survives the wreckage of his age by grasping to the same awakening as the victims. In Roth's idiom Gabe quits his pulpit, finds a way to live outside the jurisdiction of the court. In an interview Roth states that he views "Gabe Wallach, Alexander Portnoy, and David Kepesh—as three stages of a single explosive projectile that is fired into the barrier that forms one boundary of the individual's identity and experience" (RMAO 85). Roth goes on to say, "Gabe Wallach crashes up against the wall and collapses" (RMAO 85). Though he collapses, Gabe's story has not ended, for that collapse signals a beginning, the first advance of an ever-moving projectile. Everyone else lay dormant on land while Gabe tests the tumultuous waters, the deceptive and changeable sea, a reflection of a self's variety. His is finally an acceptance of the dual presence of mind and body, an acceptance of the concentrationary universe's ambiguity as it is expressed inside himself, an acceptance of two forces struggling within, attacking and responding to one another.

Descartes allows for this interaction by creating an organ he labeled the "pineal gland," the link chain between mind and body (15). Roth's protagonists feel doubled, cut in two, one part a "stimulus response device" and one part a "thinking thing" (236). It is how they respond to this split that tests their character: Do they become, like Martha, Paul, and Libby, one thing devoid of instinct or of rationality, or do they, like Gabe, allow the pineal gland to exist, allow two selves to occupy them, to navigate and torment them with their contradictory messages? Do they adopt a pulpit or do they forswear pulpits, preferring tension to simplicity? These philosophical and internal questions take on a new imperative in the new world. The legacy of the Holocaust is fear, fear of the carnal, fear of the rational, and fear of meaninglessness; yet it is that same legacy, the terror it inspires, which moves one to look for a pulpit of the carnal or of the rational to restore a lost and imagined order. To let go of a side of self is to fail, to let go of a pulpit is to invite pain but to remain an individual, halved but more whole for a riven self.

In his review of "Goodbye, Columbus" Saul Bellow suggests that the question of "worldly goods versus the goods of the spirit" is the central conflict of the novella (78). Bellow points at the same conflict the characters in *Letting Go* must either minimize and alleviate, or accept, the conflict of need (worldly goods) and purpose (the spirit). The terms are different but Bellow notices what is the first indication of the Portnovian complaint that finds full expression in Roth's fourth book.[1]

Neil is suspicious of his heart, suspicious of its motives, of its uncanny ability to trick his mind and conscience. For Neil the true self depends on the mind's persistence, its evaluation and its dogged challenging of the heart. He is like Leo Patimkin, Brenda's father's half-brother, burdened by a bitter conscience. "Even the pleasures I can't enjoy," says Leo (116). Leo, like Neil, is beset with integrity. It is after Leo and Neil have their conversation that Neil looks down on a sleeping Brenda and wonders, "How would I ever come to know her ... for as she slept I felt I knew no more of her than what I could see in a photograph" (118). He thought that in time he would see a deeper vision of Brenda, a Brenda beneath the pretty exterior.

Neil is "split between the disapproving moralist and the acquisitive self," as Rodgers points out (45). The acquisitive self, he believes, is what draws Neil closer to Brenda, allowing her to take command of him. In his prayer Neil locates this self: "If we meet You at all God, it's that we're carnal and acquisitive, and thereby partake of You. I am carnal, and I know you approve, I just know it. But how carnal can I get" (100). He fears he will become all carnality, a virtual lust machine, his conscience unplugged. Bellow feels that "Neil's meditation is curious ... why should it please God that we are carnal or acquisitive? I don't see that at all" (78). Neil sees carnality as self-evident, a part of you given by God and therefore pleasing to God. What Neil objects to, and what he supposes God to object to, is the notion that carnality is its own power.

But what Neil reveals in his passionate prayer is more than respect and trepidation towards his carnal side. What he reveals is a hidden pulpit, the underlying urge that compels him towards the culmination of his story. Linking the carnal to the Godly ("damn it, God that is You," says Neil) is what his dream has always been (100). His romanticizing of Brenda has been a means to assert a singular self, to ascribe longing to rational goals. Neil distrusts lust and instinct and trusts finally his conscience and mind. He wants to surround his instincts with nobility, his felt urges with meaning; he wants to turn what is felt as superficial desire into a slave to the mind's ethical plan. To ascribe the body's temptation to the mind's master plan is to deny carnality its difference, its separation. It becomes the hand of God, the hand of rationality; it loses its mysteriousness, its own unique properties. Instead of accepting his lust as a separate part of his whole self, Neil wants to make it a property of his head, a messenger for the mind.

Neil's denial leads him to Boston, to a decision to marry Brenda. He must make a commitment, he feels, for he has been driven by a rational mind conscious of its actions. In order to prove to himself that it has been his head all along that has ruled him, that his body's pulsations were only the means to the intended end his head had decided upon, he resolves himself to marriage, not doubting any longer Brenda's character. He can trust his body for his body was led by a clear mind. He need no longer question himself; his pulpit has clarified all. His purpose is apparent to him; his purpose defines him.

With Brenda's unforeseen rejection Neil is shocked into a new awareness. Set up for defeat he is shaken alive. "Losing" Brenda is transformed into "winning" his doubled self back (135). After Brenda's rejection Neil wonders, "What was it inside me that had turned pursuit and clutching into love" (135). Neil had turned need (pursuit and clutching) into purpose (love) because he could not abide the idea of two contradictory parts of himself residing within, pulling him this way and that. He needed order, needed to believe that if there was no order in the desolated world outside himself, at least there was order within him, needed to see himself as one thing working methodically towards some final goal. Neil adds to his query, asking what was it inside him that had "then turned it inside out again" (135). What has turned it inside out is his reborn duality born of Brenda's submersion into the Patimkin world of need. "Whatever spawned my love for her," Neil wonders, "had that spawned such lust too?" (136). The love flourished to give credence to the unmindful lust. Neil's craving for a rational self had turned an object of pure desire into an object of pure love.

Love and lust, Neil now realizes, drive each other, confuse and undermine each other. One cannot allow either to take absolute control. To allow both to exist as separate islands within is to put limits on each. The divided self offers a test to itself, while the singular self swallows whole all questions. Neil gives up the comfort of a pulpit for the freedom of the dual-self. He ends unsure of who he is and where he will go, but more leery of the urge to unite his contrary impulses, leery of subsuming one in the other. He is still that diffusive self searching for some definition of his being, some picture of his worth, ever trying to answer the question, "What is it to be what I am?" (1-GC1).

Neil's eye is the key to his "I." He learns to distinguish shadings where others see blacks and whites. The deeper eye melds the aesthetic with the intellectual eye, the way two eyes meld together to see one thing. The deeper eye sees impressionistically, knowing that what it sees cannot be trusted. "I am certain that I am, but what am I? What is there that can be esteemed true?" Descartes asks at the beginning of the "Meditations," a question Roth introduces and remarks upon when speaking of David Kepesh and his transformation into a 150 pound breast (RMAO 71). Does the "I" that the eye reveals define a self, or is there more, and what constitutes that more, that full self? This is the question that links Neil to Kepesh, Kepesh to Tarnopol, Tarnopol to Portnoy, Portnoy to Zuckerman, and Zuckerman to Roth. Descartes's preliminary query is the query Roth and his protagonists enmesh themselves in. Am I this body or this mind, both, neither, something else entirely? Am I what I feel or what I know, what I see or what I am blind to? Neil's eyes tell him a more profound story than the paper-deep Patimkin's eyes tell them, but how far, he wonders, will those eyes take him, what are their limits, what myopia lay undiagnosed, unseen, and untreated? How much blindness is implicit in one's character, how much can be overcome? Like Descartes's doubts, there is only so far one can take oneself out of one's own limits, out of the manner one sees or thinks. There are limits impossible to traverse, knowledge that study will not pull to the surface, presuppositions that hold back clarity. Descartes's "blank slate" is an impossible goal for the mature human, conditioned already by so much.

Neil throws his pulpit aside, cognizant of his own haziness, his own murkiness, but more aware that that very haze is not only a facet of being lost but of the possibility of discovery. Roth's character's lostness is a condition more to cherish than that of Patimkin-like satisfaction. Loss, like exile, is predicated on possibility, on a future, on a constant renewal and reinterpretation of vision, lost but to be found.

Like Neil, "Kepesh is lost," explains Roth, lost "somewhat the way Descartes claims to be lost" (RMAO 71). He is alive, of that he is sure, but to what end, to what purpose? It is a question which, in his convalescence, Kepesh considers and agonizes over, but it is not a question born of this unlikely metamorphosis, rather it is a question which suffuses David's life from his earliest days, a question which occupies David throughout not only his narrative of disaster, *The Breast*, but throughout his narrative of temptation, *The Professor of Desire*.

David Alan Kepesh wrestles with the Cartesian dilemma long before he is torn from any empirical sense of himself as human, as a man. His "overarching desire," as Roth says, is to "somehow achieve [his] own true purpose" (RMAO 70). The desire Kepesh discusses, then, is not simply the manifestation of sexual longing but a deeper, more penetrating, instinct towards self-knowledge, towards some kind of graspable truth. "I am one thing or I am the other," Kepesh declares (12). "Than, at twenty, do I set out to undo the contradictions and overleap the uncertainties" (12). His interior battle between need and purpose is complementary with his battle with the world's opaqueness. The concentrationary world is rife with indecipherability, with unanswered questions. Kepesh acts out his interior battle in hopes of finding a clarity of vision not only of himself but of the world as well.

Instead of viewing himself as an amalgam of roles, with an amalgam of influences, he maintains an either/or perspective on identity, hoping to fit into the role of "scholar" or "rake" (17). Literature becomes not an avenue for awakening and selection but an avenue to find a true self. Kepesh turns to "archetypes" for self-revelation (37). To be a literary man is to depart from the body, silence its caterwauling, sweep everything under the rug of scholarship. His description of himself as a "Stellian man" points out not only that he is "a man never at home, never at rest, never satisfied, always a stranger," as Rodgers claims, but that he is desperate for fulfilling a pulpit, a definition in which to encase his disordered self (162). Literary models are embedded within Kepesh and it is from them that he interprets the world. To be a literary man, then, is to let the well-defined role Professor—someone who stands aside and observes dispassionately—overtake one's individuality, to become a title, to become whole through a negation of a part of oneself.

In his introduction to his comparative literature class Kepesh outlines the goal for his narrative: "Above all," he imagines telling his class, "I hope by reading these books you will come to learn something of value about life in one of its most puzzling and maddening aspects. I hope to learn something myself" (184). Through literature he is to learn who he is. "What a church is to the true believer, a classroom is to me," he admits (185). He seeks through works of the imagination a churchly truth, a pulpit.

His preface to his unseen students provides the clues to the two antipathetic directions he will look for that truth. He states: "As you may have already surmised ... the conventions traditionally governing the relationship between student and teacher are more or less those by which I have always operated" (182). Conventions underlie his teaching style. He teaches according to a code of conduct. He wears "a jacket and a tie" and removes his watch at the start of class placing it in its traditional spot on the table top, a sign of professionalism, of seriousness and continuity (183). And yet he asks his students to refrain from talking about "'structure,' 'form' and 'symbols' ... to try living without any classroom terminology at all, to relinquish 'plot' and 'character' right along with ... 'epiphany,' 'persona,' and, of course, 'existential' as a modifier of everything existing under the sun" (183). He both embraces conventions and wishes to undo conventions, recognizing them first as ties to a solid past and then as an impediment to free thought, a hazard and a cause of lazy-thinking. In his lecture, and nowhere else, Kepesh unites his two selves, holding them together. “I am devoted to fiction,” he concludes, “but in truth nothing lives in me like my life” (185). The realms are distinct but they are both present, both part of him, Kepesh asks for a “referential relationship” between life and art, a conjoining of the world of language and the world of action, the world of form and formlessness (185).

That conjoining is only possible in the classroom. “To my mind there is nothing quite like the classroom in all of life” (184). Contradictory elements can only exist side by side in an unreal enclosure, not in the concentrationary world of “unrelenting forces” and “debilitating experience” (185). The role of professor fits seamlessly over him but it is a role that offers little sustenance outside the “bright and barren little room” (184). “I want to cry out,” Kepesh writes, “Dear friends, cherish this!” as if the classroom were the last Eden, the last gasp of innocence before reality remakes everything (184). What Kepesh fails to grasp is the reason for the placidity of the classroom, namely its retention of his own duality, the duality he fights against so hard in his life away from students. There is a tension alive in the classroom that feels to Kepesh like wholeness, a balance created which promises not closure but changeability. Kepesh enunciates this tension without holding fast to it.

In his dream of Kafka’s whore this same lesson is spoken quite directly and again it disappears with its utterance. What Kepesh learns in the schoolhouse and in his sleep eludes him in his life. In that dream David is invited to “inspect her pussy” (191). After deliberating he tells himself, “But why not? Why come to the battered heart of Europe if not to examine just this? Why come into the world at all? Students of literature, you must conquer your squeamishness once and for all! You must face the unseemly thing itself!” (191). In that moment, in the safety of his dreams, he has touched the heart of the shadow that has terrorized him, the darkness that demands he not allow the body or the mind full possession of him, that demands he accept his duality, his fragile self, his weak body and his merciless mind. But what he enacts in his dreams he cannot enact in life, unwilling to look at the nakedness of his world.[2]

David’s sleeping realizations fail to reach his waking self, for that self is surrounded by a pulpit so strong that it pushes awareness deeper inside the body’s shell. Kepesh is labeled Professor of Desire, but what does that label signify? he wonders. Should he subvert “Desire” with professorial control or subvert “Professor” with raw passions? One or the other he insists, till the end, till the change, must be his true self. One role, his pulpit tells him, will ease the uncertainty and heal the anguish. in his essay, “Man in a Shell,”

Kepesh writes about Chekhov's characters, who are held back by their learned conventions and their natural drives, ever imprisoned, trying "in vain to achieve that sense of personal freedom" (158). The essay tells of "longings fulfilled, pleasures denied, and the pain occasioned by both" (157). Pain is a product of both need and purpose, and of their interaction, but pain is existence, blood, survival, and Kepesh's search to deny pain is finally a search to deny life, to deny experience. He wants essences, wants, in Kant's words, to turn "phenomena" into "noumena," to turn appearance into solid truth, to make life as interpretable as fairy tale books. "Literature got me into this and literature is gonna have to get me out," he might say, echoing another Rothian man, Peter Tarnopol, who is no less intent on uncovering a literary identity, an identity reified by language (MLAM 194).

Both Kepesh and Tarnopol are unable to find the error inherent in their search for what Roth calls "a description" of themselves, without the aid of a disaster (CWPR 80). Kepesh's transformation is his avenue to growth and Tarnopol's many years spent with Maureen Johnson Tarnopol is his own horrible path towards enlightenment, away from the pulpit of certain literary truth. Kepesh is transformed in *The Breast* but transformed not from animate, productive teacher to fleshy, inhuman beast but from victim to autonomous individual. His physical metamorphosis is imposed upon him while his more elaborate and more important metamorphosis he achieves for himself.

Though both men's narratives are recollections, each is written with a different intention. Tarnopol uses writing to understand and reinvent himself, to locate the cause of his misfortune, and Kepesh uses his narrative to impart wisdom, to replay his experience from the vantage point of awareness. Kepesh, in effect, gives a lecture, self-implicating and self-aware, calling for a throwing down of the pulpits of understanding. Kepesh, as a breast, forgoes the pulpit of interpretation. Opening his mind to doubt, Kepesh finds himself anew. He is not only a body part, or, as he imagined himself, all brain, but both intermingled within the 150 pound thing that lies docile in its huge harness. His vision opens, his invisible eyes see.

The language of doubt, of revision, is David's new language. The language he spoke of in his introductory lecture has come to life. And it is not a language of defeat but of revitalization. Kepesh escapes what few others are able to escape, the paradigms that rule life and constrict freedom.. And freedom is this century's most persistent dilemma; the need to be free implodes from within, from an inheritance of freedom's antithesis.

Kepesh holds fast to desire as it is defined by Rodgers, "perpetual and undiminished longing" (101). As a breast satiation and culmination are out of the question. As a breast "there is no orgasmic conclusion to my excitement,"

Kepesh explains, "but only this sustained sense of imminent ejaculation" (45). No closure, no epiphany. What Kepesh is left with is promise. He reaches a point of friction, a taught hold between need and purpose. He is both a Professor and an unquenchable quivering organism of desire. He moves, now, with hardly a transition, from "contemplation of the higher things" to "contemplation of the lower" (84), from "delusions of grandeur" to those of "abasement" (82), from a belief in that which is "simple and clear" to an acknowledgement, even a welcoming, of arbitrariness and mutability (82).

A language beyond the pulpit of interpretation, beyond the confines of literary criticism allows both drives and conscience to interact simultaneously, to battle and to engage each other, for language need not be in league with any overwhelming truth. Kepesh's realization is a restatement of Tarnopol's claim that words can only approximate reality. Words need not be allied to a pulpit, need not reverberate with absolute meaning or with absolute meaninglessness. A pulpit clouds the mind, throws a shadow over thought.

When Tarnopol decides to marry his nemesis, Maureen, he is in the throes of a pulpit-enhanced delirium. Recounting the maguffin of his story, the turning point of his life, the moment of self-surrender to the duplicitous enemy, he calls a halt to his narrative to reflect upon the factors which have led him to enact this act of self-destruction, this act so inimical to his best interests. "It seemed," he writes, "then that I was making one of those moral decisions that I had heard so much about in college literature courses" (193). Literature surrounds his every action. For Peter literary models serve as exemplars for his own life. He looks upon the great books and the great masters with awe, viewing their words reverentially. "Perhaps," he wonders, "if I had not fallen so in love with these complicated fictions and moral anguish, I never would have taken that long anguished walk to the Upper West Side and back, and arrived at what seemed to me the only 'honorable' decision for a young man as morally 'serious' as myself" (194). These quoted words work messianically upon Tarnopol's actions, moving him in a direction anathema to his desires.

His intellect works against his instincts, his sense of purpose undermines his needs. Transforming his life into a fiction of Nathan Zuckerman, Peter writes of Nathan's attraction for Lydia Ketterer. Zuckerman admits that regarding Lydia he was "utterly without lust" (69). But lust has come, to Nathan, to signify nothing less than frivolity, childishness, moral-pubescence. His own quest, he feels, has taken him beyond simple visceral lust. His insistence on putting, as he says, "my tongue where she had been brutalized," is an act of literary grandiosity, not of desire, performed as if that act "could redeem" him, an act which parallels the writer's willingness, his need, in fact, to touch the horror that he was spared, to look for redemption where there is none (72).

To look at the first words of each section of *My Life as a Man* is to watch Tarnopol's progression towards a quitting of his pulpit. "Salad Days" begins with the words, "First, foremost," words of surety and definition (3). They introduce a writer and a character who believes wholeheartedly in language, who believes in word's perfectibility. "Courting Disaster," contrarily, begins with a negation, "No" (33). It introduces Tarnopol's other half, the half that Susan attracts, the side drawn to meaninglessness, which distrusts all words. These first two fictions describe a numbed self, numbed not by actual menace, as it was for Delbo, but by the memory of that menace, by its inheritance. "My True Story," however, begins with a question, "Has anything changed?" (101). Tarnopol moves through the two extremes of need and purpose, the two ends of his pulpit, to reach a median, a position of questioning and not of surrender.

There is pain in balance, the pain Zuckerman felt in *The Ghost Writer*. The burden of duality is a human burden, a burden of the times carried by so many of Roth's men and women. The Portnovian dilemma is introduced in his early story "Defender of the Faith." "Sergeant Marx," Roth tells Jerre Mangione, in a 1966 television interview, "doesn't know how far to go to stop [Grossbart]. He's very hesitant to be savage, very hesitant. to be openly cruel. He really can't deal with his cruelty" (CWPR 5). Marx is stymied by an inability to act against his morality, to trust his blood; he is made impotent by all he knows from his time in Europe. Like Helen, in *The Professor of Desire*, "moral repugnance" intervenes (218). "How far do you go?" asks Roth (CWPR 6). When does morality inhibit action, when does the moral code act against self-interest, he asks himself? And, then again, when does need inhibit morality, when does an instinctual response damn and debase a man?

To ignore these questions is to dehumanize oneself. No character, then, is more human than Alexander Portnoy, who lends his name to these questions, who pronounces them with every word in his long session with Dr. Spielvogel. Portnoy is "torn by desires repugnant to my conscience and a conscience repugnant to my desires," as he says (132). Is he, he asks, the "Assistant Commissioner of Human Opportunity," the public servant to morality, or "Commissioner of Cunt," a slave to desire and immorality? (204). He must be one or the other, an eater or a talker, "base and brainless" (204) or "A hundred and fifty-eight points of I.Q." (204), an "ignoramus" (204) or "Albert Einstein the Second" (4). His "spellbound" reading of Freud's "Contributions to the Psychology of Love" has convinced him that one current of feeling—need or purpose—must be subsumed in the other for a Freudian illumination to take place (185). Portnoy's pulpit begins with Freud. Freud's words are truth to Alex. He comes to Spielvogel not as a naive and problemed layman but as a sophisticated reader of psychoanalysis.

He narrates his own story as a Freudian case study, imposing Freud's theories and semantics on his actions, looking to Freud to solve the problem of living in the post-Holocaust world. And yet his reading of Freud is faulty. Portnoy puts great emphasis on Freud's suggestion that for catharsis to take place it is necessary that "two currents of feeling be united: tender, affectionate feelings, and the sensuous feelings" (PC 185–86). Portnoy reads union to imply stasis. He reads Freud's essay as making the case for the dissolving of disharmony rather than for fostering its continuation. Portnoy seeks a blending, a melding of his duality, blaming his impotence on division and dissonance. With Freud as guide, Portnoy waits for one current to fall to the other.

Freud's essay does state the need for a "confluence of the two currents," but confluence, even more than union, suggests not a subduing of either but an intermixing, a continuing flux between the two (56). The currents remain separate, individual, distinctive, but rise together like waves, pushing and pulling at one another. Later Freud writes, "In times during which no obstacle to sexual satisfaction, existed ... love became worthless" (57). When needs are unrestrained love loses its value. Love, Freud goes on, "developed greatest significance in lives of the ascetic monks, which were entirely occupied with the struggles against libidinous temptation" (57). Where conscience intervenes with desire sexuality and love become more valued, more intensified. "Instinctual desire is mentally increased by frustration of it," Freud argues (57). Instinct comes alive when its is challenged by conscience, conscience finds its meaning in its collision with desire. Both are enlivened by the presence of the other, not by one's subjugation of the other. What Freud asks for is not a victory of need over purpose, or purpose over need, but their constant belittling interaction.

But Portnoy, heedful of *his* Freud, rejects interaction and continues searching on for the Freudian gem that will lead him to his own Palestine. Freud's insistence on language, on talking, further animates Portnoy's journey. For Alex there are two types of language, civilized discourse and animal howling, and they are synecdoches referring to his internal contradictions. Need is joined with ungrammatical declarations, noise, the screams of pain or pleasure, while purpose is joined with eloquence, pure argot, perfect syntax. He is drawn to both the "pitiful and pathetic" (206) writing of the Monkey and the "cutesy-wootsy" innocent language of the Pilgrim's speech (233).

Portnoy believes that in one linguistic sphere he will find his tone, his meaning. He derogates one and then the other, alternating in his distaste for sophisticated words—"babble-babble"—and for the nonsensical mouthings of his "slimy ... Dionysian side" (79).

Portnoy's search for a woman is consistent with his search for a language, with his search for wholeness. "This one has a nice ass," he says, "but she talks too much" (103). One woman's language undermines her physical attributes. "On the other hand," Portnoy continues, "this one here doesn't talk at all, at least not so that she makes any sense—but, boy, can she suck" (103). Her sexual prowess seems to spring from a faulty vocabulary. Portnoy divides the world as he divides women; linguistic agility is linked with sexual limitation and linguistic coarseness linked with sexual know-how. One precludes the other, and Portnoy must choose which sphere he must anchor himself in.

The dichotomy in *Portnoy's Complaint* matures into the modern philosophical battle of speech and writing, the pulpits of Plato and Derrida. Speech is allied with purpose, with language in its purest form, while writing comes into an inheritance of anarchy, noise, the primeval voice of chaos. Plato's privileges speech, verbal communication in which words and their meaning are locked together, in which words spring from the mouth fully formed, perfect. "Plato," argues Jasper Neel, "undeniably condemns writing," while Derrida condemns Platonic speech (1). Derrida celebrates writing for is gaps, its non-referentiality, its free-floating, always alternating formlessness, its incompleteness, its rejection of truth. For Derrida there is no transcendental meaning, no signified, only play, traces, difference.

Derrida and Plato occupy the far perimeters of the dialectic of language, comparable to Portnoy's division of the Monkey's impure writing and the Pilgrim's pure speech. And Plato and Derrida are both indicted by the Holocaust. Plato's privileging of absolute truths anticipates Hitler's sure pronouncements, and Derrida's slipperiness makes guilt impossible; the truth of the horror becomes deconstructed.[3] To which, finally, will Portnoy and the text show allegiance? What Roth has created is a novel about speech (the spoken narrative of a patient to his analyst) and infused it with the properties of writing (irony, tropological uniformity, depth, plot). As Hermione Lee argues, "Roth is turning an oral tradition into a written one" (PR 33). Roth unites Derrida and Plato, allowing the two to mesh. The arguments against writing are made in writing, the arguments against speech made in the voice of an eloquent speaker. There is a search for closure but that closure is always deferred. Roth presents a narration that doubles Portnoy's dilemma and offers a way out of that dilemma.

When Alex states, "Words aren't only bombs and bullets—no they're little gifts, containing meanings," he touches upon the union which he has resisted (222). Words are both the provinces of the heart and of the head, of aggression and of love, of sense and of senselessness. Words are both

Platonic gifts and Derridian bombs. The dissonance of Portnoy's monologue is the dissonance of these two discourses dueling. Language leads to the catharsis of screaming, screaming informs the considered prose. The tension produced, both in the speaker and in the text, is the tension that animates both, that creates the agony expressed and the comedy which offers a bridge from despair.

Neel defines "successful rhetoricians" as those who "keep Plato and Derrida at work at all times ... but never subordinates them ... so that neither the Platonic search for truth nor the Derridian strategy of deconstruction overwhelms the process" (205). Roth, always heedful of the philosophical implications of the Holocaust, is the quintessential writer of this middle ground, the ground between need and purpose. Neel views this kind of rhetoric to be an attempt "to liberate ourselves from philosophy" (211). What Neel means by philosophy can be understood as the pulpit. To liberate our pulpits is to neither be a slave to any one theory or to the idea of theory at all.

To liberate ourselves from all philosophical systems, though, would be to turn from knowledge, from questioning, and from the past. In Roth, philosophy and fiction are present in each other. Roth's novels are dialogues across time and history, across disciplines. Descartes defines the split that Roth rewrites. The Cartesian split between mind and body is transferred into the felt division In Roth's characters. Roth seizes on Descartes's doubt and his iconoclasm as central principles for his own work. But Descartes's final supposition—that the body and soul are distinct and that the soul can exist beyond the body's disintegration, that God has decreed this and so it is inherently so—falls to convince Roth. Where Descartes's doubt leads him to a pulpit of religious certainty, Roth's leads him to further doubt.

Descartes maintains that he is a being "which does not require any place, or depend on any material thing in order to exist" (236). The soul is incorporeal and lives on after death. Roth takes up these further Cartesian questions briefly in *The Anatomy Lesson* and in *The Counterlife*. What is the body's purpose? Zuckerman asks. Is it merely a mechanism outside the mind, or is the mind part of the body? Is the body a means to salvation or an appendage to be forsaken? Zuckerman feels he must choose between the Lawrencian esthetic of the body or the Sadian esthetic, one which preaches that the physical is the means towards the spiritual and the other which embraces pleasure for its own sake.

In *The Anatomy Lesson* Zuckerman is consumed by his body, by his materiality, hobbled by pain, unable to forget his corporeality, even for a moment. His pain is located "in his neck, arms, and shoulders" (3). He has a "spasm in the upper trapezius," an "aching soreness to either side of the dorsal spine" (6), his "rib cage was askew," his "clavicle was crooked, his left scapula winged out at its lower angle like a chicken's," his "humories was too tightly packed into the shoulder capsule and inserted in the point on the bias" (8). He is "laden with an upper-torso," "saddled with fifteen pounds of head" (10). He has a "denuded scalp, fleshy hips, hone, softening belly" (32). He is burdened with himself, with his body, and wants only escape. No one can be more longful to believe Descartes's dictum then Nathan. To exist without the body would seem an answer to his anguish.

But his body is also the avenue of illicit, unfathomable pleasure, the joy provided by the many women who surround him, satisfying him endlessly. And though he wishes for a "release from self" he is unsure of what that release entails (274). The body, he understands is both distress and nirvana. What is life without the body? Zuckerman's rambles teach him that he is his body. "Your tongue lives in your mouth and your tongue is you" (278). There is no existence outside the body. "Illness is a message from the grave," Zuckerman contends, "Greetings: You and your body are one—it goes, you follow" (254). If he must still decide which definition of the body to live with, he must at least admit that his corpus is him, from that fact there is no escape.

"The body and the mind are one," claims Shuskin in *The Counterlife*, and Zuckerman admits, "No disputing that" (52). And yet the structure of *The Counterlife*, the dream-like quality of its story, suggests a moment of wistful doubt. For though Henry dies in chapter one he comes alive again in chapter two, and though Nathan dies in chapter four his ghost visits Maria in the same chapter, and he is alive again in chapter five. The novel denies logic, denies a final ascension to any pronouncement. Doubt follows even to this point. Roth is neither a Descartian not a materialist. He moves back and forth between belief and disbelief, as his characters move back and forth between need and purpose, always transforming, always in tumult.

Descartes's ability to heal the mind/body dilemma is a product of his time. In Roth's post-Holocaust world to assert the soul's non-physicality is to too simply heal the pain of the Holocaust's losses. For if the victims of the slaughter still exist beyond their bodies, their tragedy loses some its force. To accept Descartes's thesis, for Roth, would be to turn from the facts that call not for simple idealistic solutions but for examination.

Descartes's separation of the mind and the body becomes an important facet of the Nazi attack. Rationalism—the organized, logical, fastidious, organ of the death-camps—is deprived of its salubriousness. And irrationalism—the illogical, instinctual actions of the murderers—too becomes bereft of its attractiveness. Separated, as Descartes would have them, and as the Nazi would employ them, they leave each other to reek their own havoc, unharnessed by their opposite. What transpires inside the individual has its analogue outside. To simply throw a pulpit over the battle between need and purpose is to excuse oneself from the hard facts of the concentrationary universe. For Roth this is not only a personal but a societal failure.

Like Henry, who "was somehow not quite course enough to bow to his desires, and yet not quite fine enough to transcend them," Roth is not quite believing enough to accept the soul as immortal and separate and yet not quite nihilistic enough to give up all hope (CL 54). Caught between the two currents of feeling Roth hangs his very human hat on no pulpit.

Notes

1. Marilyn Fowler calls Neil the quintessential "Rothian protagonist," and sets her definition in a Portnoy-like dichotomy. Klugman is "a blend of the ethical Jew and the more conventional male" (107). What Fowler means by conventional male can only be surmised but ethical Jew is a less slippery appellation first found in Roth's 1974 essay, "Imagining Jews." The young and confident Roth takes to task no less than Bellow and Malamud for presenting Jews only as "actors in dramas of conscience where matters of principle of virtue are at issue" (RMAO 280). Roth complains that Malamud and Bellow employ their own pulpit when writing about Jews, making their Jews into caricatures, men without flesh, without desire, men defined only by questions of mind. Their Jews are drained of blood in an effort to protect the Jewish image after the Holocaust, to posit Jews as moral and intellectual paragons undaunted and untempted by drives beneath the shoulders and waist. Fowler's conventional man, then, must be the ethical Jew's antithesis, the man cut off from conscience, grounded only in desire, in the need for accumulation and pleasure.

2. The dream exposes Kepesh's dilemma. Read as an attempt to demythologize Kafka and as "a desecration of Kafka's image" which "subverts the lectures attempt to reconcile the conscientious dedicated life of the mind with the shameful secret life of the body," it is more accurately seen as Kepesh's subconscious realization of his need to resist paradigms of either need or purpose (Quart 70). It is an attempt to redirect Kafka from the realm of the imaginary and replace him in the real, to view Kafka in the light of the Holocaust, to rescue him from hagiography and return him as flesh and blood, as dual, halved, human. In the dream Kepesh states simply, "Franz Kafka was real" (188). If Kafka is real, containing both body and mind, then, as David admits, "so am I real" (188).

3. The case of Paul de Man is instructive here. de Man's Nazi past was denied by his deconstuctionist followers, by declaring his pro-Nazi writings to be not what they most assuredly were. de Man was freed of guilt by a belief in language's ambiguity. If nothing is true, if the author is not responsible for his words, no guilt follows the anti-Semite. The attractions, then, of deconstruction are self-evident for a man with de Man's history.

ALAN WARREN FRIEDMAN

The Jew's Complaint in Recent American Fiction: Beyond Exodus And Still in the Wilderness

On the appearance of that recent cultural phenomenon known as *Portnoy's Complaint*, Philip Roth said that right now this work "is an event. In two years it will be a book." It is an event that happens at a time when more than the usual number of American myths and idols lie under attack or already shattered, not in embassies abroad but in the streets of America herself, those streets that hordes of eager immigrants once knew were paved with gold, and which are now peopled by a radical and convulsive skepticism that finds the past not a history play but a tragedy—or worse, a farce. In *Waiting for the End*, Leslie Fiedler writes of a simpler time, the relative innocence of the late 1950s, when the enemy was still without, and when "the Jew who thinks he is an American, yet feels in his deepest heart an immitigable difference from the Gentile American who thinks he is a Jew, need only go abroad to realize that, in the eyes of non-Americans, the difference does not exist at all"[1]—because both are equally hated, equally berated, by angry crowds shouting in front of our embassies, "Americans go home!" Increasingly during the 1960s and now the 1970s, Americans who put each other on trial in Chicago and elsewhere for what they think as they cross state lines are reduced to shouting such slogans at themselves—and then having to confront the fact that they *are* home.

From *Critical Essays on Philip Roth*, edited by Sanford Pinsker © 1982 by G.K. Hall & Co.

"Land of equal opportunity," "land of the free and home of the brave," "manifest destiny"—like those of us who grew up in the fifties, and then had to do so again in the sixties, all the grand and noble truisms by which we were taught American history in high school have lost their innocence and, like Roth's Portnoy, we spend our time trying to define what has replaced it. The latest truism to go is "the melting pot"—that overheated, cracking vessel filled with its congealing, lumpy mass incapable of becoming a chemical combination through any process known to man—when ethnic is in, who values a melting pot?

Jews, and Roth's are only among the most recent exemplars, know all about the ambiguous consequences of attempted assimilation. Like other people, only more so, the Jew remains a cultural schizophrenic, a concatenation of past and future haunted by a sense of his own uniqueness, and simultaneously blessed and burdened by his heritage and his vision. The heritage teaches him that he is something special, a creature umbilically linked to a historical grandeur and sense of destiny that, however, best manifests itself through the suffering of its exemplars and which defines them whether or not they seek to escape it. His vision is that of his Promised Land, the land of milk and honey that seems always to lie just beyond his reach.

Bernard Malamud's *The Fixer*, Yakov Bok, who defines history as "the world's bad memory" and being a Jew as "an everlasting curse," says, "We're all in history, that's sure, but some are more than others, Jews more than some" (pp. 314–5). The Jews enter history, of course, in Egypt, when Moses promises them freedom and salvation, and they go with him, reluctantly, against their better judgment, out of their centuries-old comfortable slavery in the stranger's land that gave them roots, out into the wilderness and history. The Biblical account of Exodus (as opposed to Leon Uris' pop-heroic version) reads like the saga of an unhappy marriage or of the generation gap, for it tells of a God, in a manner foreshadowing Roth's Portnoy and his problems, constantly trying to prove to a doubting people that he exists, that he knows his own identity, that he has relevance—first with his flat Cartesian assertion to Moses: "I am that I am," and then his increasingly tangible but still somehow unconvincing magical tricks. He turns rods into snakes, makes plagues descend, holds back and unleashes waters, slakes the thirst of the multitude demanding, "What shall we drink?" He rains manna on them when they cry out for food—"Would to God we had died by the hand of the Lord in Egypt ... for ye have brought us forth into this wilderness, to kill this whole assembly with hunger"—but like the stereotyped Jew lusting for food, they then insist on meat instead of manna: "and the children of Israel ... wept again, and said, Who shall give us flesh to eat? We remember the fish, which we did eat in Egypt freely; the cucumbers, and the melons, and the leeks, and the onions, and the garlic: But now our soul is dried away: there is nothing at all besides this manna, before our eyes." And they get a response they did not anticipate, though they certainly should have. God tells Moses: "Say unto the people, Sanctify yourselves against tomorrow, and ye shall eat flesh: for ye have wept in the ears of the Lord ... : therefore the Lord will give you flesh, and ye shall eat. Ye shall not eat one day, nor two days, nor five days, neither ten days, nor twenty days; But even a whole month, until it comes out at your nostrils, and it be loathsome unto you: because that ye have despised the Lord which is among you ... and while the flesh was yet between their teeth, ere it was chewed, the wrath of the Lord was kindled against the people, and the Lord smote the people with a very great plague."

God's refrain throughout the exodus is, I shall do this or that or the other thing, "and ye shall know that I am the Lord your God." But except when directly confronted by overwhelming power, no one seems to take Him very seriously. This chosen people, reluctantly bearing the burden of that dubious distinction, continues its unending series of complaints and demands, which stimulates God, alternately, to indulgence and ungovernable fury. One can't help wondering about His inner needs that he compulsively keeps seeking to satisfy them through this agnostic, earthy people who have little ultimate use for Him. No wonder he keeps punishing them—for like a good Jewish mother, he is frustrated at having devoted himself, squandered himself, even sacrificed himself, to keep them fed, to give them opportunity to better themselves, to see that they have a decent life and don't consort with *goyish* idols—and they have the effrontery to be less than fully grateful.

The continuing problems of the Yahweh–Israeli relationship explain the long period of exile; for, even on foot, it really doesn't take forty years to get from Egypt to Jericho. But arriving at Canaan and realizing they are expected to fight for it, predictably, "all the children of Israel murmured against Moses and against Aaron: and the whole congregation said unto them Would God that we had died in the land of Egypt! or would God we had died in this wilderness! And wherefore hath the Lord brought us unto this land, to fall by the sword, that our wives and our children should be a prey? were it not better for us to return into Egypt? ... And the Lord said unto Moses, How long will this people provoke me? and how long will it be ere they believe me, for all the signs which I have showed among them?" Only Moses' plea saves the Jews from extinction, but they are doomed to the forty years of exile, until such time as a new generation shall have grown up among a presumably chastened people. But, as God knows best of all, they are incorrigible, "stiffnecked": "And the Lord said unto Moses ... this people will rise up, and go whoring after the Gods of the strangers of the land ... and will forsake me, and break my covenant which I have made with them.... For when I shall have brought them into the land which I sware unto their fathers, that floweth with milk and honey; and they shall have eaten and filled themselves, and waxen fat; then will they turn unto other gods, and serve them, and provoke me, and break my covenant."

There is, then, a kind of foreordination to the fact that the modern Jew, the Jew beyond Exodus, remains in the wilderness. He too doesn't really expect eternality *and* absolution *and* milk and honey *and*—well, peace and joy and youth and beauty; but to hunger for verities and encounter only reality, who needed to journey across a lifetime of wilderness and arrive at journey's end only to discover more wilderness and more lifetime? The Promised Land for the Jew, then, is a place in which to die as well as live, and although it has been given to him he must work to earn it, to produce the milk and honey that exist only insofar as he creates them (and usually having to do so without cows or bees); and though it may be called a place of respite, of cessation of wandering, it is still a wasteland—and one puts down roots there at his own risk, tentatively, circumspectly, for the indifferent arid sand will starve, burn out, bury whatever encroaches and attempts to grow there. And so the Jew, trembling and chosen, trembling *because* chosen, simultaneously enacts and unintentionally parodies the world's success story—the alienation and feebleness, the dream, the struggle, the achievement—and then the wondering if it is all worth it, especially since he achieves nothing permanent and stable, but only more struggle and uncertainty.

It should be no surprise, especially to Jews, who have been there before, that, beyond Sinai, lies more of the same, a Negev Desert of the mind offering an unceasing challenge for man's questing spirit—necessarily questing because rootless. Exodus defines man's condition as process, a constant becoming. The Jew knows, though he often forgets and needs life to remind him, that the Promised Land too is a process and not a goal, a place where one goes to eat forbidden fruit (as Portnoy takes great delight in graphically demonstrating) because such an act at least proves you're alive and in a position to make things happen—even if only for the worse. In general, the Christian view, looking towards Judgment Day and eternality beyond, says that being of the Elect means you've got it made, if not immediately then ultimately. The Jew's already been to his Promised Land, and he finds that it's not so great, in fact seems a little steep at the price; and he would like to know if maybe there isn't something just a little fancier in stock, perhaps something a little more like what the *goyim* are getting over in their neck of Paradise.

All of this is not to say that the Jew does not acknowledge the existence of his God and the possibility of a divine superstructure; he does acknowledge these—at least if pressed hard enough. But he's not only not obsessed by them, he also doesn't spend much of his time looking in that direction. The Jew lives in and of this world, for of all Western religions Judaism is the most secular and agnostic, the least concerned with considering this world as a stage in some larger process and pointed towards some otherworldly ultimate. The Jew knows that God is not a man and that he must try to be one, and so he looks within and builds what he can with the inadequate raw material he discerns there. His agnosticism and secularity lead him to humanism, to an intense concern that the day to day events of the here and now he lived in compassion and consideration, in love and peace—all the tender and lost virtues rarely actualized in a world basically indifferent to the human moment. The Rabbi's eulogy over Morris Bober, the finally-worn-out grocer in Malamud's *The Assistant*, makes the same point in more concrete terms.

> The rabbi gazed down at his prayer book, then looked up.
> "When a Jew dies, who asks if he is a Jew? He is a Jew, we don't ask. There are many ways to be a Jew. So if somebody comes to me and says, 'Rabbi, shall we call such a man Jewish who lived and worked among the gentiles and sold them pig meat, trayfe, that we don't eat it, and not once in twenty years comes inside a synagogue, is such a man a Jew, Rabbi?' To him I will say, 'Yes. Morris Bober was to me a true Jew because he lived in the Jewish experience, which he remembered, and with the Jewish heart.' Maybe not to our formal tradition ... but he was true to the spirit of our life—to want for others that which he wants also for himself. He followed the Law which God gave to Moses on Sinai and told him to bring to the people. He suffered, he endured, but with hope.... He asked for himself little—nothing, but he wanted for his beloved child a better existence than he had. For such reasons he was a Jew. What more does our sweet God ask his poor people?" (p. 180)

The Jew come to America feels doubly estranged—a continuing anomaly, an outsider in the wilderness which is the gentiles' Promised Land. "It is not surprising that he becomes, in Isaac Rosenfeld's phrase 'a specialist in alienation.'"[2] In *Making It*, Norman Podhoretz writes of his father:

> A skeptical, reticent, highly private man, he never got caught up, as so many of his contemporaries did on their journey from East European orthodoxy to Western-style modernity, either in socialism or in any one of the organized varieties of ideological

> Jewish nationalism. He was sympathetic to socialism but not a socialist; he was a Zionist, but not a passionate one; Yiddish remained his first language, but he was not a Yiddishist. He was, in short, a Jewish survivalist, unclassifiable and eclectic, tolerant of any modality of Jewish existence so long as it remained identifiably and self-consciously Jewish, and outraged by any species of Jewish assimilationism, whether overt or concealed. (pp. 297–30)

The attitude here is ambiguous, for the father is surely to be admired for his insulation from the "ism" of the moment, for his immunity from the follies of his fellow Jews. Yet the detachment also implies a lack of commitment, a continuing sense of outsidedness. Leslie Fiedler has written that

> All flights, the Jewish experience teaches, are from one exile to another; and this Americans have always known, though they have sometimes attempted to deny it. Fleeing exclusion in the Old World, the immigrant discovers loneliness in the New World; fleeing communal loneliness of seaboard settlements, he discovers the ultimate isolation of the frontier. It is the dream of exile as freedom which has made America; but it is the experience of exile as terror that has forged the self-consciousness of Americans. (*End*, p. 84)

Paradoxically, then, the Jew is also right at home in America, for alienation is a deeply American theme. He is divided between adhering to the old ways and fully adopting the new—as in the true and typical story of the immigrant who had been a rabbi in the old country; in America, unable to speak English, he naturally finds no job as a rabbi—so he becomes a rich furniture salesman. And the polarizing pressures function all the more traumatically because they are inherent, inherited rather than acquired, products of dual stereotypes: the Jew as Shylock the evil money-grubber or the *nouveau riche* at their crudest and most flagrantly ostentatious; and the obsessive scholar, ashen pale, totally oblivious to material concerns and mere physical functionings—the product of "the Einstein syndrome," which proclaims (as any Jewish mother will tell you) that all Jewish boys are born brilliant.

In another sense, the Jew in America is no longer the anomaly he once was—that of one more written about than writing. Back in the 1920s and 1930s there were not only no major Jewish writers, there were (with a scattering of exceptions like Lionel Trilling and Ben Hecht and Mike Gold) few who were significant at all. With specific reference to the thirties, Fiedler—an archetypically brilliant Jew with the usual problems and then some—has written:

> Even in the creation of the Jew, a job the Jewish writer in the United States has long been struggling to take out of the hands of the Gentiles, there is no Jewish writer who can compare in effectiveness to Thomas Wolfe. Just as Sherwood Anderson and Hemingway and Fitzgerald succeeded in making their hostile images of Jews imaginative currencies in the twenties, Wolfe succeeded in imposing on his period a series of portraits derived from his experiences at New York University; enamelled Jewesses with melon breasts; crude young male students pushing him off the sidewalk; hawk-beaked Jewish elders, presumably manipulating the world of wealth and power from behind the scenes.[3]

Clearly a major change has transpired between those earlier decades and the fifties and sixties; Jews today, though they may not be more certain of their own identity than anyone else, have nonetheless asserted their right to the dubious privilege of writing about themselves—and, in fact, of telling the *goyim* who *they* are.

Several recent commentators have suggested that, to the extent that such processes have locatable origins, the place to begin is with Hemingway's *The Sun Also Rises*, with its stereotyped Jewish antagonist named Robert Cohn:

> Less than a decade after the war that signified the end of Protestant supremacy in American culture, white Protestant Hemingway was able to control the destiny of his Jew with complete confidence, outfitting him with all the Jew's cliché characteristics (doesn't drink, doesn't know when he isn't wanted, is a wet blanket, is too intellectual and unspontaneous, and so on), using him to set off the Protestant types who are the code followers. Hemingway thoroughly humiliates Cohn through his Jewish pugnaciousness, and then dismisses him.[4]

Jewish writers of the fifties and sixties, Fiedler suggests—writers like Bellow, Malamud, and Roth—though under Hemingway's influence for a time, are not descendants of him and his at least literarily anti-Semitic contemporaries, "but are rather anti-Hemingways, avengers of the despised

Robert Cohen [sic], Jewish butt of *The Sun Also Rises*" (*End*, p. 64). They claim Hemingway's caricature as a legitimate character, embrace him as their own, and place him at the center of their still geocentric universe. He has been transformed into the modern equivalent of the hero, someone whose existence somehow matters because he radiates intensity and because, like it or not, he bears the seeds of his culture.

The book that permits the exorcism of Hemingway's ghost for the Jewish writer is Bellow's *Henderson, The Rain King*. Bellow had already made the attempt once. On the first page of his novel, *Dangling Man*, his protagonist denounces the Hemingwayesque "code of the athlete, of the tough boy.... If you have difficulties, grapple with them silently, goes one of their commandments. To hell with that! I intend to talk about mine, and if I had as many mouths as Siva has arms and kept them going all the time, I still could not do myself justice." The exorcism, however, was not to be so easily accomplished, and it was not until 13 years later that Bellow made the more extended and successful effort in *Henderson, The Rain King*. Though its protagonist is not Jewish, it is the parody of Hemingway that all right-thinking American-Jewish writers had unconsciously been awaiting. The title character, who shares Hemingway's initials, is a middle-aged American millionaire who fails to find happiness or peace by trying to raise pigs or cope with his family. He flees to Africa, rejects the safari approach to seek out the natives, becomes a kind of local deity through no talent of his own except brute strength and sheer stupidity, discovers that one is akin to the kind of animal one identifies with, has his vision, and then flies safely out of Africa and back, presumably, to connubial bliss and domestic tranquility—an ending whose very hopefulness, especially cast in such a form, mocks those achieved by Hemingway's protagonists, and of course by Hemingway himself.

Concerning being Jewish and an American and young and an intellectual in the 1930s, Lionel Trilling writes that it had nothing to do with religion or Zionism—for he and others like him had rejected the religion and were generally either indifferent to or actually opposed to the founding of what is now Israel (in the mid 1940s Alfred Kazin called Zionists "dreary middle-class chauvinists")—"our concern with Jewishness was about what is now called authenticity ... that the individual Jewish person recognizes naturally and easily that he *is* a Jew and 'accepts himself' as such." Writing from the vantage point of 1966, Trilling is able to say that

> Nowadays one of the most salient facts about American culture is the prominent place in it that is occupied by Jews. This state of affairs has become a staple subject of both journalism and

> academic study—for some years now the *Times Literary Supplement* has found it impossible to survey the American literary scene without goggling rather solemnly over the number of Jews that make it what it is; foreign students have withdrawn their attention from the New Criticism to turn it upon The Jew in American Culture.[5]

To make the same point in a slightly different way, Fiedler quotes Gore Vidal—an *au courant* writer but, alas, not Jewish—as writing "in mock horror (but with an undertone of real bitterness, too) ... : 'Every year there is a short list of the O.K. writers. Today's list consists of two Jews, two Negroes and a safe floating *goy* of the old American Establishment ...' " (*End*, p. 88).

This is not to say that Jewish writers (any more than their co-religionists in other fields) have completely taken over the scene—though sometimes it does seem as if such is the case—or that we even know what we mean when we speak of Jewish writers today. In the thirties, Trilling says, "we undertook to normalize [the Jewish present] by suggesting that it was not only as respectable as the present of any other group but also as foolish, vulgar, complicated, impossible, and promising."[6] Trilling was, of course, ahead of his time; for it is only after the apocalyptic events of the thirties and forties, only in the context of the fifties and sixties, the context of, on the one hand, the civil rights movement spearheaded to a large extent by young Jews and, on the other, that of the scandals associated with non-Jews like Billie Sol Estes, Bobby Baker, and others, that the necessary merging of stereotypes can occur so as to produce an Abe Fortas—a classically brilliant Jew driven by greed—and result in a hue and cry throughout the land that is not a ritualistic witch hunt, does not even hint at a condemnation on the grounds of Fortas' being a Jew. And on a slightly different level a Norman Podhoretz (himself a living variation on the Portnoy theme of outsidedness as "in-ness") can come along and make a fortune by writing openly about "making it" in this country. He writes that "the immigrant Jewish milieu from which I derive is by now fixed for all time in the American imagination as having been driven by an uninhibited hunger for success. This reputation is by no means as justified as we have been led to believe, but certainly on the surface the 'gospel of success' did reign supreme in the world of my childhood." Yet today it is far more significant, he adds, that American culture itself both embodies materialistic values and seeks to deny them, instilling in us curiously contradictory feelings

> toward the ambition for success.... On the one hand, we are commanded to become successful—that is, to acquire more ...

> worldly goods than we began with, and to do so by our own exertions; on the other hand, it is impressed upon us by means both direct and devious that if we obey the commandment, we shall find ourselves falling victim to the radical corruption of spirit which ... the pursuit of success requires and which its attainment always bespeaks.... On the one hand, our culture teaches us to shape our lives in accordance with the hunger for worldly things; on the other other hand, it spitefully contrives to make us ashamed of the presence of those hungers in ourselves and to deprive us as far as possible of any pleasure in their satisfaction. (*Making It*, pp. xii–xiv)

What has happened is that America herself has become a Jewish mother surrogate, supreme creator of schizophrenia in all her sons.

Thus, Trilling's implicit notion, that "beyond alienation"—to borrow the title of a recent book by an American-Jewish critic named Marcus Klein—lies assimilation for the Jew who wants it, seems a truism. For the contents of the broken melting pot have escaped and covered the land; and who shall be an outsider, an alien, when everyone is? The individual Jewish writer, then, like the Pole and the Italian and the Irishman before him, but unlike the black who follows him, is at last free to seek his own orientation and direction, to write Christian allegories like Nathanael West or obsessive moral fables like Bernard Malamud or middle-class suburban exposés cast in the form of a Jewish joke like Philip Roth. Contemporary Jewish writers, then, are neither monolithic nor univocal; they speak with many voices though they share the same tongue and the same questioning attitude towards the equivocal world their variety of protagonists try gamely to survive in.

Salinger's half-Jewish protagonists, for instance, are kids of all ages, adolescents (like Holden Caulfield) and brittle post-adolescents like the aptly named members of the Glass family; like miniature Hemingway heroes, they are at once tough and wide-eyed, sophisticated and sentimental, persistently expectant and disappointed—which is appealing and moving when the characters are young, but which becomes cloying when they remain unchanged through puberty, marriage, parenthood, religion, insanity, menopause, suicide, and so on. And yet they have their visions of fulfillment, as when Zooey Glass offers his sister the inescapable Fat Lady of the typical radio or television audience ("the eternal vulgarian," Ihab Hassan calls her[7]) as Jesus Christ himself. Malamud offers us the opposite: narrow, suffering Jews, unwilling victims of a heritage they thought to reject. In the short story "The German Refugee," for example, the title character flees to America from Nazi Germany and his non-Jewish wife, and then commits suicide after learning that she embraced Judaism and was executed in the gas chambers. Malamud's characters are old, even the young ones—old and tired and bitter and complaining about a world set against them by definition and which asks them to endure more of the same and keep on shrugging benignly. And, surprisingly, mostly they do, and achieve in the process a crummy but miraculous dignity which allows life to go on going on and meaning to remain a potential.

Bellow's early protagonists are young seekers somewhat akin to Salinger's. (Augie March, for instance, says, "I have always tried to become what I am. But it's a frightening thing. Because what if what I am by nature isn't good enough?") His later and more interesting ones are middle-aged ex-athletes rebelling against a kind of male menopause that seems to threaten them with an eternity of their present condition unless they break immediately and violently out of their inertia through the conquest of untamed jungle (as in *Henderson, the Rain King*), or of women (in *Herzog*), or of self (in *The Last Analysis*). At the beginning of their works it appears that they have already been wherever it is they are going to get, are too blind to know this, and so in a frenzied, picaresque manner strive to attain or recapture a world and a way irrevocably gone. Yet they end, oddly enough, like Malamud's characters and like *Portnoy's Complaint*, at a beginning, or at least a stasis, a still point in the turning world where, if anywhere, beginnings are still possible.

Though the level of formal education varies greatly, the typical protagonist for all these writers—and Roth's Portnoy may be the paradigmatic personification—is highly intellectual and articulate. Unlike Robert Cohn who is mocked because he talks too much, the protagonist of the modern American-Jewish novel takes pride in being an obsessive self-confessor whose verbal diarrhea is, he thinks, preventive medicine against the constipation he will surely inherit from his father. But unlike their fathers, such characters know too much to remain passive, stoical, and silent, and too little to discover ultimate consoling responses to the unending questions they feel constrained to ask about the inadequacies of their world and its strange inhabitants—themselves most especially. Tragic heroes they're not; they don't suffer grandly, they just sort of have aches and pains all over. Tragic heroes are psychotic, possessed of a monomaniacal sense of grandeur; but the Jewish hero like Portnoy is neurotic—and he whines about it (and why not? it hurts just as much whether he's made to suffer by others or himself), but his whining itself is often a thing of glory, so brilliant that it impresses him, dazzles him—and he revels in it, drinks (non-alcoholically) to it, indulges himself in it, plays it for all its worth before whatever audience he can capture by mesmerization or money, whether it be Portnoy's analyst, Zooey Glass's Fat Lady, the group of psychiatrists gathered to watch the closed-circuit performance in Bellow's *The Last Analysis*, or the myriad recipients, living and dead, of Herzog's endless letters.

And on top of everything else, to add to his joy and his woes, the Jew has a mother. As a rule tragic heroes do not have mothers. One who does, Shakespeare's Coriolanus, a huge-statured military commander, causes major problems for the critics because of his dominating mother (appropriately named Volumnia) and his uncomfortable relationship with her; they don't know whether he is superman or, as Aufidius the rival general calls him, a boy of tears. Now any Jew with a mother will recognize immediately that Coriolanus' duality is the quite normal consequence of his trying to please his mother who wants, inevitably, lovingly, two impossibly contradictory things of him: that he be hailed by the world for his unique achievements and that he fulfill himself according to *her* vision of human greatness; that is, that he be totally independent—"As if a man were author of himself" (*Coriolanus*, Act V, scene iii, line 36)—and simultaneously totally dependent upon the self-sacrificing mother who has given him the best years of her life, worked her fingers to the bone for him, scrimped and went without, and asks for nothing in return—except that he be exactly what she needs him to be. If we see Coriolanus, then, as a precursor of Portnoy, a kind of "my son, the Roman tyrant," it all makes perfect sense. Volumnia will do literally anything to have her son achieve her definition of his role, but God help him if he attempts to strike out on his own. The moral, I suppose, is that if you're going to have a mother you'd better be Jewish—at least then you'll know where your troubles are likely to originate.

Oedipus and Hamlet also had mothers, and, at least in the case of Oedipus, in both senses of that phrase. But Jocasta and Gertrude are not only embodiments of political power, they are also good-looking, sexy females, worth murdering kings to possess. The Jewish mother is, on the other hand, the tender and dumpy seat of domestic authority, by definition harassed, middle-aged, long suffering, and simultaneously so emasculating towards any handy husbands or sons and of such delicate sensibilities that even the vaguely risqué, the barest hint at anything having to do with that dirty of dirties, the ultimate four-letter word if it only had the money to buy one more—S-E-X—that one can't help but wonder where all the Jewish kids keep coming from—certainly not from such mothers as these.

Like Malamud's characters, Roth's are Jewish all the way, only their humor has turned to feverishly pitched self-deprecation rather than bitter resignation. Here is Portnoy, who has just been warned by his mother, yet again, about eating French-fried potatoes out because "*tateleh*, it begins with diarrhea, but do you know how it ends? With a sensitive stomach like yours, do you know how it finally ends? *Wearing a plastic bag to do your business in!*" (p. 32). Portnoy's response is typical of his theatrical exasperation:

> Where was the gusto, where was the boldness and courage? Who filled these parents of mine with such a fearful sense of life? ... These two are the outstanding producers and packagers of guilt in our time! ... Please, who crippled us like this? Who made us so morbid and hysterical and weak? ... Is this the Jewish suffering I used to hear so much about? Is this what has come down to me from the pogroms and the persecution? from the mockery and abuse bestowed by the *goyim* over these two thousand lovely years? (pp. 35–7).

What Roth has written is a nervous Jewish *bildungsroman*, its protagonist stretched on the analyst's couch during the entire novel, circling in and around his rites of passage from innocence to neurosis, trying to define his experience as an assimilated, heritage-rejecting American Jew who still feels himself as one apart, unique, doomed to be different from the fellow Americans he longs to embrace as his own. "Look, I'm not asking for the world," he says,

> I just don't see why I should get any less out of life than some schmuck like Oogie Pringle or Henry Aldrich. I want Jane Powell too, God damn it! And Corliss and Veronica. I too want to be the boyfriend of Debbie Reynolds—it's the Eddie Fisher in me coming out, that's all, the longing in all us swarthy Jewboys for those bland blond exotics called *shikses*.... Only what I don't know yet in these feverish years is that for every Eddie yearning for a Debbie, there is a Debbie yearning for an Eddie—a Marilyn Monroe yearning for her Arthur Miller—even an Alice Faye yearning for Phil Harris.... Who knew, you see, who knew back when we were watching *National Velvet*, that this stupendous purple-eyed girl who had the supreme *goyische* gift of all, the courage and know-how to get up and ride around on a horse (as opposed to having one pull your wagon, like the rag-seller for whom I am named)—who would have believed that this girl on the horse with the riding breeches and the perfect enunciation was lusting for our kind no less than we for hers? Because you know what Mike Todd was—a cheap facsimile of my Uncle Hymie upstairs! And who in his right mind would ever have believed that Elizabeth Taylor had the hots for Uncle Hymie? (pp. 151–2).

Both Alexander Portnoy and his mother (the only Mrs. Portnoy he ever knows), are firm believers in "the Einstein syndrome"—especially as personified by Alexander Portnoy. As in *Making It*, perhaps the central theme in *Portnoy's Complaint* (and one virtually ignored by the reviews) concerns the use and abuse of the intellect and, more specifically, the ambiguous role of the intellect in Jewish culture. Traditionally, the Jews view intellect as an end in itself, a dubious but supreme sign of specialness because it bestows more responsibility than freedom; if a means to anything, then to unworldly success: the disputatious role of Talmudic scholar. But the young Jew's assertion of his *own* intellect often takes the form of a total rejection of his Jewishness—the culture, the religion, the people—as when Portnoy, age fourteen, refuses with atheistic integrity to get dressed up on Rosh Hashanah. Looking back on the scene, which hurts rather than amuses, Portnoy mocks the self-righteous younger version of himself—yet it is typical not only of a certain stage in the life of the recently bar-mitzvahed, third generation American Jew, but also of Portnoy throughout his life. For while he intends his intellect as a moral force, an instrument for improving the lot of at least those who fall within the province of the Assistant Commissioner of Human Opportunity for the City of New York if not of the entire world, it becomes a pious means for making money, fame, and females. The thirty-three-year-old Portnoy knows that the self-assertion of the fourteen-year-old Portnoy is essentially a sham: a gut-level attack on his parents cast in the form of an intellectual statement; but though Portnoy's confessional, like Podhoretz's, reveals a great deal of self-consciousness, both are still able to maintain the natural arrogance that supposedly accrues to those of superior intellect and, simultaneously, to perfect that intellect in the service of worldly success. The dichotomy leads invariably to obsessive self-deception, guilt, and a despairing need to escape what pursues from within. Portnoy's neurosis results primarily from rebelling against what he hates (and yet also loves) in his mother and finding it in himself—the prejudice against *goyim*, for example, which he compensates for by taking to bed every blond, blue-eyed, button-nosed, seemingly unobtainable *shikse* he can get his hands on, seduce, do acrobatic tricks with, abandon, and then feel guilty about—all the time striving to put "the id back in Yid ..., and the *oy* back in *goy*" (p. 209). Podhoretz quotes Freud (himself of course a Jew) on the mother–son origins of such paradoxical role-playing: "A man who has been the indisputable favorite of his mother [Portnoy on his father: 'Among his other misfortunes, I was his wife's favorite.'] keeps for life the feeling of a conqueror, that confidence of success which frequently induces real success" (*Making It*, p. 57). "Let's face it, Ma," says Portnoy, "I am the smartest and neatest little boy in the history of my school! Teachers ... go home happy to their husbands because of me" (p. 14). And yet, "When I am bad I am locked out of the apartment," and from his bed at night he can "hear her babbling about her problems to the women around the mah-jongg game: *My Alex is suddenly such a bad eater I have to stand over him with a knife*" (pp. 13, 43). Who but a Jewish mother, of whom Portnoy's is but an epitome, would sacrifice everything—even, or perhaps the word is especially, her husband—in order that her son may succeed, and then winds up revelling in her sacrifice and mocking the success? What other kind of mother makes her sacrifices with such complete and utter commitment that she can threaten the object of all her sacrificing, the pride and joy of her whole life, with immediate and total extinction if he should fail by one iota to achieve in direct proportion to the extent of her sacrificing?—an achievement which is impossible since her sacrifice knows no bounds, is always greater than one can imagine, measure, or equal. And so Portnoy, now an adult, successful and famous, is still making the same complaint:

> Whenever my name now appears in a new story in the *Times*, they bombard every living relative with a copy of the clipping. Half my father's retirement pay goes down the drain in postage, and my mother is on the phone for days at a stretch and has to be fed intravenously, her mouth is going at such a rate about her Alex. In fact, it's exactly as it always has been: they can't get over what a success and a genius I am, ... but still, if you know what I mean, still somehow not entirely perfect.... All they have sacrificed for me and done for me and how they boast about me and are the best public relations firm (they tell me) any child could have, and it turns out that I still won't be perfect. Did you ever hear of such a thing in your life? I just refuse to be perfect. (pp. 107–8)

The anguish Portnoy expresses comically here is real and intense—for he, too, would like to have achieved the all he intended when he started out, the all that lies always beyond the actual. What Portnoy will not, cannot, say is that the intensity of their involvement in his life is not only cloying but also beautiful, and valuable beyond anything he has attained by repudiating them. As Portnoy knows all too well, and has been at pains to demonstrate throughout the session that is his book, his life is immeasurably less perfect than they will ever know. And the resulting guilt—the sense of having achieved nothing of substance (though thriving as the world measures these things) and the need to maintain the façade of success—leads, naturally enough, to his taking the offensive, to his evading introspection by accusing his parents of unforgiveable acts.

For some undefined sin, Moses was barred from bringing his people into the Promised Land towards which he had led them for forty years. Where Moses failed to go there Portnoy has gone, and what he learns, among other things, is that Moses was better off—at least he could still maintain his vision uncontaminated by reality. After all the gentile girls he's had in order to prove how much he belongs *here*, Portnoy (in a section Roth ironically calls "In Exile") goes to Israel to discover that, for once, the Jews are the WASPS, and he finds that the discovery renders him impotent—first, with a small, voluptuous Israeli lieutenant and then with a beautiful idealist who reminds him of, of all people, his mother. As Portnoy puts it: "Doctor: *I couldn't get it up in the State of Israel*! How's *that* for symbolism, *bubi*? Let's see somebody beat that, for acting-out! Could not maintain an erection in The Promised Land! At least not when I needed it, not when I wanted it, not when there was something more desirable than my own hand to stick it into ..." (pp. 257–8). The girl from the kibbutz, who calls him "nothing but a self-hating Jew, ... a shlemiel," towers six feet over the prostrate, defeated Portnoy who starts to sing,

> "Im-po-tent in Is-rael, da da daaah," to the tune of "Lullaby in Birdland.
>
> "Another joke?" she asked.
>
> "And another. And another. Why disclaim my life?"
>
> Then she said a kind thing. She could afford to, of course, way up there. "You should go home."
>
> "Sure, that's what I need, back into the exile."
>
> (pp. 265–9)

And so it's back to America, the diaspora, the Promised Land for Gentiles, back to the alienation which defines him there as it defined the Jews during the forty years in the desert and throughout their history—back because a successful Jewish nation makes neither historical nor sexual sense, and because Portnoy has conceived of Israel not as process, something alive and changing—as Exodus teaches us it is—but rather as something fixed and determined. Besides, only in America can he spite his mother by seducing *shikses*, the only form of love apparently granted Portnoy's perverse penis—at least until the end and the hopeful hint of a beginning with which Roth concludes both the book and what is, after all, only Portnoy's first session of self-analysis and self-definition. The book ends with a cry for help and the possibility of a beginning, a return to process and promise. Eliot's anti-Semitic Gerontion asks, "After such knowledge, what forgiveness?" But self-willed ignorance is not the Jew's way; for Portnoy, now fully conscious heir of Jewish tradition (like Malamud's Yakov Bok), only after such confrontation and self-revelation as that which comprise his book may forgiveness, and therefore viable self-definition, possibly follow. Such endings would seem to be the only kind possible in American-Jewish novels. Perhaps they are the only kind possible in a world that remains defined by mortality and flux. Perhaps, and I suggest this with great temerity, they are (if we but knew it) the only kind we need.

Notes

1. *Waiting for the End: The Crisis in American Culture and a Portrait of Twentieth Century American Literature* (New York, 1964), p. 102. Subsequent references to this work are cited in the text as *End.*

2. Irving Malin, *Jews and Americans* (Carbondale, 1965), p. 14.

3. "The Breakthrough: The American Jewish Novelist and the Fictional Image of the Jew," *Midstream*, 4 (Winter 1958), p. 17.

4. Michael J. Hoffman, "From Cohn to Herzog," *The Yale Review* (Spring 1969), p. 342.

5. "Afterword," *The Unpossessed* by Tess Slesinger (New York, 1966), pp. 319–21.

6. *Ibid.*, p. 320.

7. *Radical Innocence* (New York, 1961), p. 283.

ROBERT FORREY

Oedipal Politics in Portnoy's Complaint

If Freud was correct, the Oedipus complex is the nucleus not only of neurosis but of civilization; that is, it is not only a negative factor creating momentous psychological problems but a positive one also, creating structure, meaning and culture. The French structuralist Jacques Lacan has elaborated and extended Freud's ideas on the Oedipus complex, particularly the central role of language and culture, in the structuring and organization of human experience. Explicating Lacan's theories, which are embedded in a notoriously dense prose, Anika Lemaire writes, "the Oedipus complex is the unconscious articulation of a human world of culture and language; it is the very structure of the unconscious forms of the society ... [Lacan's] point of view consists simply in seeing the Oedipus complex as the pivot of humanization, as a transition from the natural register of life to a cultural register of group exchange and therefore of laws, symbols and organization."[1] On the crucial role of the father in the Oedipus complex, she says, paraphrasing Lacan, the father is "the representative of the Law and a protagonist in the subject's entry into the order of culture, civilization and language. 'It is in the Name-of-the-Father that we must recognize the symbolic function which identifies his person with the figure of the Law' (*Ecrits*, 16)."[2]

At his father's insistence, the David Schearl of Henry Roth's *Call It Sleep* (1934) went to cheder and studied Hebrew, God's language. It is an indication of how far removed from Jewish religious roots Alexander Portnoy is that his father insists he learn shorthand. After all, because Billy Rose knew shorthand, Bernard Baruch hired him as a secretary. By contrast, learning Hebrew never became an issue; it apparently was a dead, useless language. Even Yiddish was nearly a lost tongue for Portnoy, or so he felt. "Talk Yiddish?" he asks. "*How*? I've got twenty-five words to my name—half of them dirty and the rest mispronounced!"[3] He suffers a similar feeling of linguistic inferiority about his English—he refers deprecatingly at one point to his "five-hundred-word New Jersey vocabulary" (p. 233).

Portnoy's feelings of linguistic inadequacy are complemented by and inextricably tied up with his feelings of sexual inadequacy, as one might expect, according to Lacanian theory. A (seemingly) small vocabulary and a (seemingly) small penis go hand in hand. Furthermore, consistent with Lacanian theory, it is the mother, Sophie Portnoy, who made the son feel ashamed of the size, and even the existence, of his penis. Never in his whole life had Alex Portnoy felt more humiliated than when his mother chided him as a boy for wanting a bathing-suit with a jock-strap in it. Her words on that occasion were inscribed indelibly in his memory: "For your little thing?" (p. 51). Another incident which Portnoy recalled from his childhood is instructive in illustrating the connection between the penis and what Lacan designates as the "Name-of-the-Father." When Portnoy Sr. urinated with the bathroom door open, Sophie scolded him for setting a bad example for his son, whom she referred to in that situation not by name but as "you-know-who." Significantly, when it came to sexuality and the penis, neither father nor son possessed a name. Recollecting the episode, Portnoy bitterly lamented, "If only you-know-who [himself, the son] could have found some inspiration in what's-his-name's [Jake, the father's] coarseness" (p. 50). What it was about his father, "what's-his-name," that Alex wanted most to be proud of and identify with was his masculinity, symbolized by his penis.

When Portnoy in describing to Spielvogel an act of masturbation in adolescence says he grabbed "that battered battering ram to freedom, my adolescent cock" (p. 35), he is simultaneously playing with language and his penis. In the scene from adolescence, as Portnoy recalls it, he was being nagged by his mother about what foods he should and should not eat. To escape from this nagging, he fled to the bathroom and behind the closed door, as was his frequent habit, began masturbating his "battered battering ram," etc. This is linguistic as well as sexual playing because Portnoy's penis in that situation was anything but a means to freedom, for the object of Portnoy's fantasies in adolescence was often his sister, who in turn was a barely disguised substitute—as other young women were later—for his mother, who in that same bathroom when Portnoy was a boy used to try to induce him to urinate by seductively tickling his penis. The sexual desire Portnoy had felt for his mother when he was a child did not disappear when he grew older; it just became more disguised and less conscious. In retreating to the bathroom in adolescence, Portnoy was not getting away from his mother; he was by sexual means attaching himself more closely to her. He was only pretending, playing, he was trying to liberate himself from her when he talked about his cock and freedom. His linguistic model in this act of self-deception was not Yiddish or even American but Anglo-Saxon. The noun "cock" has connotations, stemming from the Old English, lacking in the Yiddish words for penis Portnoy usually uses—schmuck, putz, etc. And the phrase "battered battering ram to freedom" echoes the language ("my head is bloodied but unbowed") and mood of that classic expression of Anglo-Saxon pride and courage in the period of imperial England's decline, Henley's poem "Invictus", which Portnoy had learned by heart in school. It is precisely because Portnoy was so completely in the "fell clutch" of his mother that, with his penis and language, he played games in which he pretended that he was potent, that he was getting away from, or letting go of, his mother. In reality, Portnoy was as impotent as his father was constipated; though the bathroom appeared to be the one place father and son could escape from the mother, it was actually the place where they were most clearly subject to her.

In spite of the sexual and linguistic confusion in *Call It Sleep*, the God of the Old Testament sits on His throne, looming omnipotently over David Schearl's Lower East Side, the creator of the Word and the Law. The God who presides over Portnoy's Newark, if He exists at all (which Portnoy deeply doubts), is a petty, jealous and vindictive God. In referring to Him, Portnoy adopts his mother's linguistic attitude toward his father by calling the Heavenly Father not "what's-his-name" but something very much like it: "None Other." The original kill-joy, None Other is determined that all Jews will grow up to be inhibited, neurotic and miserable, as Alex sees it. As Alex's constipated father told him, this God has a big book in which He annually writes in the names of those who are going to live for another twelve months. If you break the smallest rule, Portnoy concludes, this God will sit down in anger and frustration (like his constipated father on the toilet, he blasphemously suggests) and leave your name out of the book. Such is the meanness and authority of this God—and the control he exerts through words—that if He does not write your name down you do not continue to exist.

Nobody in *Portnoy's Complaint* better bespeaks the bankruptcy of the Law and the Word than the official representative of the God of the Old

Testament and spiritual leader for Newark's Reform Jews, Rabbi Warshaw. All of the Rabbi's limitations as a man and a Jew are epitomized, in Roth's characterization of him, in his speech; he is defined in the novel and we see and measure him primarily, perhaps exclusively, through the pretentious and condescending way in which he uses English to say nothing. The overweight and Pall-Mall smoking Rabbi is the American Jew as English gentleman. "This is a man," Portnoy says of him, "who somewhere along the line got the idea that the basic unit of meaning in the English language is the syllable. So no word he pronounces has less than three of them, not even the word God" (p. 73). In contrast to herring-breathed Reb Pankover in *Call It Sleep*, with his unkept clothes and atrocious English (but fluent Hebrew and Yiddish), the role of "Rabbi Syllable," as Roth calls Warshaw, is not to badger, exhort or instruct on God's behalf, but rather to establish through syllabification his own social respectability, in contrast to his uncouth Newark congregation with their Yiddish and East European-inflected American accents. For the effete Rabbi Warshaw, scripture is not Hebrew but "Anglo-oracular" English, perhaps the ultimate antithesis, for an American Jew, from the father's tongue.

In his quest for manhood, Portnoy turns pleadingly to the psychoanalyst Spielvogel, with his heavy foreign accent, as to another Jewish father.

> Doctor Spielvogel, this is my life, my only life, and I'm living it in the middle of a Jewish joke! I am the son in the Jewish joke—*only it ain't no joke*! Please who crippled us like this? Who made us so morbid, and hysterical and weak? ... Doctor, I can't stand any more being frightened like this over nothing. Bless me with manhood. (p. 37.)

Again, it accords with Lacan's theories that Portnoy's attempt to achieve manhood is quintessentially linguistic, as if talking to a new Jewish father (Spielvogel-Freud), whose authority with words is much greater than his own father's, can make him a man. (And note, too, in the child-like candor, Yiddish-like locutions, and intentionally bad grammar of this appeal, the pains Portnoy takes to distinguish his speech from that of the phony Jewish father, Rabbi Warshaw.) Instead of continuing his obsessive and futile pursuit of women, i.e. the mother, Portnoy through psychoanalysis in a sense goes to bed with the father. With Freud's *Collected Papers* in one hand and his penis in the other, reading the one and "kneading" the other, to quote Roth's pun, Portnoy looks eagerly for "the sentence, the phrase, the *word* that will liberate me from what I understand are called my fantasies and fixations"

(p. 186). A compulsive, determined masturbator, as previously noted, Portnoy plays religiously with his penis; he also plays with words, with English, Yiddish and psychoanalytic words, trying to get them to liberate him from his compulsions, trying to come to some understanding of the meaning of his complaint. Psychoanalytic desiderata—the truths of the secularized Jewish faith—occur to him in the form of punning slogans: "LET MY PETER GO!"; "LET'S PUT THE ID BACK IN YID!"; etc. These slogans are rhetorical therapy, part of the "talking cure" which Portnoy conducts in the form of a monologue with his Jewish father figure—Spielvogel.

Before turning to Spielvogel, Portnoy had tried to find salvation sexually through a number of Gentile women. His feelings for and against them were often related at least in part to language. The only Gentile woman he ever seriously thought about marrying was from that same Iowa family in which language was used gently, if not also somewhat genteelly. As young as thirteen Portnoy had felt the irresistible appeal of the well-bred blond shikses, but he understood even then that they lived in an entirely different world, with "grammatical fathers" and mothers named Mary ("Mary! Mother also of Jesus Christ!" he said of the Iowa shikse's mother). Another shikse, a boarding-school type from Connecticut, disqualified herself as a candidate for Mrs. Alexander Portnoy, if Alex is to be believed, because in part she spoke in an intolerable "cutesy-wootsy boarding school argot" (p. 233). Nothing could redeem her in his eyes, not even her great personal sacrifice in finally performing fellatio on him. All of his deeply problematic and ambivalent feelings about Gentile Women came to a head in his relationship with a sexually uninhibited and uninhibiting model he dubbed "the Monkey." He named her this not simply because of her passion for, as he put it, eating his banana, but also, it appears, because he had trouble calling her by her real name, Mary—the mother of Christ again. What in the end convinced Portnoy that he could not find his manhood through the Monkey, in spite of her sexiness, was his discovery that she was barely literate, as she revealed in a note she left for her maid: "dir willa polish the floor by bathrum *pleze* & dont furget the insies of windose mary jane r." Not her promiscuity or predilection for sexual perversity, but such ignorance of the language led Portnoy to the moralistic conclusion: "How unnatural can a relationship be! This woman is ineducable and beyond reclamation" (p. 206). What this rejection of the Monkey may in part signify—and other dimensions of the novel support of this point—is that the Gentile woman, Mary (the mother of Christers) is a hopeless pagan, a slut: the woman who did not get the Word. As inadequate as he, a Jew, felt linguistically, his Gentile paramour was appallingly worse; her illiteracy served to remind him of his inescapably linguistic, Jewish identity.

As a teen-ager in Newark, Portnoy had reluctantly joined some other Jewish boys in a visit to the flat of "Bubbles" Girardi, a loose Italian-American girl. Afraid of being infected or contaminated in the unkosher surroundings, he was appalled by a picture of Christ above the kitchen sink. "What kind of base and brainless schmucks are these people to worship somebody who, number one, never existed, and number two, if he did, looking as he does in that picture, was without a doubt the Pansy of Palestine" (p. 168). In Portnoy's eyes, Christ is the nice Jewish boy become homosexual messiah. By way of settling the question of whether he himself was homosexual, Portnoy answers that, amazing as it sometimes seemed to him (in view of his mother's influence), he was not; he was infected by neither it nor Christianity. We can believe that he sincerely believes he was not, and still be unconvinced that Christ, the prototypical nice Jewish boy, was not a haunting religious and sexual influence in Portnoy's life. It is quite possible that Portnoy's unexplained but deep hostility toward Christ is the result of feeling pressured all his life into becoming a nice Jewish boy or, to put it in a different light, a Jewish son-as-savior. Elsewhere Portnoy had pointed out the tendency of Jewish parents to make their children feel, on the one hand, like "evil little shits," and on the other, like "saviors and sheer perfection" (p. 119). He felt this pressure from within his own family, even after he was a grown man. Weary and feeling on death's doorstep, his father Jake looked to Alex, when the latter was thirty-three, to keep him alive. "Does he actually believe that I somehow have the power to destroy death?" Portnoy asks Spielvogel. "That I am the resurrection and the life? My dad, a real believing Christer! And doesn't even know it!" (p. 118). Jake Portnoy may not have been aware that he wanted his son to be a savior, but the Monkey, the Gentile, knows that's what she wanted, and she goaded him to live up to her expectations. "But—what, what was I supposed to be but *her* Jewish savior?" (p. 153), he asks Spielvogel. But isn't that really his secret forbidden wish, to be a "Christer," that is a Jewish son who transcends the Oedipal politics of the Jewish family, who sexually renounces not only the mother and the debased (Gentile) sexual objects who serve as her substitute, but also renounces sexuality (or at least heterosexuality) itself? Isn't Portnoy afraid that, to get out of the Jewish family, where words were weapons and language somewhat lethal, he would be willing to become anything—a savior, a Christian, a pansy or perhaps, like the ex-Jewish son ascending over the Gentile sink, all three? Until he discovered psychoanalysis, with its putatively therapeutic rhetoric, the Jewish son had only two alternatives: follow in the footsteps of Christ or become permanently trapped in a Jewish joke.

The sexual, religious and linguistic threads of *Portnoy's Complaint* are woven together in the trip Portnoy describes taking at the age of thirty-three to Rome, Greece and Israel. He went to Rome with the Monkey and the two of them went to bed with a whore in Rome, fulfilling one of Portnoy's conscious sexual fantasies, as well as, possibly, one of his unconscious religious ones. The experience proved disappointing to him, and in a recurrence of an old phobia, he became obsessed with the idea that the whore of Rome had infected him. It was in Rome that he saw clearly the futility of having looked for salvation, that is for his manhood, through Gentile women. In Greece, his next stop after Rome, he abandoned the Monkey. Given the Oedipal nature of his problems, it was an appropriate place, he himself reflects, to end the relationship. However, he was under no illusion that his Oedipal drama was Greek rather than Jewish, tragic rather than pathetic. "*Oedipus Rex* is a tragedy, schmuck, not another joke!" (p. 266), he castigates himself. The conclusion Portnoy reached in Europe was that, instead of wasting his life pursuing Gentile women, he wanted to marry a Jewish girl and raise a Jewish family. But to do that he has to feel like a man, like a *Jewish* man, the model of which he fondly remembers as the Jewish fathers who played baseball in Newark: "Because I love those men! Because I want to grow up to be one of those men!" (p. 277).

Possibly reflecting the relatively low status of the male in Yiddish culture, the Yiddish language contains a number of demeaning and deprecatory slang words for the penis. Derogatory words like schmuck, putz, shvontz, and schlong can be used to describe the penis or, alternately, a contemptibly hapless or stupid, usually Jewish, male (i.e. schlemiel). On the subject of emasculated Jewish sons, Portnoy says his mother held up to him as models to follow a number of namby-pambies who did everything to please their Jewish mothers. "'Do you remember Seymour Schmuck, Alex?' she asks me, or Aaron Putz or Howard Schlong, or some yo-yo I am supposed to have known in grade school twenty-five years ago, and of whom I have no recollection whatsoever" (p. 99). In assigning fictitious names to the boys his mother praises, Portnoy exploits the connotations of Yiddish slang words for penis to underscore the Jewish son's slavish attachment to his mother. What the penis-names Portnoy makes up reveal is the tendency of the Jewish son, in his attempt to please the mother, to become the phallus, which, Lacan reminds us, is the object of her desire. To escape becoming a mama's boy, the son must renounce those sexual feelings for his mother which tend to make him identify with the object of her desire—the phallus. To become a man and accede to the Name-of-the-Father, the son must, under the threat of castration, represented by the father, graduate from being the phallus to having it (he must lose it before he can use it), the distinction between which, Lacan claims, is absolutely crucial. If to please his mother the son persists in being the object of his mother's desire, that is the phallus, then he becomes a schmuck.

When Portnoy had fantasies of becoming a Jewish father, bringing his family up in New Jersey, he imagined them all listening each evening not to the sacred texts of Judaism (the *toroth*) but to those Jewish comics, with or without Yiddish accents, who kept Americans laughing when he was growing up in the thirties and forties: Jack Benny and Mr. Kitzel (of whose Yiddish accent the boy Portnoy could do a flawless and hilarious imitation); Fred Allen and Mrs. Nussbaum; and Phil Harris and Frankie Remly. (Omitted, by oversight no doubt, were Eddie Cantor and the Mad Russian.) The point is even Portnoy's sentimental dream of Jewish marriage and fatherhood unfolds within the context of a Jewish joke—the same Jewish joke in which he felt he had lost his manhood and from which he had pleaded with Spielvogel to liberate him. Nationalized by radio and later extended and further commercialized by popular literature, film and television, the Jewish joke become the cultural code, the linguistic mode in which the complaining Jewish son, blaming most and often all his problems on his Jewish mother, capitalized on—and became further mired in—his feelings of emotional and sexual incompetence.

Portnoy's ultimate complaint is not only against the mother; it is also against language, against the word, the traditional repository of Jewish faith. And against talk, which Michael Gold, writing in the thirties, claimed "has ever been the joy of the Jewish race, great torrents of boundless, exalted talk."[4] Some post-War Jewish-American writers, like Roth, tend to see language and talk as complaint, perhaps a specifically Jewish complaint, which they want to get away from, or at least reduce to its most elemental meaning: pain. Instead of wanting to talk exaltedly, Portnoy at the end of the novel wants simply to howl. "A pure howl," he tells Spielvogel, "without any more words between me and it!" (p. 273). (The antithesis, perhaps, to the excessive syllabification of Rabbi Warshaw.) What all this howling (or is it merely whining?) is about is the Jewish son's lack of tumidity and potency. Unable to assume the role of the father, who possesses the Phallus and the word, Portnoy is driven to cunnilingus—the tongue substituting for the phallus, sex for language. Without the word, without the phallus, the only way the son can relate to the forbidden other, the Mother, and her substitutes, is by using the tongue to complain futilely about, or orally and impotently enter into, her. In behaving like this Portnoy is lacking in culture, in Lacan's sense; he is reduced to an animal, non-linguistic level: "Maybe that's all I really am, a lapper of cunt, the slavish mouth for some woman's hole. Eat! And so be it! Maybe the wisest solution is for me to live on all fours! Crawl through life feasting on pussy, and leave the righting of wrongs and the fathering of families to the upright creatures!" (p. 270). Portnoy's rough beast can not come; his howling complaint is utter wordlessness; his argument, in its various senses, is without issue.

More complex linguistically than it may at first appear, Portnoy's complaint, i.e. the Oedipus complex, nevertheless becomes in Roth's treatment of it, a Jewish joke, a brilliant, elaborate spiel. (It is perhaps a compensation for his complex fate as a Jew that the castrated Portnoy becomes such an accomplished, cunning linguist.) The psychoanalytic dialogue turns into a Jewish monologue; the quest for *the* psychoanalytic word that would help resolve the Oedipus complex ends in a howl of frustration and painful laughter. The new Jewish father to whom Portnoy had prayed for deliverance from the Jewish joke his life had become turns out to be an "ungrammatical" father, another creature of the Diaspora and of the doctrine of historical impotency. That Spielvogel is circumscribed by and a victim of the same Jewish joke that Portnoy had prayed for deliverance from is indicated by the fact that the only words the psychoanalyst speaks, the very last words in the novel—"Now vee may perhaps to begin. Yes?"—bear the accent and syntax of a Jewish vaudevillian, and are introduced with the caption "Punchline," thus emphasizing that all that had been said up to that point was a joke, an extended vocal Jewish spiel.

Writing at a time when or in a frame of mind in which it was still possible for an American Jew to be romantic and mythopoeic about the Oedipus complex, Henry Roth called it sleep. Writing in the nineteen-sixties, in a very different frame of mind, Philip Roth reduced that monumental human complex which Freud connected with "the beginnings of religion, ethics, society and art" into a hysterically funny, a specifically, if not exclusively, Jewish complaint: the complaint of the Jewish son to the Jewish father about the Jewish mother. However, Portnoy's fundamental but unspoken complaint is language, that symbolic discourse in the complex structure of which not only meaning but manhood (the Phallus) can be either achieved or, as in Portnoy's case, lost. Roth's novel suggests that language is a Jewish and perhaps ultimately a human complaint. But language is also, structuralists remind us, the precondition of humanity, "the site of possible liberty and truth."[5] Perhaps that is the point which Portnoy, if he is to be more than a cunning linguist, must take seriously.

NOTES

1. Anika Lemaire, *Jacques Lacan* (London: Routledge & Kegan Paul, 1977), p. 92.

2. *Lacan*, p. 85. Because of the vital importance which Lacan attributes to the resolution of the Oedipus complex in the acquisition of language and accession of the subject to the symbolic realm, it is worth trying to clarify a complex point in his theory, specifically the notion that "in the quest for the Phallus, the subject moves from being it to having it." (*Lacan*, p. 95.) In the immediate, undifferentiated relationship with the mother, the son is the phallus (by which Lacan means much more than penis), which is the

object of the mother's desire. "Originally, the *infans* subject wishes *to be* the Phallus, the object of his mother's desire. This means that in order to ensure himself of his mother's presence and her complete affective support, the child unconsciously seeks to be that which can best gratify her. He seeks to make himself exclusively indispensable. This affective wish is tinged with eroticism, and the multiple phantasies elaborated by the child, who is, in a confused way, awake to his parents' sexual relations, are grouped around the phallic symbol, around the general idea of the 'Father'": and yet it is the father who "renders the mother–child fusion impossible by his interdiction and marks the child with a fundamental lack of being ... His true desire and the multiple phantasmatic forms it took are pushed back into the unconscious. This is the primal repression which determines accession to language and which substitutes a symbol and a Law for the Real of existence." (*Lacan*, p. 87.) By accepting the Law of the father the son gives up the mother, as a sexual object, and begins a quest for other objects farther and farther from the original object of his desire. The son gives up the mother but he acquires by way of compensation the whole world—that is the world of discourse and symbolic exchange, all that we designate by the term culture. If the son had not made this transition, language would have for him no referent; words and "reality," the signifier and the signified, would be indistinguishable, which is why schizophrenia is not just a sexual problem; it is also a language problem.

3. *Portnoy's Complaint* (New York: Random House, 1967), p. 224. Subsequent page references will be incorporated into the text of the paper.

4. *Jews Without Money* (New York: Avon Books, 1965), p. 70.

5. "Forward by Antoine Vergote," In *Lacan*, p. xxiii.

ALAN COOPER

The Alex Perplex

To be bad! Neil Klugman had flirted with the idea and gone back to the library. Paul, Gabe, and Lucy never got to first base with it; duty, in an age of duty, had pulled them down. It was an American ideal that traced at least to Huck Finn's glorious refusal to be civilized, and it was the underside of niceness that all "nice Jewish boys" could spot down the block or across the fence or tracks, where unparented gentile kids roved unencumbered by expectations of A's or Hebrew school or even homework.

To reveal this underside of the Jewish psyche, Roth would need release from the artistic and emotional restraints under which he had always practiced his craft. No simple matter. The writing of *Portnoy's Complaint* (1969) was a complex and indirect undertaking, a coalescence of awarenesses and events within the writer and within the age. *Portnoy's* multiple-stage process of gestation Roth would analyze in a series of interviews and responses to critics published mostly in *Reading Myself and Others* (1975); but the shocks that induced its birth he would not disclose until *The Facts* (1988). What should become clear to the ordinary reader of these works—and should have been assumed, though it was not, by all critics—is that *Portnoy's Complaint* is no spontaneous ranting by its author, although its final drafting came in a spurt of concentrated energy that helped give it that tone.

The five years Roth took after *Letting Go* to convert Maggie's oral

---

history into *When She Was Good* was the longest time he would ever take between published novels. But during that time he was also trying out stories, in different forms, based in his own background. The strain of maintaining his contrived Middle-American tone in the novel in progress could be relieved by some free use of his adolescent wisecracking tone in these other pieces: that tone he had so studiously striven to replace during years of absorbing the great tradition. And imagining Maggie into Lucy could be offset by imagining Newark's Weequahic boys into their wilder ethnic possibilities. Roth needed, he said, to work both veins at once:

> This continuous movement back and forth from one partially realized project to another is fairly typical of how my work evolves and the way I deal with literary frustration and uncertainty, and serves me as a means of both checking and indulging "inspiration." The idea, in part, is to keep alive fictions that draw their energy from different sources, so that when circumstances combine to rouse one or another of the sleeping beasts, there is a carcass around for it to feed on. (*RMAO* 35)

Early in that five-year span Roth worked up a two-hundred-page manuscript titled *The Jewboy*, based loosely and folkloricly on growing up in Newark, in which he gave free rein to wordplay and *kvetches* (*RMAO* 33–34). Pursuing an interest in drama (that shortly would win him a Ford Foundation grant to study the genre), he also worked up the draft of a play titled *The Nice Jewish Boy*—"in its way a less comforting, more aggressive *Abie's Irish Rose*"—which got as far into production as a 1964 reading at the American Place Theater, the nice, *shiksa*-involved Jewish boy being played by the then unknown Dustin Hoffman (*RMAO* 34). But though the dialogue revealed the surface conflicts of his characters, Roth was not sufficiently at home in stage drama to explore their "secret life," and so he gave up the project. He was now two years into the writing of Lucy's complaint; without knowing it, he was also in the early stages of writing Alex's. But neither the theme nor the form it would take was clear to Roth:

> ... the struggle that was to be at the source of Alexander Portnoy's difficulties, and motivate his complaint, was in those early years of work still so out of focus that all I could do was recapitulate his problem *technically*, telling first the dreamy side of the story, then the story in more conventional terms and by relatively measured means. Not until I found, in the person of a troubled analysand, the voice that could speak in behalf of both the "Jewboy" (with all that word signifies to Jew and Gentile alike

> about aggression, appetite, and marginality) and the "nice Jewish boy" (and what that epithet implies about repression, respectability, and social acceptance) was I able to complete a fiction that was expressive, instead of symptomatic, of the character's dilemma. (*RMAO* 35)

There would first be other stages to go. In 1964 Roth faced Maggie in court for legal separation proceedings (*Facts* 155), and subsequent telephone calls and other entanglements kept the real woman not far from the forefront of his mind. Writing *When She Was Good* continued to be an emotional strain. Its very writing was in part an attempt to exorcise Maggie from his own psyche, but whatever royalties it might bring would not free him from the burdens of her alimony: he had not had a great commercial success in his writing and he saw himself doomed by Maggie's refusal of a divorce and her insistence on claiming social, emotional, and financial rewards from his limited fame. Whatever relief Roth might have gotten on the couch, or in bed, his vocation was that of writer, and his instinct was to write himself free. After he completed the manuscript of *When She Was Good* in mid-1966, feeling the need to break loose, Roth "almost immediately began to write a longish monologue, beside which the fetid indiscretions of *Portnoy's Complaint* [he later said] would appear to be the work of Louisa May Alcott" (*RMAO* 36). In this manic piece, his monologist delivers a slide-show lecture on sex, the slides being of the genitalia of the famous. Roth did not finish this monologue, realizing that it was "blasphemous, mean, bizarre, scatological, tasteless, [though] spirited" and therefore unpublishable. But, Roth explained,

> buried somewhere in the sixty or seventy pages were several thousand words on the subject of adolescent masturbation, a personal interlude by the lecturer, that seemed to me ... to be funny and true, and worth saving, if only because it was the only sustained piece of writing on the subject that I could remember reading in a work of fiction. (*RMAO* 36)

This was not an attempt at personal confession, or even a deliberate attempt to explore the subject, rather an emanation from an unpublishable "writer's hijinks" that allowed Roth, he says,

> to relax my guard and go on at some length about the solitary activity that is so difficult to talk about and yet so near at hand. For me writing about the act had, at the outset, to be as secret as the act itself. (*RMAO* 37)

Roth had also embarked on still a fourth piece, an autobiographical fiction about growing up Jewish in New Jersey, to which he had assigned the tentative title *Portrait of the Artist* and for which he had invented another family living upstairs in their two-family house, based partly on families of childhood friends but drawing themes also from writings of Roth's Jewish students at the Iowa Writers' Workshop—a family he called the Portnoys.

What his Jewish students had written about—what Roth had contrasted to Harry Golden's asserted contentment in his 1961 "Some New Jewish Stereotypes"—was the phenomenon, common in his students' early adolescence, of parental smothering: being watched, forever watched, by their mothers, and envying their gentile friends their parents' indifference. That indifference to the details of a son's life afforded the gentile child opportunity for sexual adventure. As Roth had noted,

> ... in these short stories the girls to whom the Gentile friend leads the young [Jewish] narrator are never Jewish. The Jewish women are mothers and sisters. The sexual yearning is for the Other. The dream of the shiksa—counterpart to the Gentile dream of the Jewess, often described as 'melon breasted.' ... [W]hat the heroes of these stories invariably learn—as the Gentile comrades disappear into other neighborhoods or into maturity—are the burdensome contradictions of their own predicament. (*RMAO* 143)

So many of Roth's students had written variations on this story that he now confidently regarded it as a genuine folktale, "an authentic bit of American-Jewish mythology" that could transform those Portnoys upstairs into something more.

> ... here were the fallible, oversized, anthropomorphic gods who had reigned over the households of my neighborhood; here was that legendary Jewish family dwelling on high, whose squabbles over French-fried potatoes, synagogue attendance, and shiksas were, admittedly, of an Olympian magnitude and splendor, but by whose terrifying kitchen lightning storms were illuminated the values, dreams, fears, and aspirations by which we mortal Jews lived somewhat less vividly down below. (*RMAO* 39)

Roth's 1974 account of the coalescing of all these elements is pat and entertaining, though not yet complete. He had begun

> to ground the mythological in the recognizable, the verifiable, the historical. Though they might *derive* from Mt. Olympus (by way of Mt. Sinai), these Portnoys were going to live in a Newark and at a time and in a way I could vouch for by observation and experience.

This required the first person, dropping the restraining conventions of *Portrait of the Artist*, and releasing

> the Portnoys from their role as supporting actors in another family's drama. They would not get star billing until sometime later, when out of odds and ends of *Portrait of the Artist* I liked best, I began to write something I called 'A Jewish Patient Begins His Analysis.' (*RMAO* 40)

From all this experimentation Roth was almost prepared to fashion the work that, after taking the country by storm, would be criticized for being a mere personal rant. Roth's, account concludes:

> This turned out to be a brief story narrated by the Portnoys' son, Alexander, purportedly his introductory remarks to his psychoanalyst. And who was this Alexander? None other than that Jewish boy who used to turn up time after time in the stories written by those Jewish graduate students back in the Iowa Writers' Workshop: the "watched-over" Jewish son with his sexual dream of The Other. Strictly speaking, the writing of *Portnoy's Complaint* began with discovering Portnoy's voice—more accurately, his mouth—and discovering, along with it, the listening ear: the silent Dr. Spielvogel. The psychoanalytic monologue—a narrative technique whose rhetorical possibilities I'd been availing myself of for years, only not on paper—was to furnish the means by which I thought I might convincingly draw together the fantastic element of *The Jewboy* and the realistic documentation of *Portrait of the Artist* and *The Nice Jewish Boy*. And a means, too, of legitimizing the obscene preoccupations of the untitled slide show on the subject of sexual parts. Instead of the projection screen (and the gaping), the couch (and the unveiling); instead of gleeful, sadistic voyeurism—brash, shameful, masochistic, euphoric, vengeful, conscience-ridden exhibitionism. Now I could perhaps to begin. (*RMAO* 40–41)

The birthing of the novel, however, was attended by two unexpected events; one would provide Roth with a sense of destiny about himself that would surface again two decades later, and the other would both provide the final thrust into publication of *Portnoy's Complaint* and hover at the edge of Roth's fictive imagination for the next half decade. The first event was an attack of appendicitis that brought him to within two hours of death, left his stomach filled with poisonous pus, had him delirious from peritonitis, and kept him in the hospital for most of two and a half months; he had, as Albert Goldman would put it, "wrestled the *Malekhamoves*—the angel of death—to a fall" and felt prophetically charged with new life. That and his convalescence in Florida, shared time with Ann Mudge that did not allow him to write, exacerbated his itch to get back to *Portnoy*, parts of which he had brought out in periodicals. But over the project hung another cloud; the enthusiastic responses to episodes already published had sparked speculation in publishing circles that the whole work, if it were finished and brought out as a book, would pay handsome royalties. Maggie was now working in publishing, resentfully drinking, and positioning herself, through phone calls and legal inquiries that Roth had heard about, to make herself known as his muse and to turn a considerable portion of any royalties into alimony. The prospect of a custody battle over the as-yet-unborn novel was enough to protract the labor. It might take years or leave the fetus stillborn. The other event, which Roth would fictionalize six years later in *My Life as a Man* but not disclose to the public until twenty years later in *The Facts*, was Maggie's sudden death in a car accident in Central Park.

The conflict of Roth's feelings at the latter piece of news one can only begin to imagine. Commanding his responses into order and out of guilt would preoccupy Roth personally and fictively for at least two decades. But the immediate practical effect was liberation, the end of the waking nightmare. She was out of his life, and he, despite wishes and fantasies, was guiltless of her blood. Anything he published now he would own himself. No court could limit his activities. After the funeral (Jewish, at her obsessed request) and the partings from her now grown children, for whom he had done some parenting a decade before, he returned to his manuscript and within a few days made hasty reservations to lose himself in the Yaddo artists' colony at Saratoga Springs (he had gone there two years before to finish *When She Was Good*)[1] so as to bring to publishable light the text of *Portnoy's Complaint*. He went by bus—a car might, at flagging moments, tempt him out of the concentrated discipline of staying in his cabin at his typewriter—and he was at work from the time he left the Port Authority bus terminal, "rereading on the long trip up the thruway the rough first draft of the last two chapters of [his] book" (*Facts* 156). His sense of freedom, converted to total concentration, allowed him to work in isolation "twelve and fourteen hours a day until the book was done, and then [he] took the bus back down, feeling triumphant and indestructible."

Roth provided his accounts of the writing of *Portnoy's Complaint* long after publication, to answer that strain of criticism that would equate him with his protagonist and the novel with a transcript of his therapy. But the experience, he has said, liberated more than his unwritten life; it liberated him as a writer

> from an apprentice's literary models, particularly from the awesome graduate-school authority of Henry James, whose *Portrait of a Lady* had been a virtual handbook during the early drafts of *Letting Go*, and from the example of Flaubert, whose detached irony in the face of a small-town woman's disastrous delusions had me obsessively thumbing through the pages of *Madame Bovary* during the years I was searching for the perch from which to observe the people in *When She Was Good*. (*Facts* 157)

From now on his characters could sound like the Jews among whom he had been most comfortable in his youth and like those popular comics now teaching rising inflection to the general population. The most endearing among these, for Roth, had long been Henny Youngman, whom he had seen on stage at the Roxy when he was ten. Considering in 1973 whether he still viewed himself as a disciple of Youngman, he concluded:

> Also of Jake the Snake H., a middle-aged master of invective and insult, and a repository of lascivious neighborhood gossip (and, amazingly, the father of a friend of mine), who owned the corner candy store in the years when I much preferred the pinball machine to the company of my parents. I am also a disciple of my older brother's friend and navy buddy, Arnold G., an unconstrained Jewish living-room clown whose indecent stories of failure and confusion in sex did a little to demythologize the world of the sensual for me in early adolescence. As Jake the Snake demythologized the world of the respectable. As Henny Youngman, whining about family and friends while eliciting laughable squeaks from the violin (the very violin that was to make of every little Jewish boy, myself included, a world-famous, urbane, poetic, dignified, and revered Yehudi), demythologized our yearnings for cultural superiority—or for superiority through

> culture—and argued by his shlemieldom that it was in the world of domestic squabble and unending social compromise, rather than on the concert stage, that the Jews of his audience might expect to spend their lives. (*RMAO* 81)

Whether the liberation was into a discovery of his own voice and subject or out of the bonds of social contract with his people would be a subject of debate among critics for almost the rest of Roth's career. Put another way, would Roth now be using the voices and anxieties of Jews to probe their, or America's, repression or to denigrate Jewish ethical values? Should America feel for Portnoy or revile him and his author as turncoats?

Alex Portnoy wants to be bad and to be guilt-free. He manages neither. Sexually violate and curse as he may, his soul belongs to those who owned his first years; and Sophie and Jack stand for goodness. How far can he distance himself from them when his only outlet is Dr. Spielvogel, sitting silently opposite the couch, and when all his words are but a preface to dubious action? Any healing (highly unlikely) will have to take place after the novel has concluded. Behind Spielvogel looms Sophie, "the most unforgettable character," as the *Reader's Digest* would put it, Alex "has ever met," her original female musk Oedipally perfuming—and endowing with moral sanction—every woman he will meet from his first-grade teacher to the Israeli who finally wrestles him into humiliated submission. Jack, his unworthy Oedipal rival, is a nebbish with heart—but away from Sophie able to move policies and agents—who wants for Alex opportunities beyond the eighth grade and a company desk. The insurance company for which Jack sells policies to the blacks of the inner city is located off in Massachusetts, where the pilgrims still hold sway; on his company stationery a picture of the Mayflower underscores the awareness that Jack and his crew of customers have yet to land in the real America. In hopes that his son can complete the journey, he sacrifices in heat and spikes of light. But Alex can move past his father only in paroxysms of guilt, alternately ranting and weeping. "Doctor, what should I rid myself of, tell me, the hatred or the love?"

At thirty-three, now Assistant Commissioner for Human Opportunity for the City of New York, Portnoy spends 274 pages poring over the causes and effects of this ambivalence toward parents. He rehashes his attempts to free himself through sex, reiterating its failure to bring pleasure or release. He is "torn by desires that are repugnant to [his] conscience, and a conscience repugnant to [his] desires." To free himself from goodness, from being the "nice Jewish boy" that his job description appears to underscore, he would be secretly bad, sexually licentious, except that the shame such behavior engenders only intensifies the problem. He wants "to be bad—and enjoy it!" But he can't, at least not without help. Desperately he prays to the deity Spielvogel: "Bless me with manhood! Make me brave! Make me strong! Make me *whole*! Enough being a nice Jewish boy, publicly pleasing my parents, while privately pulling my putz! Enough!"

Why this need to "put the id back in Yid" at age thirty-three? Perhaps because he had not satisfied other needs earlier, especially the adolescent's defining need for separation and privacy. Alex's only chance for that had been the one venue from which he could close out his prying mother, the bathroom (though his family did not accept the closing even of this door). Another adolescent need, to be one of the guys, he could fulfill by swapping fantasies on the corner and then playing them out in that bathroom. The danger of discovery and the realization that what he was doing flew in the face of tribal taboos gave the activity zest and himself identity.

Unable to stand up against Sophie, Alex had thus learned in youth to substitute masturbation for assertion, to drown out her carping plaints with a sexy blonde voice in his head urging on "Big Boy." Then in adulthood, as he exchanged this fantasy Gentile for the real-life women he met, he reduced them similarly to stereotypes: "The Pumpkin," "The Pilgrim," and "The Monkey" were all the forbidden *shiksa* in her respective guises as Middle-American wholesome, old New England establishment, and blue-collar ex-hillbilly. Among them, in Alex's recountings, only the Monkey approaches a rounded character with needs and capacity to love. But sexually liberated, nearly fulfilling Portnoy's fantasy, she is the most threatening. Her being almost illiterate (though a highly successful professional model) and slightly whorish affronts the Jewish parents buried within him. Sophie with the breadknife lingers in the back of his mind ready to castrate as once she would cut him bread and wave away constipating French fries. Alex must cast his Monkey off. After taking her as far away from Sophie as possible, he leaves her on the ledge of an Athens hotel, threatening to jump, while he flies off to Israel, to another mythic bosom. Portnoy's assertions of penile prowess—his personal myth of the battering ram that could break down barriers—have left him alienated and lonely. "How have I come to be such an enemy and flayer of myself? And so alone! Oh, so alone! Nothing but *self*! Locked up in *me*!"

Alex's only happy memories of his Jewish boyhood are not of solitary but of participatory activity. His most religious experiences, though, had nothing to do with *shul*. Flying into Israel, in the chapter ironically titled "In Exile," Portnoy daydreams of what had been for him the perfect Jewish homeland, the Weequahic neighborhood field where on Sunday mornings he had watched the "men" play softball. They were Jews of every station, and teachers of the art of kibitzing, and he had supposed that he would always be there, even when grown, to complete his Sundays after *his* participation with *his* own wife and children and family meal and radio shows, in a Jewish national home where he would be totally American. Alex was too young then to ask whether this ball field was any different from those that had nurtured the heroes of his bubble-gum cards. But the "men" were communal parents. His own father had not played, had been able only occasionally to be a spectator; but through membership in this circumcised Weequahic tribe, Alex felt connected to the larger Jewish peoplehood.

Alex's apprenticeship for being one of the "men" was served in two illusory worlds of safe haven, a sunny world of center field and a misty world of fat and sweat. On weekdays after school Alex had played baseball, the most self-defining of team sports, and once a month he had gone with his father to the Turkish baths. These totally male spheres, with their initiations and ceremonies, had provided respite from the suffocation of Sophie. Baseball represented the opportunity for individual grace. Unlike other team sports where one could be lost in the huddle or the whirl of bodies, baseball focused instant after instant on the solitary player. The grace of the ball player is a common theme in Roth, beginning quite early. In "You Can't Tell a Man by The Song He Sings," the sixth story in the *Goodbye, Columbus* collection, it is relative prowess in baseball that distinguishes the doer from the talker among school-yard kids, and in "Recollections from Beyond the Last Rope" Roth mused on the ball player's poise and sense of control, which he as a child had practiced in his cellar winters at Newark to impress the girls of summer at Bradley Beach.

> I practiced not only throwing but standing, waiting, retrieving. I knew exactly what I wanted to look like; and it was some years after I'd stopped vacationing at Bradley that I saw in Florence what I'd had in mind—it was Michelangelo's David. He would have knocked the girls at Bradley for a loop. Imagine that what he is holding up to his breast is not a sling, but a glove; imagine in that throwing arm, loose but ready at his side, not a rock but a baseball; see the way each joint picks up the weight from the one above; see how he peers down for the signal beneath those brows. See all that, and you'll see what I was trying for in my cellar all winter long. (45)

That same sense of poise and control Alex Portnoy had known in center field. There everything was clear. He knew who he was and what he had to do; practice let him do it without endless thinking about moral consequences. And since Sophie knew nothing about its mysteries, there was no question of pleasing or disappointing her, or need—or opportunity—to disappear within the team. "Is it me?" was not at war with "Is it us?" A center fielder had sovereignty over his life. Portnoy tells his doctor, "there are people who feel in life the ease, the self-assurance, the simple and essential affiliation with what is going on, that I used to feel as the center fielder for the Seabees." Those people, at ease under spacious skies, were Americans.

Another escape into a purely male world had been Portnoy's monthly visit with his father to the local steam baths, a return to a primeval pre-Portnoy era, "some sloppy watery time, before there were families such as we know them." Here Jack is relaxed, in charge of himself; and Alex not only feels the warm physical bond to his father in a "natural" domain "without *goyim* and women" but also "... lose[s] touch instantaneously with that ass-licking little boy who runs home after school with A's in his hand...." Like the ballfield, this haven from oppression remains a dream, a time out from his two nemeses. Not only from women, tainted by Sophie, but also from *goyim*, tainted by Jewish suspicion: for beyond the bounds of Weequahic, in headlines and table talk, is gentile America, and Gentiles make the country unkosher. Alex may continually assert to Spielvogel that he is more than a "nice Jewish boy," that he "*happen[s] also to be a human being!*" but neither principled egalitarianism nor all his familiarity with the America of movies and radio can make "natural" the Gentiles his parents have taught him to distrust. Interludes in the bath house could expunge them from consciousness, but afterward—and long after—it was he who would be the alien. Seeing himself at the mercy of the *goyim*, he could approach them only obliquely through their daughters: he could "*conquer* America" by debasing "Thereal McCoy" or her nicknamed variants.

But it is he who is subdued—as a man, as an American, as a Jew. He runs to Israel to see if he can regain two out of three. He finds that he cannot. If America was "Thereal McCoy," Israel is Sophie (or Naomi, the soldier who looks like her), taboo and therefore impregnable to conquest by sex. Naomi's rejection, first driving him into a frenzied attempt at rape, leaves him impotent. Portnoy recoils, no more at home in Israel than in New York or soon-to-be *judenrein* Weequahic. The Jew in him, cultivated by fear, had prevented his entering fully into America; the American had all but eviscerated the Jew. Powerless to assert a self, he is unmanned. The obscenity of his situation leaves him on the couch unpacking his heart like a whore with words. What words can they be but obscenities?

If this sounds as grim as the conflicts of *Letting Go*, perhaps it is because the sound so far described is incomplete. That novel had presented the anguish of young men trying to achieve manhood by doing good; this, of one trying hopelessly to achieve manhood by being bad. For a Jew of their upbringing, the second quest is harder because it is perverse. And being perverse, being a total inversion of normal expectation, it is comic. To have to try, to strive, to be bad is on the surface absurd, yet for Jews of this upbringing—and for many readers—licentious behavior would have required a willful effort (that some were putting forth). What made a whole country laugh was an absurdity recognizable. Not the daring (for its time) language, not just the "Jewish joke" in which Portnoy complains of being trapped—even though the novel ends in a punch line. This is a comically absurd novel because Portnoy's moral anguish threatens the reader in a way Gabe's did not. The reader shares Portnoy's surrender of illusions about a higher moral plane, about sacrifice being noble. That illusion had been stripped away between 1962 and 1969. (Roth would come to speak of the sixties as "the demythologizing decade" [*RMAO* 86].) Along with Portnoy, the reader must also flinch; and among the legion of theories about what constitutes humor, laughter as a way of handling pain has some application here, as much for the reader as for poor Portnoy. Roth would say a few years later that in this novel "comedy was the means by which the character synthesized and articulated his sense of himself and his predicament" (*RMAO* 75). It was also the synthesizing means for the reader. Roth's conversion in discipleship from James and Flaubert to Jake the Snake and Henny Youngman was also attended by a new respect for Kafka's sense of "guilt ... as a comic idea" (*RMAO* 22). Burlesquing remorse and victimization might, by its very excess, render the most painful self-recognition bearable. Mixing the burlesque with passages of awakening sexuality and adolescent burden could render a complaint like Portnoy's sufferable in howls of resignation. The less curable, the more likely such a disorder is for Kafkaesque treatment, whose very essence is hopelessness. And Alex's monologue—Roth's novel—is only an introductory statement, the opening exposition of patient to analyst. Nowhere does it proceed into the treatment itself, still less near to a cure.

Nor was the sickness just some exotic Jewish complaint. The fictive dictionary definition of *Portnoy's Complaint*, which precedes the title page begins; "A disorder in which strongly-felt ethical and altruistic impulses are perpetually warring with extreme sexual longings, often of a perverse nature." The bedrock of this comedy was an inconsistency between ethics and longings felt throughout American society. In the 1960s not only liberated Jews were trying to live by a fate-thwarted conflict of codes; so was the nation. Camelot, as the Kennedy administration had been dubbed, called into service idealistic young men like this Assistant Commissioner for Human Opportunity to uphold the family—those home movies out of Hyannisport and the White House—and pour their energies sacrificially into civic amelioration. But Camelot also offered them partying at night, glamor and movie stars, the license to experiment with forbidden sexual pleasures, the right to fulfill their most primitive instincts and passions. Like King Arthur's "city built to music" it depended on a harmony of idealism and trust, and when the music stopped, shattered by assassination, divisive war, and the cynical foreclosures of the new Mordreds, it left not only the best and the brightest but a whole once-idealistic nation suspended in anger and impotence. Needing defenses against the compromised notion of good, the young had begun celebrating the natural life. A capacity to experience that life to the full might be a proof against the despairing consequences of their parents' values. There might be hope in the joy of badness. Comedy is built on tensions of inconsistency, comedy of the absurd on thrashings amidst hopelessness. America in 1969 knew Portnoy's basic conflict. You didn't have to be Jewish to feel the schizophrenia of the age.

After Roth returned from Yaddo, as he tells in *The Facts*, his agent arranged for a landmark contract with a huge advance from Random House. From the receptions to those episodes earlier published in *Esquire*, *Partisan Review*, and Theodore Solotaroff's incipient *New American Review*, the book, he knew—and publisher Bennett Cerf knew—would be a blockbuster.

Indeed, the sensation caused by this publishing event has never been duplicated. It was the perfect emblem of a turning point in American history from which there would be no going back. This was February 1969. Hippies, flower children, the Beatles, rebellion against the older generation were the order of the day. Major elements of that rebellion were freedom of language and openness about sex. The cover once off, the subject would never startle so again, nor would its language. Nixon had been in office less than a month. The events of the election of the previous fall had left the nation angry, the generations at war. *Portnoy's Complaint* would be a national cathartic (a function, though, that would cast a shadow over the novel's status as a work of literature). Even the anticipation was part of the event. Review copies were out to the periodicals (as is usual) weeks before the February 21 publication date, and reviewers were now jockeying to be first into print. Geoffrey Wolff, writing in the February 10 *Washington Post*, spoke for many when he said that "Roth has composed what for me is the most important book of my generation." In the February 7 *Life*, the nation's family magazine, a review by Albert Goldman prepared America for Alexander Portnoy with a long piece largely about his creator. Its two-page opening spread, seven eighths occupied by pictures of Roth and, as his shadow, Franz Kafka, was introduced with the announcement, "'Portnoy's Complaint' by Philip Roth looms as a **Wild Blue Shocker** and the American novel of the sixties." The opening portion of Goldman's article was not a piece of criticism but a piece of history:

> The publication of a book is not often a major event in American culture. Most of our classics, when they first appeared, met with disappointing receptions, and even the much-balleyhooed best-sellers of recent years have rarely cut a great swath, outside the lanes of publicity and journalism. But this year a real literary-cultural event portends and every shepherd of public opinion, every magus of criticism, is wending his way toward its site. Gathered at an old New York City inn called Random House, at the stroke of midnight on the 21st of February in this 5,729th year since the creation of the world, they will hail the birth of a new American hero, Alexander Portnoy. A savior and scapegoat of the '60s, Portnoy is destined at the Christological age of 33 to take upon himself all the sins of sexually obsessed modern man and expiate them in a tragicomic crucifixion. The gospel that records the passion of this mock messiah is a slender, psychotic novel by Philip Roth called *Portnoy's Complaint* (the title is a triple pun signifying that the hero is a whiner, a lover, and a sick man). So great is the fame of the book even before its publication that it is being hailed as *the* book of the present decade and as an American masterwork in the tradition of *Huckleberry Finn*.

Apparently, Jewishness had arrived: for all America, 1969 could be 5,729 and sexual adventurers could be circumcised. Goldman's article went on to tell that parts of the novel had already been passed around at fashionable parties where guests had been invited to read sections serially at table, "Portnoy" being the password of the day, and compared the publisher's final cutting and binding of pages to the secret cutting of heroin for injection into the national veins. What with book club contracts and advances on softcover and movie rights, the novel had "earned almost a million dollars prior to the first press run." That run of 150,000 copies would be tripled and 420,000 hardcover copies sold within a year. *Portnoy's Complaint* would give Roth financial independence and the opportunity to write about whatever he chose for decades.

Yet for Roth's career as a writer all the personal fame and notoriety was less important than the responses of serious critics and of the organized Jewish community. And the Jewish reaction was important more for the material it would give him than for any immediate concern about pleasing a constituency. The popular media quickly identified Alex with Roth, and the talk was as much about masturbation as Jewish mothers and more about both than about ethical angst. Jacqueline Susann quipped that she would invite him onto a talk show but she would not want to touch his hand. (This from the author of *Valley of the Dolls*!) The press had him secretly engaged to Barbra Streisand, whom he had never even met. Nor was engagement what Roth sought. He shortly broke off the relationship with Ann Mudge, despite her having seen him through nightmares of marital war and peritonitis delirium. It was not just that she was unable comfortably to introduce the arch-Jew into her patrician WASP family or that she shared with Maggie, for all their social differences, a reaction against her origins that made Philip a cause as much as a person (*Facts* 133, 158). He was determined, for the foreseeable future, to give no more hostages to fortune. Not even Streisand could have stood a chance.

The literary and pulpit reactions to *Portnoy's Complaint* were mixed but never mild. It seemed as if everybody bought the book, everybody laughed, and then everybody sat down to decide whether, having bought the book and having laughed, they had acted correctly. Part of that decision would depend on age. When Wolff spoke of the novel as "the most important book of [his] generation," he was speaking roughly for Roth's contemporaries. So did some of the younger rabbis, at least those of a somewhat liberal persuasion. Rabbi Eugene Borowitz, a few years Roth's senior, finessed the issue by neutering high praise with an observation: the titled complaint, in its psycho-medical sense, while astonishingly true for his and Roth's generation, was quickly becoming a piece of history, no longer affecting Jewish children because they were now being spoiled rather than repressed.[2] Borowitz does not use these as relative terms—as if "spoiled" were not what Roth's Jewish Iowa Workshop students must have seemed to their unwatched gentile friends—rather, in his zeal to affirm Roth's "moral earnestness," Borowitz treats a cultural heritage as if it could transform itself overnight by adopting new child-rearing fashions. But beyond changing fashions was burgeoning size: the very numbers of the young fostered both change and continuity. The sixties baby-boomers were a larger group than all who had come of age in the preceding several decades: combined. Not only were they overwhelming their parents with a culture of their own, but their ways of assimilating the traditions of their parents were often obscure, even to themselves. They protested too much to acquit themselves entirely of being papa's and momma's continuators. In 1992, playwright Donald Margulies, considering the forces that contributed to his writing *Sight Unseen*, testified:

> I was 15 when I first read "Portnoy's Complaint" and for all the wrong reasons; I was scanning for tales of sexy shiksas, but what I found were stunning insights into what it meant to be a Jew and a man. Even though he was nearly a generation older, Roth and I seemed to have grown up together, surrounded by many of the

> same relatives, sharing many similar experiences. He opened a window for me and let fresh air into a stuffy Brooklyn apartment and gave me (and still gives me) the courage to write what I know.[3]

The children of Borowitz's readers, it seems, had not been so unaffected, or so homogeneous, after all. But in 1969 it was grownups, ranging in age and affiliation, who were voicing official opinion.

Surprisingly, many rabbinic and other Jewishly affiliated reviewers knew Roth's critical essays of the early sixties and were prepared to parry them. His insistence that a novel is not a position paper and that mature readers do not require clichés of Jewish saintliness was to them smoke and mirrors. These spokesmen would identify Portnoy's vilifications as Roth's deep-harbored anti-Semitism. In supposed essays in criticism, many argued circularly from premises accepting such identification to conclusions proving it. The conflict for these makers of opinion was often that the literary distinction was a luxury a culture under attack could not afford, and this Jewish culture, now under attack from its own children, would eventually be under attack from traditional enemies who would use against it this testimony of one of its own sons. Some of the less fearful dismissed the book as a mere collection of gags, asserting that the motive for trying to satirize Jewishness, if it was not anti-Semitism, was vulgarity, the venting of low impulses in comic *shtick*. Any work this frenetic in its accusations of Jewish practices, they said, could not be respectable literature; and Alex's anguish belied Roth's alleged artistic distance. Many, in many moods, identified the problem as *galut*—the Diaspora. But swept up in Zionist solutions, Jewish leaders often declared the remedy to be *aliyah*, missing the satirical reference to Israel as "The Exile" for an Americanized Jew. The least accusatory detractors just felt that Roth lacked an abiding faith in the peoplehood of the Jews and that perhaps his satire had consumed itself and could be considered done (Already!).

As to the argument that *Portnoy's Complaint* posed an external threat to the Jewish people, it had at its core an analogy. Portnoy's lusts for *shiksas* were precisely what the traditional anti-Semite said all Jews felt, what the Aryan accused the would-be-defiling Jew of trying to perpetrate. Marie Syrkin raised the decade-old Julius Streicher and Joseph Goebbels references (they had appeared after *Goodbye, Columbus*) in her *Midstream*[4] review:

> ... under the cartoon of the Jewish joke leers the anti-Jewish stereotype. Portnoy polluting his environment is one such. When he graduates to the fascination of female "apertures and

> openings," his penis never loses its Jewish consciousness. Like Julius Streicher's satanic Jewboy lusting after Aryan maidens, Portnoy seeks blonde *shikses*.... [In the] baleful stereotype ... [which] ... emerges from under the banter... [t]he dark Jew seeking to defile the fair Nordic is standard stuff... [T]here is little to choose between [Goebbels'] and Roth's interpretation of what animates Portnoy. In both views the Jewish male is not drawn to a particular girl who is gentile, but by a gentile "background" which he must violate sexually.

Syrkin quotes raunchy text (with dashes in place of the four-letter words) to support each claim. She scores the "Jewboy," but does not assess the "Nice Jewish Boy" at war with him. But her main fallacy is the one inherent in all reasoning by analogy: the analogy goes only so far and then the two subjects being compared part company. The parting here comes at the point of motive. Streicher's and Goebbels's motives, we may say (at least for these purposes), were clear. But Roth's purpose in giving these thoughts to Portnoy is the bone of all the critical contention that was emerging. Portnoy, here before Dr. Spielvogel, is not proud of these urges. They are part of his sickness. He would rid himself of them as well as he would rid himself of the parental inhibitions that have magnified them in his unconscious. That his whole background has made him anti-*goyish* is also a serious problem. He laughs over his having been an investigator who helped expose the WASP hero of the quiz-show scandals:

> Yes, I was one happy yiddel down there in Washington, a little Stern gang of my own, busily exploding Charlie's honor and integrity, while simultaneously becoming lover to that aristocratic Yankee beauty whose forebears arrived on these shores in the seventeenth century. Phenomenon known as Hating Your Goy And Eating One Too. (233)

Syrkin extends her accusation of Roth to embrace Portnoy's sick glee in recollections such as this. To have Portnoy admit to these vindictive feelings and to sharing his father's exhortations about the absurdity of the whole Christian premise—feelings shared by a huge proportion of his Jewish readers!—is from Syrkin's point of view dangerous to Jewish life in a pluralistic society. (To the dedicated labor-Zionist in Syrkin, the reminder about the Stern gang was not very helpful either.[5]) Yet in assigning to Portnoy thoughts that resemble Nazi stereotypes Roth needed no more vicious a motive than a wish to underscore a main conflict of Diaspora life:

that the conditions of living as a minority create urges to assimilate into the majority and that guilt over those urges creates anger directed against what is seen as the oppression of the majority. That aspect of being "bad" is part of Roth's subject, not as an endorsement of enemy propaganda but as an issue of identity and freedom.

Perhaps the most outright condemnation on grounds of comforting enemies came from Gershom Scholem, writing in Hebrew in Haaretz. Scholem begins with the premise that "anti-Semites [having] long dreamed of defaming the Jew by producing literature intended to reveal his degeneracy and corruption, particularly in matters of sex," but failing for want of "authentic knowledge of the Jewish way of life," are now handed their model by "a brash young Jew who knows that way of life in all its essential atmosphere, and does their work for them."

> Here in the center of Roth's revolting book ... stands the loathsome figure whom the anti-Semites have conjured in their imagination and portrayed in their literature, and a Jewish author, a highly gifted if perverted artist, offers all the slogans which for them are priceless.

Scholem will not be deterred by arguments about literature.

> Let the Pollyannas not tell us that what we have here is satire.... The fact is that the hero of a best-seller, avidly acquired by the public, proclaims (and lives his proclamation) that his behavior is shaped by a single lust which becomes the slogan of his life: to get "*shikse* cunt."

For this, "the book for which all anti-Semites have been praying," Scholem says, all Jews except "the author who revels in obscenities" will pay.

> I daresay that with the next turn of history, not long to be delayed, this book will make all of us defendants at court.... This book will be quoted to us—and how it will be quoted! They will say to us: Here you have the testimony from one of your own artists ... an authentic Jewish witness. This is the man whom you have summoned to the dialogue between Israel and the Diaspora. This is the man whose hero finally complains about the *chutzpah* of the kibbutz girl, the Jewess emancipated from the oppressive nightmare of Judaism, because she will not do him the honor of

> serving as his Jewish *shikse*. This is the man who pours out his heart to the public, whom he mockingly calls by the name of his analyst, Dr. Spielvogel.
>
> "I wonder what price *k'lal yisrael* [the world Jewish community]—and there is such an entity in the eyes of the Gentiles—is going to pay for this book. Woe to us on that day of reckoning!"

An American reader might well have wondered whether Gershom Scholem was serious. An Israeli psychiatrist found his fears "more ridiculous than any one of Portnoy's absurd fears or all of them put together ... [for] ... [t]he Goyim who want to hate us will, with or without Portnoy, never run out of ammunition...."[7] But Scholem was deadly serious. Whatever he might say elsewhere about trial of the Jewish soul by sin in a mystic, remote age, this book and this man, he avers, is a contemporary threat. To Scholem it is hardly a novel; it is a tract. Portnoy and Spielvogel are mere devices for Roth's spewings into the public ear. Scholem does not even read the book as an American phenomenon. Or if he does, he reads America as vulnerable to—or possibly responsible for—all the effects to come of the Nazism he had known in his own life in Europe.

When respondents to the *Haaretz*[6] piece objected that Scholem's article confused literature with history or that these were an aspect of Diaspora responses that it was well worth knowing about, Scholem reiterated his position. He had been talking, he said, about the effect of the book—worse than *The Protocols of the Elders of Zion* because insider evidence—for which "the Jewish people are going to pay a price...." Toward the end of this defense of his earlier remarks, he includes a quotation (changed slightly in its double translation back and forth across the ocean) from Roth's "Writing About Jews" and curiously mixes a concession to literature with a sense of doom.

> I recently read that Roth's book has now appeared in German translation. Marvelous news indeed!
>
> It is quite correct that we need hide nothing for fear of, "What will the Gentiles say?" I have repeated this obvious and simple truth in some of my articles condemning Jewish apologetics. But we have to know and acknowledge that for speaking such "truth", even this kind of "truth from America", the full price will have to be paid. He who states this fact should not be blamed for doing so.

It is impossible to know whether Scholem's jeremiad has had any prophetic merit. It does not seem so. The very pursuit of the question would require investigative techniques that Kafka could hardly imagine. There seemed to be no sudden surge or overt demonstration occasioned by the publication of the novel in Poland in 1986 as "Kompleks Portnoya," whose 50,000 copy first printing sold out immediately and won for its translator, Anna Kolyszko, the annual award of the Polish Translators Union. Nor was there any reaction but laughter and praise when an avant-garde Lodz theater presented the translation as a play—here Portnoy unshaven in hospital pajamas delivering a ninety-minute monologue—to a "captivated" audience in 1988.[8] Whether anti-Semitism (as distinguished from traditional Jew hatred on grounds of religious objection) is prompted by behavior or competition from a threatening Jewish presence[9] or arises as an echo whenever there is social unrest even in the relative absence of Jews,[10] it tends to be ignited by effects other than those of fiction. And the new nationalisms need no *Portnoy's Complaint* to justify their surging xenophobia.

The rationale of the less frightened but merely revolted critics was that the vulgarity proceeded from infectious self-hatred. Syrkin's review embraces both objections. Alongside its concern with a clear and present danger, it is representative of many reactions of the Jewish reviewing core in its shifts of grounds within standard terms of literary criticism. Syrkin reasons frequently by definition. She identifies a category that the novel is allegedly striving to fill and then shows how it fails to meet the criteria for that category. She calls the book bad satire because it cannot make up its mind; she calls Alexander Portnoy "unconvincing" as an emancipated Jew because—she blithely generalizes—"an emancipated Jew does not invariably refer to gentile girls as *shikses*; his vocabulary and imagination are more flexible." She posits a restricted category called "human being" and denies Portnoy membership because "no trace of any intellectual or social concerns is permitted to smudge the contour of Portnoy as sketched by Roth." That Portnoy is speaking in pain in an analytic first session, unloading his whole Complaint, does not influence Syrkin's appraisal:

> His scholastic excellence and the post he occupies do not serve as amplifications of his personality; instead they are further Jewish demerits hung on him like tags: Jews may be smart students and be interested in social causes but beware what is within. Roth's scalpel exposes not only the dirt behind the respectable facade of the Jewish family, but the wretched creature cowering behind the much-touted Jewish intelligence and devotion to liberal causes. At any rate Portnoy never voices an idea or expresses a generous

> emotion. A total phony, presumably, and a rebuke to all those Jews who get high grades and profess to be socially involved.

Is the book, then, in Syrkin's view, an attack on the phoniness and hard-heartedness of Jewish intellectuals? Even Syrkin acknowledges that that is not its intent, just its effect. But, she asserts, Roth's intent to make Portnoy's condition a "disorder" (in the words of the fictive medical definition of the **Complaint**) fails its own test of complexity:

> Where is a single scene in which the patient suffering from this conflict [between strongly felt ethical and altruistic impulses and extreme sexual longings] appears as an ethical or moral being? The reduction of Portnoy to a series of compulsive sexual practices dehumanizes him, and the author's chief way of redeeming his hero from anonymity is to label him "Jewish."

But, one may ask, how does someone "appear as" an ethical or moral human being in a complaint? Only through the recounting of deeds, hopes, fears, impulses. All his life Portnoy had done his homework and followed the rules, and now he has seen others who had flouted them achieve success and fame. What, if not "ethical impulses," is it that keeps him from enjoying being bad? Syrkin's only answer is that when he cries out that he has become "'the son in the Jewish joke,' he is chanting Roth's themesong."

Another category Syrkin raises is the false comparison some critics have made with Bellow's *Herzog*. She has known Herzog, and Portnoy is no Herzog. One is a "human being" presented with "rich humor"; the other a "caricature" in a "farce." When Portnoy gets his comeuppance from the Sabra in Israel, Syrkin sees him writhing "unchastened" on the floor. Her proof is Alex's own words: "Ow, my heart! And in Israel! Where other Jews find refuge, sanctuary and peace, Portnoy now perishes! Where other Jews flourish, I now expire!" A less angry Marie Syrkin might have seen a kind of chastening here. She knew her English literature well and could quote at length from the poets. Surely, had she no program of her own, she would have recognized the echo of Byron's Childe Harold pronouncing on his exiled self in the third person. And perhaps in that and in other variations of tone she might have begun to see something else going on besides Roth's chanting his theme song, perhaps Portnoy's author faintly mocking him, taking him less seriously than Syrkin's righteousness would allow. In failing the novel for not *being* another *Herzog*, Syrkin never raises the question of whether Roth *intended* another *Herzog*. Clearly he was limiting himself by the form of the introductory analytic session—and its controlling anger—to a narrative point of view that could not explore the many sidedness of character and situation that *Herzog* encompasses.

As to the range of Roth's intents, Syrkin is easily guided by her own responses. And in this she is typical of many critics over the years. If Roth presents a double point of view on any subject, they will type him with the more stridently expressed side and see any characters who oppose what they take to be Roth's point of view as mere surrogates for themselves. Syrkin sees such inclusion as a deliberate debating point, not as pan of the fiction. In this case, she decides, Roth is warding off anticipated criticism by putting the obvious accusation of Portnoy as a self-hating Jew into the mouth of the sabra, giving Roth the appearance of being above the battle. As if there were no sound fictive reason for having Naomi seal the doom that sends Portnoy packing to seek Spielvogel, Syrkin reads the episode as a strategy in Roth's war with her and her colleagues. They cannot seize on Naomi's words since "[t]o quote Roth against Roth would be a reductio ad absurdum." But Syrkin can expose the stratagem and reduce the reductio.

Syrkin also scores what she sees as Roth's obvious intent to shock in introducing into literature all the four-letter words that Syrkin apologizes for being unable to quote. Having declared the motive, she pronounces its failure: the language is not new. Witness Joyce and Lawrence. What is new is its obscene use. *Ulysses* had been cleared of obscenity charges because the words in question were not used as "dirt for dirt's sake." Lawrence had used them in *Lady Chatterly's Lover* "romantically rather than obscenely." Syrkin's own last words on the subject are an attempt at a literary distinction.

> Intense sexual passion circumstantially described is not obscene, as any number of literary works demonstrate. Obscenity is achieved when the writer shows not human beings animated by emotion but merely organs in friction. This contemptuous dismemberment of personality Roth aims for and achieves *ad nauseum*.

"Merely organs in friction" may be the distinguishing feature not of obscenity but of pornography. Certainly in obscenity intent is also an issue. And Portnoy's graphic re-creations for his analyst have something to do with verifying his need for help. But even the pornographic does not apply. Roth's purpose is hardly titillation: there is not a passage in the book that Portnoy, himself, would take to the bathroom. And only the most unsympathetic reading would find Portnoy, or the Monkey, never "animated by emotion." If Roth is writing out of contempt, one may ask of what he is contemptuous. Syrkin's cryptic answer is, of "the sty under the abstention from pork," that is, of all that keeps Jews from assimilating guiltlessly into the gentile culture. But that is the whole issue of Diaspora, and one Jew's questionings may be another Jew's vilifications. Nowhere does Syrkin acknowledge that Portnoy sees his flight from Jewish compunctions as trying to be "bad" or that its opposite, the "good" from which he would fly, has him hooked.

In Syrkin's and others' reviews Roth's failures to satisfy imposed categories of critical judgment become reductions of the novel (and its unique mode) to everything from mere failed first draft,[11] to a series of stereotypical stand-up gags, to a comic strip, to an attempt to normalize Jews by a "paradoxical effort to help the Jews by reviling them."[12] Critics regularly accuse Roth of misrepresenting Jews because Sophie would not intend the breadknife to threaten castration or because Jack, as presented, would never be unfaithful with a secretary—ignoring the fact that these are clearly Alex's fantasies, about which not accuracy but anxiety is the issue in an analysis. Portnoy is called a failed *schlemiel* because he does not conform closely enough to the tradition of *schlemiel*dom. He is said to draw upon the Sabbatarian tradition of rebellion in the Jewish community, "the impulse to violate, to light fires on the Sabbath, deny the existence of God, destroy the purity of the family, the desire to expose and destroy rather than to create and revere." But, the accusation continues, he is no Sabbati Zevi, his world no *Satan in Goray*, because he is just an imp, not to be taken seriously. "Indeed," says this last analysis, "if we take him seriously, we are lost."[13] Even the defense that this whole monologue is a therapeutic session with requirements of its own evokes analyses of the analysis to prove that that will not do. Okay, says this line of argument, there are works where we are tipped off that we cannot trust the internal narrator's accounts. "[W]e can trust his report of what happened but not his interpretation of what it means. In Portnoy ... the reader is never given an objective view of events from which to measure the narrator's version."[14] Such a reading, that misses the fixation in Portnoy's hyperboles or the love-hate in his accounts of his parents, has either very fixed criteria for the device of the known-unreliable narrator or is too put off by the subject to allow itself to do the reader's job. Roth gives the book only one narrator—though he modulates that voice in moods created by the memories—but the reader is never intended to take Portnoy on face value. Certainly Spielvogel doesn't. The reader has a role to play. And even if Alex's analyses are wrong, does that render him without any meaningful complaint? Experts from Bruno Bettelheim[15] down were tempted to analyze Alex's analysis to show that from this or that school's perspective, he was not so sick—maybe just spoiled by an immature author, or by an author needing to make *aliyah*.[16]

One did not have to be a psychoanalyst to hold the point of view. It was shared by many in the lay core of traditional Jewish opinion makers. For Trude Weiss-Rosmarin, the book was just immature filth. Weiss-Rosmarin, editor of *The Jewish Spectator*, had a long-held set position. She had written at the time of the publication of *Goodbye, Columbus* that the question: Who is a Jew? akin in many ways to the predicament of modern man's uncertainties of identity, is a product of "negative identification" that comes from the fragmentation of *galut* existence.[17] She was impatient with Americans who sought or fought this fragmented Jewish self when they perhaps belonged in Israel. In her non-review of *Portnoy's Complaint*, what she calls a "no-book," she begins by telling she did not really read it. Her tone is almost self-exonerating, as if to have really read it were to have been an accessory to some crime. She says she speed-read twenty pages and found it boring, with its juvenile repetition of four-letter words, conceding that she might have liked it in her teens, but assuring that she is not given to vicarious titillation or to being "a voyeuse of the Peeping Jane type."[18] She goes on to aver that "I am not doing therapy so why should I be privy to *Portnoy's Complaint*?" She draws a contrast between the sexually starved who reduce sex to a certain four-letter word and the sexually sophisticated who can appreciate "The Song of Songs" and mentions a rabbi friend who was unable to review the novel from the pulpit because he considered it "disgusting." Roth, she goes on, "speaks for a certain segment of alienated Jewishly ignorant Jews who write and teach." In contrast, she draws on a leading critic to raise another question:

> I do not think *Portnoy's Complaint* will become the definitive statement on "the Jewish condition of the modern Jew." After all, as Alfred Kazin concluded his review of this no-book, if "the complexity and moral depth of Jewish experience, which may look reducible to a mother, a son, a shriek, a cry" were just that, "as a subject it would have been exhausted long ago."

Weiss-Rosmarin's editorial dismisses the novel but not its social effect. Seventeen years later, collecting the fifty most telling editorials, one each from fifty years of *The Jewish Spectator*, she reprinted it as her most significant editorial of 1969.[19]

Kazin's question was introduced by "if." But Roth did not intend to reduce or exhaust "the complexity and moral depth of Jewish experience"; he intended merely to show a dimension of it elicited by the new freedom—and perhaps to portray the frustrations of any psychological entrapment. He well knew that "freedom" was no mere absence of legal or physical restrictions, that the "hook" one might still be on can cut far deeper into the flesh. Roth would continue to explore the effects of feeling trapped in his next few works of fiction.

Debate within Jewish circles—magazines to pulpits—was almost as feverish as sales of the novel. Like a giant Rorschach test, it allowed the passionate reading in of every mind set. Rabbi Borowitz's review could have stood in part as an answer to Trude Weiss-Rosmarin's. He calls *Portnoy's Complaint* "one of the great moral documents and Jewish books of our time" for its portrayal in modern terms of the traditional problem of "the *yetzer hara*, the urge to do evil," always associated with sexuality. And though the traditional rabbis would have objected to Roth's *nibbul peh*, his filthy mouth, it is for our time honest language:

> To use euphemism or be delicate would simply reinforce the old cerebral defenses. We do not lust in detachment.... The gutsy language makes the book a visceral experience ... [of] a universal malady of civilization, the inability to integrate a schizoid yetzer.

The humor, Borowitz asserts, is right as a device to make one not just "crack up" but "crack open," a "very Jewish" use of humor that "heals more than it hurts." And it is fitting, not insulting, that Portnoy is Jewish, for

> who better than the Jew should serve as a symbol of mankind's aspiration to morality—more, mankind's obsession with morality despite what nature and history have taught! [Alex's] ... commitment to the ethical ... is as strong as his sexuality for it derives from centuries of doing mitzvot. [Finally, Portnoy's] sense of Jewishness/community [is] one of his human ideals ... he loves his Diaspora Jewishness and sees it as a key means to his humanization. [In short] ... here in the guise of humor, much of Judaism's most serious message about being a man has been given modern and effective voice.

Rabbi Borowitz did not remain unchallenged by pulpit rabbis. Rabbi Arthur Lelyveld, who saw Borowitz "playing Akiba to Philip Roth's Bar Kochba," could not buy the characterization of the book as uniquely Jewish or profound.[20] "Oedipus and Electra were not Jewish." Portnoy, says Lelyveld, may be a stereotype, but he is not a type. Nor will it do to say that Portnoy is no more intended to be typical of Jews of his class than Emma Bovary of Frenchwomen of hers (an argument that Roth had made about some of his earlier protagonists). Portnoy shares, rather, the faults (as Lelyveld sees them) of Shylock and Fagin who "are *less than true to life*" because they are "besmirched by the prejudices of their time." This interesting statement, fraught with contradiction, contains a premise that has been advanced and countered endlessly in Jewish critical writing. It is the chicken-and-egg game of all social stereotyping in literature.[21] Certainly the besmirching effects of anti-Semitism in Shakespeare's and Dickens's days were part of their characters' reality, gave them the distortions of point of view that their authors observed. In an analogous example, though the taint of bastardy did not make every bastard in Shakespeare's day act like "a bastard," it made enough of them do so to allow Edmund's "Now, gods, stand up for bastards!" to ring true in *King Lear*. If Lelyveld means that the writers themselves were so blinded by prejudice that they could not compose believable characters, then he is declaring Shylock and Fagin to be grotesques that have brought down the works containing them—patently not so. But Lelyveld denies and affirms the "Portnoy type" all in one statement:

> One can find Alexander Portnoy "hilarious" or revealing of a repressed self, only if one is able in some way to identify with him. I have great pity for those who do so identify with Alexander Portnoy. They have evidently failed to find in their lives that genuine meeting with another which is true relationship.

The logic here is a double bind. The "way" that fiction creates identification is by drawing on elements already within readers. Men can identify with oppressed women because men have experienced similar powerlessness as children. But to Lelyveld, Jews who identified with Alex Portnoy were displaying not capacity for sympathy but failure of living. In equating "identify" with "being identical to" and gilding the equation with a show of pity, Lelyveld wishes away a significant part of his congregation. But, then, older critics were quicker to deny the believability of Alex Portnoy than Alex's peers. Like Weiss-Rosmarin and, (in some respects) later, Irving Howe, Lelyveld's declared reactions "progressed from shock and disgust to compassion and finally to boredom." What is even less understandable is Lelyveld's declaration that neither Portnoy nor Spielvogel can be real because they are comic figures or that guilt as a comic idea cannot work because the suffering character is driven to turn against his true Jewish self in asserting that he is "*also a human being!*" Lelyveld finds himself, as defender of the faith, compelled to reason that "[e]xposing self-hatred as a neurosis, the book also characterizes Jewishness as a neurosis." Such zealous refusal to separate the book from the character might be expected to elicit declarations like Lelyveld's next lines:

> At this point I must respond with every fiber of my chauvinist, separatist being. I have no will to be just like everyone else—whatever that means. I want to identify with Jewish triumph, with Jewish wisdom, as well as with Jewish suffering.

"I want" is the cry of Portnoy, and also of Tarnopol and Kepesh and a few more of Roth's protagonists to come. The rabbinic "I want" and Alex's "I want" are both recognizable cries in the real world, but they do not meet on the plane of literary criticism. Roth has not said "I want." He has said that "Portnoy wants," as, had he chosen to write a novel about the frustrations of being a rabbi in 1969 America, he could have had his suffering hero declare "with every fiber" of his being that *he* wants his congregants to know their heritage and forget their petty complaints. Or he might have had his wild-eyed rabbinic hero excommunicate everyone he considered Jewishly ignorant and found himself mumbling to God about his principled unemployment. But would such a rabbi have been more Jewish than Portnoy?

Lelyveld is missing something else in his reading of Portnoy's outcry. Alex, this professional assister in "humane" affairs, equates "Jew" with "humane." When he asserts that he is not just a Jew but also a "human" being, he is partially contrasting "humane" and "human." The "humane" side of him has kept at bay his "human" needs, whose visceral dimensions emerge from beneath his repressions unsatisfied and shaming. At thirty-three Alex should be able to balance—and satisfy—both dimensions as a man.

Five years later, another rabbi, Robert Saks, wrote an essay on Gershom Scholem's *Sabbatai Sevi*, focusing on its discussion of "the paradoxical concept of holiness coming out of sin."[22] Saks, apparently unaware of Scholem's own pronouncements against *Portnoy's Complaint*, reminds his readers that Scholem defines Judaism as a religion encompassing wide varieties of conduct, the belief *of* Jews not just a belief *for* Jews. For Scholem a Jew is to be defined in large part by one's sincere belief that one is a Jew. In his own work, Scholem thus treats cravings and appetites not as drives foreign to Judaism, needing only to be repressed, but as indicators of a striving for holiness. Saks, interpreting Scholem on this conflict, says, "In Sabbatian terminology ... where the holy spark of peace and freedom from craving is hidden in a shell of longing and temptation, a person should enter the shell—do the forbidden act—and thus break the shell's power from within." In this regard, says Saks, *Portnoy's Complaint*

> can be read as a satirical comment, from a Sabbatian perspective, on Jewish law. Portnoy is a Jewish boy with a healthy libido, the

> son of the most repressive of Jewish mothers. Roth, I believe, makes it very clear that the Jewish Mother, the Jewish God, and the Jewish laws are of one mold for [Portnoy].

To prove his point, Saks quotes Alex's diatribe on the dietary laws, concluding with Alex's speculation that maybe in breaking them, he found the wherewithal to break a sexual taboo:

> Now, maybe the lobster is what did it. That taboo so easily and simply broken, confidence may have been given to the whole slimy, suicidal Dionysian side of my nature; the lesson may have been learned that to break the law, all you have to do is—just go ahead and break it! All you have to do is stop trembling and quaking and finding it unimaginable and beyond you: all you have to do, *is do it*! What else, I ask you, were all those prohibitive dietary rules and regulations all about to begin with, what else but to give us little Jewish children practice in being repressed? Practice, darling, practice, practice, practice. Inhibition doesn't grow on trees, you know.... (79)

Saks ends his essay shortly after this quotation, letting it speak for itself without analysis. His Jewish readership would know the echoes: practice, practice, practice was to make them all Yehudi Menuhins or Artur Rubinsteins; what didn't grow on trees was money—controlling echoes applied to the very subject of control. Portnoy's point, of course, is that the sinning didn't work. The floodgates once opened, further practice in the forbidden didn't inure him to guilt but only pushed it under awhile until it returned to overwhelm him. "Why is a little turbulence so beyond my means? Why must the least deviation from respectable conventions cause me such inner hell? When I *hate* those fucking conventions! When I know *better* than the taboos!" (124). Roth presents the irony of supposing one can reason himself into freedom. Saks thinks "a satirical comment, from a Sabbatian perspective, on Jewish law" can illuminate the Sabbatian danger: Portnoy is within "the shell of longing and temptation"; it remains a question whether Spielvogel can help him break its power from within. For twentieth-century American Jewry a next question might be: if Portnoy can break the power, will the longing, the temptation, and the suffering have been worth it? It is a question only for one who takes the book seriously.

Critics implicitly debated whether *Portnoy's Complaint* is a Jewish book. One answer is an implication of Scholem's distinction of a Jew. If Alex's sincerity *is* his authenticity, then he is every bit a Jew and his problems a

Jewish problem. His being Jewish does not turn on the extent of his knowledge of the tradition, but on his personal response to whatever he knows of the tradition. His father, as Sanford Pinsker points out, embodies the conflict too: "... Jake Portnoy speaks for thousands when he takes his brilliant, rebellious son to task:

> Tell me something [Jake demands], do you know Talmud, my educated son? Do you know history? ... Do you know a single thing about the wonderful history and heritage of the sages of your people?

Alexander, indeed, does not, but then again, neither does his father. And for all the passionate denials, neither do most American Jews."[23]

Pinsker is, of course, right. Nonetheless, the "passionate denials" of their ignorance by American Jews are a form of self-identification, even if their tradition is largely a set of echoes replayed as origins. American-born Jack Portnoy (Alex calls him "Jake" only when fantasizing the old man's independence of Sophie—for example, *shtupping* his *goyische* secretary) had gotten through the eighth grade, without Talmud, on the bounty of the State of New Jersey. What he knows as Jewish, and has passed on, includes a respect for learning of all kinds. Roth, giving Jack that ironic cross-examination of his son, does not let young Alex respond by questioning his father's authenticity. Even on Spielvogel's couch he recounts the episode more in anger than in a reasoned challenge to his father's Jewishness. Jack Portnoy's respect for the learning he lacks is part of his personal identification as a Jew. Part of Alex's conflict with his father is his guilt about the old man's uncompleted emancipation. Grateful for his sacrifices but ashamed of his relative lack of education, Alex feels responsible for completing that education and bringing its benefits home: "... in my liberation would be his—from ignorance, from exploitation, from anonymity." Here is some of that ethical striving and moral conscience, indeed, the generous emotion, that Marie Syrkin denies.

Portnoy's sense of responsibility for helping his father to continue learning is part of the inverse Diaspora heritage (Roth owns up to the same feelings in *Patrimony*). It need not be demeaning to father or son, provided the father has dignity in his home. But Alex's counter-feelings for his father arise from another aspect of their transformed heritage. The father's achievements outside the house pall next to the mother's need for recognition of her accomplishment. In their Jewish value system, that accomplishment is Alex, the only son. Departing from his own family model (Roth has an older brother), he makes Alex's one sibling an older sister. This choice of personae, which allows Alex in the bathroom to obsess over her drying underwear, also leaves the boy with the burden of being Sophie's major project. He has to be good and be brilliant and be more. Two generations back, in *shtetl* society, women earned much of the living keeping store or sewing dresses, and men spent much of their time in respected study. But women no longer had outside occupations or large families to diffuse their energies, and among men study for its own sake was no longer respected. Alex's brilliance could have value only to the extent that he became somebody in the world and brought dividends, including children, back into the home. Implicit in Alex's complaint is resentment about the reduced role of the father created by the new Jewish need to gratify a home-centered mother. (From the Freudian standpoint one might say that Jack is not competitor enough.) But Alex also resents the burden of goodness that the new focus has placed on the son, the burden of being the superachiever.[24] Being watched so, he feels emasculated. Roth lets the overwrought Alex sum up this trap in his burlesqued detail of Ronald Nimkin, the fifteen-year-old pianist-suicide, who had been dubbed by the women in the building "Jose Iturbi the Second," found hanging from the bathroom showerhead with a note pinned to his well-laundered shirt:

> *Mrs. Blumenthal called. Please bring your mah-jongg rules to the game tonight.*
>
> *Ronald.*

At the same time, Alex resents Jack's having been reduced and made ridiculous. How easy, and how betraying, to go beyond him. This was, indeed, a Jewish subject.

That Jewish America, outside the closed world of yeshiva orthodoxy, was as ignorant of Talmud and the Jewish sages as were Jack and Alex Portnoy may account for the pious tones of some of the reviews and sermons directed at the book. More musing tones were not available for use with this audience. Congregational ignorance had taken some of the old-world play out of rabbinic communication. Irony requires a knowing audience; the cryptic remark requires freedom from misunderstanding. Without that common wavelength between rabbi and congregation, reasoning with becomes talking to; parable becomes preachment. Sermons on the trendy *Portnoy's Complaint*, the prerogative of senior rabbis, tended to be negative because most senior rabbis were looking for moral content and finding it in the short passages rather than the whole text. These defenders against the new liberation were unlikely to find, under apparent insults to Judaism, satire on goodness. Rushing to keep up with the hubbub about the book, many noted its surface for the sake of the sabbath sermon. But few could identify Roth's subject. They could address the problem of values, the problem of assimilation, the problem of self-hatred, even the problem of sexual freedom, but they could not address the *problem* of goodness, except to deny it existed.

But goodness was being devalued all around, evoking cynicism to conceal its loss. For more than another two decades America would openly expect not the best but the worst from its politicians, its athletes, its parents and children. Psychiatrists and evangelists would be seen as Mercedes-Benz charlatans; athletic heroes, as cool millionaires; captains of industry, as leveraged buyout artists. The corrupting octopus of the 1980s, BCCI, would embrace governments at all levels and on all points of the political compass. "Ozzie and Harriet" would have long given way to "Married with Children"; the hit song of the late eighties would be Michael Jackson's "I'm Bad," with only a pale afterflash of the ironic inversion in that term long understood in the black community. But in 1969, after Camelot, the idea that goodness could be a burden felt intensely by Jews was an idea less worthy of ironic reflection than of pulpit denunciation.

A few Jewish periodical reviews saw the book as more than a rant or psychological case study or confession, saw it as comic parody of that mode or even allegory, which requires, for heightening, the typecasting other critics condemned. Helen Weinberg saw it as an allegory of the Jew in Diaspora America, of

> ... the restlessness, the near-feverishness, the anarchistic itchiness of the young American Jew, burdened with the remnant of an authentic tradition of justice, law, reason, and righteousness, while forced to live in the mad, illogical, meretricious world of American culture.

Taking seriously Roth's view that fiction cannot outdo the wild American reality, this view sees Roth's sensibility naturally turned to satire—not the objective, distancing satire of the eighteenth century, but one that had to be peculiarly subjective to get at an elusive unreality partly created out of the satirist's inner self. Put another way, this is not the satire that can stand aside and sneer at the unworthiness of institutions to fulfill their own ideals. This is satire in which the victim rages at the victimizer who has become the victimizer partly through the licensing admiration of the victim. Part of Portnoy's "Complaint" is the lover's complaint, satire of which goes at least as far back as Chaucer's "complaint to his empty purse," but the other—sorrowful—side of the lover's complaint is also to be found in Alex's compassion. Unlike Syrkin and Weiss-Rosmarin, Weinberg finds that

> [t]here is as much compassion as there is anger in his complaint, though the anger is noisier, more attention-getting; and, since the total thrust of the book is comic and satirical, the anger is more in keeping with the wished-for final tone. But the compassion is undeniably present and cannot be avoided: the scenes in the mother's hospital room; the private discussion between Alex and his sister about the Jews of Europe; on the baseball field; of the hours of a brief feeling of real love during the love affair—all of these scenes, and several others, reveal Portnoy's deep tenderness toward all that appears to enrage him the most. His compassion—or "suffering" in the broad sense—is what really threatens him. He is likely to lose his free self if he loves the Jews, or his parents, or his girl friends too much. And so he does not love them, and is angry with himself and them.

Satire on goodness cannot be Swiftian satire. Who but a devil would really have moral objections to goodness? But the impotence of goodness to overcome the paradox of America is an impotence legitimately expressed in self-mocking rage. That paradox, so heightened for the Jew, is an integrated self to be created out of the WASP and the transported European-Jewish senses of self without mutual denigration. To get a handle on it, one would have to be comparatively, perhaps enragingly, secure.

Alexander Portnoy is not secure, and many of his grievances are myopic: The Jews are not the only conscience- or custom-repressed group in America. The *goyim* are not one homogeneous mass. Venturing outside one's ethnic group for sexual adventure or proof of individuality marks a wider American conflict than just a Jewish one. Not only Jews value education and intellect. Self-mockery and invective are not exclusively Jewish arts—as Alex might have learned had he attended an Irish, Italian, or Puerto Rican softball game. With one or more of these conflicts most people everywhere can identify. Their peculiar combination may constitute a Jewish syndrome, but it is the Jew's belief that it is only his problem that makes it a Jewish subject. And that belief is a reality. Goodness wed to exclusivity needs to be examined—best through the permissive light of satire. Roth, unbound from Jamesian sobriety, was secure enough to examine it. But Roth had no intention of, or illusions about, making the psychoanalyst's couch a new subgenre of the novel. He could take liberties in the form but once. Some of its tones might apply to fiction dealing with entrapment and to satires in different forms, but as a mode this novel of the couch could neither pass nor fail tests of comparison. For Roth's future considerations of the American-Jewish problem, the reaction of the Jewish establishment to *Portnoy's*

Complaint would be more interesting than Roth's limited attempt to portray the demigods of Weequahic.

NOTES

1. Albert Goldman, "Wild Blue Shocker," 63.

2. Eugene Borowitz, "Portnoy's Complaint," *Dimensions* Summer 1969:48–50. This is a publication of the Union of American Hebrew Congregations.

3. Donald Margulies, "A Playwright's Search for a Spiritual Father," *New York Times* 21 June 1992: H5.

4. Marie Syrkin, "The Fun of Self-Abuse," *Midstream* April 1969: 64–68.

5. Syrkin once urged this writer sympathy for all those who had subordinated their art to the Zionist cause, mentioning specifically Meyer Levin. As a supporter of the Labor Party and the early work of the *Hagganah*, she was not at all proud of the Stern gang.

6. Scholem wrote two pieces, one ("Some Plain Words") in answer to a May 22, 1969, review by Robert Weltsch, and one ("Social Criticism—Not Literary") in counter-reply to objections to his first essay by Dr. Benjamin Kadar and Daniel Gedanke. The essays were translated by Edgar E. Siskin and published as: Gershom Scholem, "Portnoy's Complaint," trans. E.E. Siskin CCARJ (Central Conference of American Rabbis) June 1970: 56–58.

7. H.E. Retik, "Postscript to *Portnoy's Complaint*," *Israel Magazine* Summer 1969: 40–42.

8. "Poles Hear *Portnoy's Complaint*," Associated Press story from Lodz, Poland, 11 February 1988.

9. See Jacob Katz, "Accounting for Anti-Semitism," *Commentary* June 1991: 52–54.

10. Robert S. Wistrich, "Once Again, Anti-Semitism Without Jews," *Commentary* August 1992: 45–49.

11. Judah Stampfer, "Adolescent Marx Brothers," *Jewish Heritage* Summer 1969:13.

12. Peter Shaw, "Portnoy & His Creator," *Commentary* May 1969: 77.

13. Stampfer, 15.

14. Shaw, 78.

15. Bruno Bettelheim, "Portnoy Psychoanalyzed, *Midstream*," June-July 1969.

16. See Retik, 42.

17. Trude Weiss-Rosmarin, "On Jewish Self-Definition, "*Reconstructionist* XXV, 2.6 March 1959: 22–25.

18. Trude Weiss-Rosmarin, "Portnoy's Complaint" (editorial), *Jewish Spectator* April 1969: 6.

19. Jewish Spectator Winter 1985/Spring 1986: 46–47. When I asked Weiss-Rosmarin why this dismissive piece was the most important editorial among all the issues of 1969, she answered, perhaps cryptically with triple underlying of the year, "I thought that this 'dismissive review' was appropriate in *1969*."

20. Sermon delivered March 7, 1969, at Fairmount Temple, Cleveland, Ohio. Reprinted with omissions as Arthur J. Lelyveld, "Old Disease in New Form: Diagnosing 'Portnoy's Complaint,'" *Jewish Digest* Summer 1969: 1–4.

21. In *The Ghost Writer* the question, "Do you believe Shakespeare's Shylock and Dickens's Fagin have been of no use to anti-Semites?" becomes one of Judge Wapter's "Ten Questions for Nathan Zuckerman." (102–3).

22. A shortened form of this review, with the references to and quotations from *Portnoy's Complaint* here used omitted, appeared in *The Jewish Spectator* for Fall 1974.

23. Sanford Pinsker, “Surviving History: Updated notes on the American-Jewish Dream,” *Jewish Spectator* Summer 1988: 21.

24. Franklin Zimring, “Portnoy’s Real Complaint,” *Moment* December 1980: 58-62.

25. Helen Weinberg, “Growing Up Jewish,” *Judaism* Spring 1969: 241–45.

MARTHA A. RAVITS

The Jewish Mother: Comedy and Controversy in American Popular Culture

The comic stereotype of the Jewish mother, from domineering to grotesque, is a cultural construct developed by male writers in the United States in the 1960s, the era of political turbulence that coincided with the second wave of feminism in this country. Among other objectives, feminists hoped that their efforts to expose the misogyny behind negative stereotypes would help to end them. Yet the representation of the Jewish mother both as a nagging guardian of ethnic identity and the embodiment of its worst traits continued to pour forth in newly minted versions from the pens and comedy routines of Jewish men. Some feminist writers like Erica Jong attempted to fight humor with humor while others in novels, screenplays, and essays tried to add complexity and nuance to the image of the Jewish mother. The history of the stereotype thus follows a jagged pattern of vilification and vindication, of male action and female reaction, of call and response, that left the caricature firmly ingrained in popular imagination. Overall, feminist responses to men's comic devaluing of the Jewish mother failed to disrupt the persistence of the image. But in recent decades, as Jews' concerns about assimilation have decreased and new cruxes of female identity and vocation have arisen, the expansion of women's roles outside the family has gradually defused the comic exaggeration of the overprotective mother. Not direct critique by feminists and social commentators, but the indirect effects of

From *MELUS* Vol. 25, No. 1 (Spring 2000). © 2000 by *MELUS*.

shifting social expectations and goals have brought solace to the stigmatized figure of the Jewish mother.

Feminist critics of several schools of thought have developed ideas about women's laughter as a means of disrupting the structures of patriarchal discourse and ideology. They stress women's creative energy and humor as distinctive features of feminist writing with the potential to unsettle the logocentrism of male authority. Hélène Cixous in "The Laugh of the Medusa" metaphorically describes women's verbal spontaneity, generosity, and *jouissance* as part of a defiant, liberating stance. Julia Kristeva, from a psychoanalytic perspective, writes that a pre-Oedipal phase linked to the maternal *chora* can resurface in texts to interrupt the symbolic order of the father. Similarly, the disruptive power of laughter is treated in Patricia Yaeger's "theory of play" as having political as well as cognitive effects. Contemporary feminist theory, then, valorizes the transformative potential of humor and language to subvert male dominance and regulation of social norms.[1] When the ranks seem to close in around a personification like the Jewish mother, comedy itself can refurbish and redeem her image. This essay, in tracing the gender wars fought over the stereotype of the Jewish mother, examines how that negative image became rooted in popular culture in the 1960s and the difficulties women writers faced in their attempts to intervene and revise it.

The myth of the manipulative Jewish mother is a complex formulation, ranging from affectionate to hostile, that grew to color perceptions of Jewish womanhood in a way that shows the triumph of comic expediency over social reality, even within a minority group that generally considered itself tolerant and liberal. Whether the Jewish mother is represented as protecting her children or demanding their loyalty, she is seen as exceeding prescribed boundaries, as being excessive. Her claims to affection, her voicing of opinions, her expressions of maternal worry are perceived as threatening in part because she acts as a free agent, not as a subordinate female according to mainstream cultural ideals. Even when she is represented as self-effacing, cast as the martyr, she is interpreted as being manipulative or passive-aggressive, secretly striving to impose her will on others. The Jewish-mother stereotype is fraught with contradictions that have not served to deconstruct it, but rather to let critics of the mother have it both ways. Jewish-mother jokes functioned to undermine women's attributes of power, to put the noncompliant older woman in her place. Through humor and ridicule, the stereotype acts to silence ethnic women by warning against their zealous energy and hidden agendas.

The indictment of mothers in American culture did not, however, originate in Jewish or ethnic humor. There was a time at mid-century when maligning the mother took a more generalized form. Maxine L. Margolis attributes the "old standby" of mother blame to the gendered division of labor in our society that makes child-rearing strictly a maternal task: "If anything goes wrong, it must be the mother's fault" (260). Margolis cites as evidence the 1943 book *Maternal Overprotection* by David Levy, who charged that women had "made maternity into a disease" (260). Also during the 1940s, Philip Wylie's attack on "Momism" in *Generation of Vipers* became a best seller. Wylie went so far as to denounce mothers for weakening the social fabric of the republic and donning "the breeches of Uncle Sam" (201). The menace of the maternal eased in the 1950s as conformism and the comforts of suburban living isolated middle-class women in the domestic realm away from public affairs. It was during the social and political strife of the 1960s that trouble for the mother erupted again. The emergence of the women's movement added to the revolutionary tenor of the times. Along with the popularization of notions of Freudian psychoanalysis (the so-called "Jewish science"), Jewish entertainers crossed over to mainstream popularity and made further inroads into dominant culture. Humor is often an instrument and indicator of social change. Lois Leveen stresses the positive function of ethnic humor in mediating social acceptance of minorities. She calls it "a volatile and subversive force that proves liberating to the ethnic despite its self-deprecating elements" (44). Often Jewish comedians and writers chose the Jewish woman, the wife and mother, as a target of satire in their repertoires for mainstream audiences. Thus the figure of the domineering mother in America came to be labeled specifically as a "Jewish mother" in public consciousness.

The stereotype indicates the sensitive spots of transition and social change for Jews. In elaborate caricatures, Jewish male writers crafted an overbearing woman, who lived vicariously through the son she pushed toward material success, while she herself unwittingly undermined his progress by her ignorance of the dominant culture. All the embarrassing baggage of ethnicity—unassimilated habits, Yiddish accent, incomplete understanding of American mores—was projected onto the mother, a representative of outmoded values. Her ethnic manner and gaucheness did not keep pace with the rapid assimilation and adaptation of her Americanized son. Her backwardness threatened to prevent his acceptance in wider social circles. Therefore, the mother, by virtue of gender and generation, functioned as a scapegoat for self-directed Jewish resentment about minority status in mainstream culture. Paula Hyman explains that historically, "faced with the need to establish their own identities in societies in which they were both fully acculturated and yet perceived as partially Other because they were Jews, Jewish men were eager to distinguish themselves from the women of their community.... The negative representations of women that they produced reflected their own ambivalence about assimilation and its limits" (169).

By the 1960s, most Jews were comfortable enough in America to reflect upon their historical adjustment from immigrant status to "native sons" through the lens of humor. The liminal position between tradition and adaptation has been described by Ralph Ellison as the quintessential American identity (Leveen 41). Jews felt most conflicted about Otherness and the desire for acceptance when they could look over social fences and see the opportunity to blend into the dominant group, if only they could shed traits of ethnicity regarded as inferior by non-Jews. The idea of "being too Jewish" was an indefensible concept that smacked of internalized anti-Semitism, but male writers used it with impunity when personified in the mother. What better strategy for dealing with prejudice than to deflect it into misogyny? The outward features of Otherness—Old World backwardness, loudness, vulgarity, clannishness, ignorance, and, materialism—were heaped onto the mother.

The most memorable and fully elaborated caricature of the Jewish mother was produced by Philip Roth in his 1969 novel *Portnoy's Complaint*, a best seller that made his reputation.[2] While some male critics lauded Roth's narrator as "a spokesman for aggrieved Jewish sons" (Kiernan 35), Jewish women felt betrayed. Charlotte Baum recounts a meeting of a Jewish women's reading group shortly after the publication of *Portnoy*. The women were outraged over the characterization of the mother that distorted their own memories of the hard work, labor organizing, and sacrifices of their mothers and themselves: "if anyone had complaints to make, it was they!" (Baum, Hyman, and Michel x–xi). Tillie Olsen in *Silences*, her classic essay on the lack of realistic portrayals of women in literature, repeats this story and poignantly asks: why have Jewish women writers not given voice to their own experience of the mother? (183). Some women writers, in fact, did take up the challenge, but compared to the highly successful male attacks that fired the popular imagination, defenses of the Jewish mother received little attention. As a satirical harpy the Jewish mother became a comic icon, while reinterpretations of the character by women writers failed to generate interest. Rehabilitating the image of the Jewish mother proved a thankless task, in part because the stereotype dovetailed so effectively with archetypes of the dangerous female, usurper of patriarchal power, just when women seemed on the verge of becoming newly dangerous and politicized through the women's movement.

The archetype of the domineering, meddling woman persists in folk motifs and literature throughout history and across cultures. Vilification of the woman was neither new nor exclusively Jewish. As a transgressor, she is found in Biblical warnings against the shrewish wife in the Book of Proverbs; in ancient Greece she is enshrined in the works of Hesiod and in the legend of Socrates's wife Xanthippe. Literary examples include the object of the Roman poet Juvenal's Sixth Satire, Shakespeare's bloodthirsty Lady Macbeth and untamed Kate, and the henpecking wife of Rip Van Winkle, inscribed by Washington Irving in the beginnings of our national fiction.

She has been more violent, she has been less comic, but the twentieth-century version of the domineering woman in literature and popular culture is distinctly an invention of Jewish-American humor. Canonical literature in the United States until the 1960s, in fact, is notable for the virtual absence of the mother figure. For most of literary history, young male protagonists are characterized as orphans. Forced to become rugged individuals early in life, they embody the Emersonian trait of self-reliance: Ishmael, Huck Finn, Nick Adams. Even Holden Caulfield in the 1950s (created by Jewish novelist J. D. Salinger) returned home to find his mother conveniently absent. It is ironic, therefore, that when a mother enters the American literary scene in the 1960s, she enters through the side door of ethnic literature and turns out to be a Jewish mother, by definition excessive in her mothering.[3]

Her image combines the misogyny of both the American and the Jewish patriarchal traditions. As an ethnic woman, she bears what feminists call double oppression and surplus visibility: she is Mother writ large. Along with exaggerated maternal concerns, she personifies garish ethnic manners and materialistic, middle-class pretensions. She is a virtual grab bag of contradictory vices: she is aggressive, parochial, ignorant, smothering, crass, selfish but also self-martyring. Most dangerously, she is accused of "Filling the patriarchal vacuum"! (*Portnoy* 45). Her power, therefore, is ascribed both to self-aggrandizement and to a weakening of male dominance; she becomes a site of displaced anxiety about the subversion of gender roles in America.

Riv-Ellen Prell, in *Fighting to Become Americans: Jews, Gender, and the Anxiety of Assimilation*, analyzes the ways in which gender has served to symbolize Jews' relationships to nation, family, and the consumer economy. Undesirable qualities, often both American and Jewish, were coded as female. Ridicule through female stereotypes emphasized Jews' desire for upward mobility and acculturation along with their worry about prevailing attitudes of the non-Jewish community toward them: "The relationship between Jews' growing access to the wider culture and the increasingly strident images of Jewish women suggest that Jews may well feel that the price of admission to America is a rejection of critical aspects of oneself as a Jew. Projected onto mothers, wives, lovers, and partners are the loathsome and unacceptable qualities of affluence constantly represented as Jewish rather than middle-class" (13).

Concerns about appearances to the outside, gentile society (encapsulated in the phrase "*shonda* to the Goyim" or "embarrassment in front of non-Jews") were heightened by minority status and sensitivity about old prejudices about Jewish greed dating back to medieval moneylenders. The ambition to rise on the economic ladder functioned as both positive motivation for modern Jews and a shameful reminder of negative stereotypes. The situation was especially perplexing because of the crux of ambivalence in American culture itself about materialism, which was celebrated, on the one hand, as a route to national progress but was suspect, on the other, for violating Christian warnings about filthy lucre. According to Prell, "scholars of ... stereotypes understand them most often to be projections onto the minority of the dominant group's fantasies about its own needs and desires" (12).

The caricature of the transgressive Jewish mother, in short, became a convenient Rorschach test open to multiple interpretations and contradictions. Her social construction helped ease the tensions of cultural transition for second and third generation Jews. Although it was the father's economic position that signified the status of the household to those outside the ethnic group, it was the mother's position inside the family that signified shifting attitudes and quandaries about ethnicity within it. In the decades after World War II in the United States, satirical portrayal of the Jewish mother became an accepted outlet for Jews' feelings of pride about their gains through assimilation and also for self-doubts about the resulting erosion of group identity and cohesiveness.

The negative stereotype of the Jewish mother casts so large a shadow in the later part of the twentieth century that it obscures previous images of the mother in Jewish literature and lore. The Jewish mother, in fact, cut a very different figure in American immigrant literature, where she was drawn in loving, sentimentalized portraits by sons in Yiddish and Jewish American novels, autobiographies, and plays. Melvin Friedman points out that, in *Call It Sleep* by Henry Roth, *A Walker in the City* by Alfred Kazin, and *Making It* by Norman Podhoretz, "the self-effacing mother and wife ... reacts with extreme courage to poverty and displacement. She is a true figure of the diaspora, with a built-in sense of suffering and survival" (158). Al Jolson's film *The Jazz Singer* in 1927 presented her to mainstream audiences as a loving and forgiving mother, whose loyalty to her son and acceptance of his assimilation overcame the wrath of the father.

The history of Jewish women in America also shows that, contrary to the stereotype of the backward mother, in the major waves of immigration around the turn of the twentieth century, women adapted quickly to urbanization and the customs of the New World. In the shtetls of Eastern

Europe, Jewish women had served their families by conducting business in the marketplace so that their men were free to spend time in study and prayer. In America, the concept of appropriate gender spheres was different, and as soon as family finances permitted, the woman stayed at home to concentrate on domestic duties and childrearing. Thomas Sowell interprets the Jewish mother's maternal worries as vestiges of Old World habits carried over to America. In the Pale of Settlement (the area of Poland and Russia from which most Eastern European Jews came), virulent anti-Semitism meant that Jews lived under the constant threat of violence and pogroms. Even in the best of times, Jewish boys were in danger of being kidnapped to be Russified by "six years of training in Greek Orthodox schools, followed by the twenty-five years of military service to which all Russian males were subject" (Sowell 78). (My own paternal grandfather emigrated at the turn of the century to escape this conscription.) The image of the ever-vigilant, overprotective Jewish mother, Sowell notes, is "understandable in view of the Jewish experience in eastern Europe, where Jewish children who wandered off might never be seen again.... The life pattern of centuries was not readily broken in America" (82).

Thus, maternal anxiety in Jewish comedy, like the tear in the voice of Al Jolson's jazz singer, is a reminder of a darker past. When growing prosperity in America enabled Jews to move out of the ghettos into less crowded neighborhoods and eventually into the suburbs ("the gilded ghettos"), the more affluent, middle-class lifestyle meant increasing isolation and a narrowing of gender roles for a woman. If previously she had worn a heroic face to sons of the first generation struggling in America, in the postwar period she rapidly lost prestige as her son gained it. Her departure from the workplace and public sector, along with American subordination and idealization of the fragile, sheltered woman, weakened her role. When she spoke out to question male decisions or to voice maternal concerns, she was scorned as too loud and aggressive, lacking in gentile refinement and manners. The victim of gender bias was labeled the transgressor.

With the introduction of her comic incarnation in the 1960s, the Jewish mother became the favorite target of the Jewish son, the parent who could be blamed for his own sense of vulnerability, accused of jeopardizing his American male birthright of untrammeled freedom. When American myths of masculinity push the son to strike out for the open road, his Jewish mother's pleading draws him back and reminds him of obligations to home and family. Her enjoinders embarrass him by subverting his stance of machismo and independence, threatening his mental composure (if not mental health), and arousing anxiety and (that word most associated with her) *guilt*. She refuses to observe the boundaries between proper parental concern and overprotection. For her, there are no boundaries in relation to her child. Her voice overflows with unsealed emotion and verbal excess. She is charged both with expressing too much love, thus delaying the son's individuation, and with expressing too much criticism, thus undermining his self-confidence.

Several Jewish writers make the joke that no Jewish male can become an adult while his mother is still alive. This barb echoes the anti-Semitic charge in Ernest Hemingway's *The Sun Also Rises*, in which the sensitive male, Robert Cohn, is mocked as "a case of arrested development" (44). Jewish writers absorb the fear and resentment of the outer society's hostility to them and transfer it to the inner family circle where it can be laid safely at the feet of the woman because of her lower status in the patriarchal pecking order. Prell writes that "intercultural stereotypes shape intracultural ones" (18). Humorists from Philip Roth to Woody Allen delight in tracing male feelings of inadequacy back to the mother. She is held responsible for both the outside world's misunderstanding of the Jewish male and for his own anxieties about a lack of requisite masculine toughness. The Jewish mother stereotype in popular culture refocuses a generalized uneasiness about female desires to "civilize" and tame the wayward male, thus emasculating him by making him a "mama's boy." At the same time, it activates specifically Jewish fears about the high price of ethnicity in a reluctantly pluralistic society. The mother's presence is an uneasy reminder to the Jew of his own secondary status, his lingering worry that anti-Semitism will eventually catch up with him.

A confluence of social factors in the 1960s resulted in a series of books by male writers that popularized the Jewish mother as "a new culture monster" who found "considerable resonance in the public imagination" (Altman 109). Philip Roth refers to the 1960s as a "demythologizing decade" because of the political disillusionment created by the Vietnam War and the Civil Rights Movement, but he fails to connect the mythologizing of the Jewish mother to the radical youth culture and the male response to the women's movement ("Reading Myself" 404–417). Jewish writers drew upon the routines of stand-up comedians to privilege the son and recast the mother as his comic antagonist: Bruce Jay Friedman in *A Mother's Kisses* (1964), Dan Greenberg in *How to Be a Jewish Mother* (1964), and, at decade's end, Wallace Markfield in *Teitlebaum's Window* (1970). But it was Roth's depiction of Sophie Portnoy in *Portnoy's Complaint* (1969) that set the standard. While both parents come in for solid rounds of criticism in the novel, Roth's caricature of the Jewish father has faded over the years while his caricature of the mother survives in robust health. The mother's exaggerated demands and worries made her a perfect target for Roth's linguistic energy: her verbal excess mirrors the son's own. The narrator-son laments that his mother has ruined his life by "scolding, correcting, reproving, criticizing, faultfinding without end" (45).

Locked behind the Venetian blinds of her scrupulously cleaned house, a woman like Sophie Portnoy lived according to a strict gender system that offered few outlets for her talents and ambitions. Small wonder that women were forced to live vicariously through the sons and husbands they sent out into the world. Betty Friedan diagnosed their plight in *The Feminine Mystique* (1964) as "the problem that has no name" and helped to found the National Organization of Women in 1966, one year before Sophie Portnoy made her debut in the pages of *Esquire Magazine*. Women's calls for greater equality, opportunities, and redress of grievances ran headlong into resistance from Jewish male writers, a group that often prided itself on attitudes of liberalism and tolerance. By portraying women as uppity, excessively verbose, and demanding, men implied that there was little reason to take women's complaints seriously. The attack on motherhood, traditionally the female role of greatest influence, further undermined women's social and political credibility.

Feminists who objected to the stereotype and attempted to rectify it ran into formidable obstacles. Eventually the backlash against feminism called feminist thinkers strident and lacking in humor. Women were damned if they defended the mother, damned if they didn't. When they pointed out the overt misogyny of the personification, they were dismissed as spoilsports. Yet, the stereotype arose at a juncture that created a particularly painful bind for Jewish women, who often felt assailed on all sides. Feminism was pushing them to venture into the "real world" beyond the domestic sphere, where they had long relied on their roles as wife and mother for a sense of identity and cultural validation. At the same time, Jewish men were mocking their ethnicity, thus scorning their sense of cultural commitment in upholding Jewish values and religion.

Into this milieu of ingratitude stepped Grace Paley in the mid-1970s with an essay in *Esquire* entitled simply "Mom." Paley defends the Jewish mother and poignantly calls up childhood memories from the immigrant generation of a woman who fell victim to a "mocking campaign" that Paley traces as far back as the 1930s and ultimately to Freud. "The chief investigator into human pain" had looked into his book of "awful prognoses" and sealed her fate. Paley is pessimistic about a daughter's ability to revive the image of the loving Jewish mother after the ravages of male scorn: "Unfortunately, science and literature had turned against her. What use was my accumulating affection when the brains of the opposition included her son the doctor and her son the novelist? Because of them, she never even had a chance at the crown of apple pie awarded her American-born sisters." Instead the Jewish mother "was destined, with her meaty bossiness, her sighs, her suffering, to be dumped into the villain room of social meaning and psychological causation" (85–6).

For Jewish male writers, the "villain room of social meaning and psychological causation" proved a fruitful workshop. The low estimation of the mother in psychoanalytic paradigms from Freud to Lacan to contemporary theorists allowed Jewish writers to vent comic spleen as they dissected the contradictions and psychopathology of their own everyday lives. The techniques of obliqueness and irony suited their purposes. Alex Portnoy's frustrations about growing up Jewish in Newark, New Jersey, during the Depression are deflected onto his parents: "The guilt, the fears—the terror bred into my bones! What in their world was not charged with danger, dripping with germs, fraught with peril? ... Who filled these parents of mine with such a fearful sense of life?" (37).

The comic question suggests a serious answer, of course, one grounded in Jewish history, that long chronicle of economic deprivation and violent anti-Semitism. Jews' worries about matters of survival eased in the United States, but were replaced by a different, more subtle set of insecurities. Their feelings of vulnerability were complicated and intensified in the aftermath of the Holocaust, just when the goal of acceptance by mainstream America seemed within reach. Sensitive issues about assimilation, religion, class, and gender were reactivated for Jews. Internalized feelings of insecurity and difference became yeasty material for writers. As the social and economic rewards of merging into the mainstream enticed the Jewish son away from ethnic origins, he assuaged feelings of disloyalty by blaming his mother, keeper of his Jewish conscience (or Freudian "superego"), for holding him back.

Thus the Jewish mother was devalued and stigmatized as a regressive force during the very period when she might rightfully have expected to share credit for the elevation of her children in economic and social status. As Jews rose in the professions and business, writers and comics used self-mocking humor to chide the mother for the very values that were keys to their success: the drive for education, aggressiveness, and social ambition. Furthermore, the stereotype of the Jewish mother was developed and perpetuated in fields where Jewish culture made its greatest impact on dominant culture: stand-up comedy, literature, and film. As Jewish humor evolved from a medium of intragroup cohesiveness into a popular performance for those outside the group, the satiric portrayal of the Jewish-mother was sharpened. Gladys Rothbell writes that when negative caricatures are considered "sympathetic in-group humor," the bias against women is easily ignored (123). Then, when those jokes cross over into mainstream popularity, the misogynistic humor becomes "not only a social construct but also a successful commercial commodity." The anti-Semitic stigma of the stereotyping is tolerated along with "the basic classist, ageist, or sexist nature" of the Jewish-mother jokes (127). A more positive interpretation of ethnic jokes is offered by Lois Leveen, who argues that humor allows the joke teller to display knowledge of ethnicity that makes common cause with the object of the mockery. Thus, "ethnic jokes may indicate that it is not the ethnic individual who is laughable, but rather the stereotype—and those who believe the stereotype to be truthful and accurate—at which the joke teller and the joke listener laugh together" (43).

I suspect that humor serves multiple purposes and is more polymorphously perverse than any single approach or explanation can describe. It may reinforce resentments across gender lines but also relieve them. It may openly denigrate ethnic traits but also obliquely praise them. Some portraits of the Jewish mother criticize her mothering techniques while paying backhanded tribute to their effectiveness. The contradictory knot of character traits in the stereotype suggests affection for a figure who lavishes watchful attention on her child *and* resentment of the power she wields. In *Jewish Humor: What the Best Jewish Jokes Say About the Jews*, Joseph Telushkin cites as paradigmatic a story about a worried Jewish mother who takes her adolescent son to see a psychiatrist. After several visits, the doctor informs the woman that the boy is suffering from an Oedipus complex. "Oedipus, Shmedipus," she replies, "as long as he loves his mother" (30). The woman's uneducated response reveals not only her ignorance of psychoanalytic theories, but also her embarrassing inability to recognize the boundary between healthy filial affection and incestuous excess. Her Jewish inflection and malapropism are comic vestiges of backwardness that nonetheless emphasize her assertion of the primacy of the mother–child connection.

Ambiguity and doubleness, affection and resentment of the mother, shape familiar conflicts in the Jewish son's perspective in literature and film. Vignettes about the damaging Jewish mother offer classic Oedipal explanations of male development that on the surface seem to alleviate male self-blame yet can ricochet to expose male deficiencies. In comedies by Philip Roth or Woody Allen, the psychoanalytic framework is often used to highlight the son's befuddled condition. In these melodramas of beset Jewish manhood (to twist Nina Baym's phrase), the protagonist's central struggle is not with the outside world but with the self embroiled in the family romance. His efforts to separate from the mother and the ferocity of her resistance, an unexpected switch from conditioned female passivity, propels the comedy.

Portnoy's Complaint, in fact, began in its first installment as an extended variation on the Jewish-mother joke. In free-association discourse delivered on the psychiatrist's couch, Alexander Portnoy at 33, the age at which Jesus was crucified, lambastes his mother for her faults and his own, real and imagined. The epigraph to the novel is a mock definition from the Diagnostic Statistical Manual of Psychiatric Disorders, a description of a new complaint "in which strongly felt ethical and altruistic impulses are perpetually warring with extreme sexual longings, often of a perverse nature. [M]any of the symptoms can be traced to the bonds obtaining in the mother–child relationship." This synopsis squarely places blame for the patient's neurotic suffering on the mother, disregarding paternal influence and the son's free will. Yet as Portnoy protests about maternal overprotection, his self-serving discourse illuminates the recesses of his own mind. His monologue covers a range of anxieties about individuation, ethnicity, and femininity, including male fear about feminine aspects of the self. "There's more here than just adolescent resentment and Oedipal rage," Portnoy warns (71), and that "more" is the telltale premise of psychological investigation and literary interpretation.

The opening chapter, titled "The Most Unforgettable Character I've Met," introduces the mother through the young boy's eyes, a lens of magical realism that shows a dangerous fascination with her:

> She was so deeply imbedded in my consciousness that for the first year of school I seem to have believed that each of my teachers was my mother in disguise. As soon as the last bell had sounded, I would rush off for home, wondering as I ran if I could possibly make it to our apartment before she had succeeded in transforming herself. Invariably she was already in the kitchen by the time I arrived, and setting out my milk and cookies. Instead of causing me to give up my delusions, however, the feat merely intensified my respect for her powers. And then it was always a relief not to have caught her between incarnations anyway. (1)

Torn between indebtedness to the mother and resentment of her, Portnoy grows increasingly hostile as he ages. With the onset of male puberty, the mother's greatest power becomes her ability to influence her son through guilt, which Charlotte Baum, Paula Hyman, and Sonya Michel define as "that most exquisite instrument of remote control" (236). It is the mother's struggle to restrain her son's libido and the son's efforts to free himself that fuel Portnoy's story. Indeed, once Sophie Portnoy with her countless admonitions and suspicions is left behind, the novel loses comic force.

There's no place like home in Portnoy's narrative because that's where the mother is, "the most unforgettable character" the reader meets in the text.

To escape the mother's gravitational pull and assert his independence, Alexander Portnoy uses a tactic familiar to readers and observers of Jewish sons in American comedy: he seeks as a love object the non-Jewish woman or *shikse*, a woman who is the antithesis of the mother in appearance, culture, and mental attitudes. Thus, the mockheroic drama of Jewish humor combines the male erotic quest with the quest for assimilation. From Alex Portnoy to Woody Allen to Jerry Seinfeld, love in the arms of a non-Jewish woman symbolizes the embrace of the gentile world. The struggle for filial autonomy is equated with the quest for mainstream acceptance that requires repudiation of both ethnicity and the ethnic mother in the pursuit of a mate.

By the 1970s, when Tillie Olsen issued her call for a defense of the Jewish mother, two feminist responses had already appeared: one was Grace Paley's meditation on "Mom," discussed above (published, ironically, in the same magazine that carried Sophie Portnoy) and the other was Erica Jong's comedy, *Fear of Flying* (1973), which contains a pointed rebuttal to *Portnoy*. Jong's iconoclastic, ribald, and scathingly funny novel became the sexual manifesto of the women's liberation movement and established her as a spokeswoman for her generation. It won praise from critics Henry Miller and John Updike. Bookstores had a hard time keeping it in stock. In the novel, the protagonist Isadora Wing is a journalist, poet, and former analysand, who travels to Europe to report on a psychiatric conference in Vienna with her psychiatrist husband. Unfortunately, but not surprisingly, amidst the sensationalism of Isadora's disclosures about sexual affairs and erotic fantasies (including the "zipless fuck"), her reflections on the Jewish mother received scant attention.

Jong's portrait of the mother, in a chapter entitled "Pandora's Box or My Two Mothers," is a deliberate attempt to complicate and revise the reductive image of the Jewish mother crafted by male writers. Jong's narrator makes duality the key to her conflicting feelings about her mother as a good and a bad parent, in short, a mother who defies stereotyping. Indeed, Isadora Wing's mother is introduced as a direct rebuttal to Portnoy: "I envy Alexander Portnoy. If only I had a real Jewish mother—easily pigeonholed and filed away—a real literary property" (161). Wing's stereoscopic view of the mother may fall into the trap of binary categorizing shunned by later feminist critics, but it rightfully condemns the male view of the mother as an oversimplification. By satirizing the distortion and commodification of the Jewish mother in male comedy, Jong underscores the need for the corrective vision of female experience.

Socio-economic differences admittedly separate Isadora's privileged

German-Jewish mother, Judith Stoloff White, from lower middle-class Sophie Portnoy, with her eastern-European roots and accent, but Jong tries to pry the mother figure away from stock expectations. Her feminist reconsideration urges the view that between the extremes of the mother-as-cipher in mainstream fiction and the mother-as-monster in Jewish male fiction lies a range of possibilities to be explored. Judith Stoloff White is but one sketch of a literary alternative to combat the prevailing stereotype. Yet, in Jong's highly allusive prose, she is significantly nicknamed "Jude" for the patron saint of lost causes.

Jude is a tour de force, a refashioned version of the Jewish mother as a bohemian, a rebel against convention who critiques mainstream culture. Isadora Wing begins her description with a set of paradoxes. Applying the Catullan formula *odi et amo* to the mother, the daughter complains that "My love for her and my hate for her are so bafflingly intertwined that I can hardly *see* her" (Jong 161). Jude was never retiring or inhibited, as Isadora points out, but a forceful, artistic personality. She bears none of the crassness of the formulaic Jewish mother but maintains, instead, an air of cultivation, mystery, and aloofness. She is a free spirit who embarrasses her child not by her backwardness but by her progressiveness, her individualistic way of dressing and behaving. She has been a communist, an artist, a hippie, and is a devoted mother who has given up "poetry and painting for arty clothes and compulsive reupholstering" (162). She frustrates her teenage daughter's "passion for ordinariness" (161) by dressing for Parents' Day at school in "tapestried toreador pants and a Pucci pink silk sweater and a Mexican serape" (163). As an educated, assimilated woman, Jude Stoloff White has the self-confidence to defy decorum and to teach her child to question authority. Ultimately, Jude challenges the American double standard of social freedom for men (including sexual freedom) but rigid control for women. Her daughter's later rejection of conventional sexual mores in favor of sexual liberation can, therefore, be attributed in part to maternal influence.

For Jude the Jewish mother instills not fear in her child, as Sophie Portnoy did, but social daring. She offers two cardinal rules:

> 1. Above all, never be *ordinary*.
> 2. The world is a predatory place: Eat faster! (162)

These injunctions satirize the aggressiveness and food fetishism of the Jewish mother stereotype, but also offer in condensed, secularized form a feminist satire of the law (or decalogue) of the father. Jong appropriates the son's Oedipal rebelliousness and recasts it from a female perspective. The "two mothers" of Isadora's narrative are contrasting yet complementary halves of maternal representation: the demanding, directive mother of ethnic humor and the idealized, companionable mother of mainstream culture who is supportive and fun-loving, a woman who takes her daughters ice-skating on the pond in Central Park.[4]

As the good mother, Jude laughs at her daughter's jokes as if she were a composite of Milton Berle, Groucho Marx, and Irwin Corey, an overt reference to the female humorist's apprenticeship to Jewish stand-up comedians. The mother regards Isadora as a literary prodigy at age eight and later encourages her daughter's "adolescent maunderings" (167). Therefore she stands in stark contrast to the critical, emasculating mother of male humor as a woman who instills artistic confidence and psychological self-sufficiency in her child. She is the mother as presiding genius of the female artist's literary career. But even her good side baffles her child, for Isadora, like Portnoy, is enmeshed in the task of self-definition and ripe for rebellion. Yet any form of rebellion that Isadora can imagine—her choice of a Chinese-American spouse, for instance—can be interpreted from another angle as a departure from the "ordinary" and therefore as a fulfillment of her mother's first cardinal rule. "Surely no girl could have a more devoted mother, a mother more interested in her becoming a whole person, in becoming, if she wished, an artist? Then why am I so furious with her? And why does she make me feel that I am nothing but a blurred carbon copy of her? ... That I have no freedom, no independence, no identity at all?" (168).

The impulse to blame the mother thus re-emerges as a female method of defining selfhood, but with important gender differences. Jong's novel, which appeared five years before Nancy Chodorow's *The Reproduction of Mothering: Psychoanalysis and the Sociology of Gender*, embodies in comedic form theoretical insights about the continuity of female identity and a daughter's complex attenuation of relational bonds with the mother. Isadora frets that the umbilical cord which connects her to her mother has never been cut. Like other women writers who stress filial attachment, Isadora asserts, for better or worse, along with Anne Sexton, that "A woman *is* her mother" (77).

Jong's heroine theorizes, in psychoanalytic fashion, that somehow the puzzles of heterosexuality are the crux of her otherwise inexplicable fury at the mother. "Sex," she confesses, "was the real Pandora's box." The daughter's sense of entrapment and release is expressed in a mythological metaphor that (in addition to the obscene pun) is drawn from outside both Jewish and Freudian frames of reference. The allusion to Pandora invokes a female figure of Greek mythology who is blamed for unleashing all evils and illness upon the world. In reclaiming this misogynistic myth, Jong taps the subversive nature of female creative and sexual forces. She, like Cixous, links her views of female autonomy and erotic desire to a revisionary construct that is mythic yet female-centered, classical but not explicitly Freudian. Jong makes the mother–daughter relationship part of an experiment in female laughter that interrupts male paradigms and works to liberate both the Jewish mother and daughter from falsification.

But comedy often trades in stock types. It is hard to fight oversimplification and stereotyping with more nuanced interpretations. Jong's attempt to widen the frame of imagery failed to spring the Jewish mother from the trap of comic conventions. In the following decade, the 1980s, an increasing number of works by women took up the cause and treated the Jewish mother with new seriousness and respect: Lee Grant's film of Tillie Olsen's *Tell Me a Riddle*, Anne Roiphe's novel *Lovingkindness*, and Laurie Colwin's novel *Family Happiness*. Grant's film depicts the memories and death of a defiant, aged radical. Roiphe represents the Jewish mother as a feminist professor who resists the urge to try to control her daughter's life, despite the girl's conversion to a sect of Jewish orthodoxy that the mother despises. Colwin in her novel creates a sympathetic protagonist who juggles the responsibilities of the so-called sandwich generation as she struggles to be both a dutiful mother and a dutiful daughter, even while seeking her own erotic fulfillment. And in a poignant story, this time called "Mother" (1985), Grace Paley again focuses on the underappreciated subject of her title, a deceased woman who in life seemed to occupy a place only on the margins of her daughter and husband's attention.

But this constellation of works about Jewish mothers who are not domineering did little to efface the cultural imprint of the negative stereotype. Women writers continue to repudiate the charge that Jewish mothering is bad mothering. A mother's ambition for her child may be exaggerated into a comic flaw, but, when interpreted sympathetically, can also testify to maternal desire for the child's best interests within a highly competitive, materialistic society. How a child internalizes such messages varies according to the child's individual character. The actual influence of Jewish mothering as a component in achievement has received more comic attention than serious study. Despite the mother's prominence in *Portnoy's Complaint*, Roth's own mother is barely mentioned in his autobiography, and surprisingly little has been written about the mothers of twentieth-century Jewish intellectuals Freud, Einstein, or Bettelheim.[5] Ironically, it is John Updike, the WASP literary giant of American letters, who champions the Jewish mother. He creates a tender portrait of her beneficent influence on her son the writer in *Bech: A Book* (1970). In the final chapter, Bech recounts the day his mother took him out of school to witness the awarding of medals to literary luminaries at a theater in New York. Years after her death, when he receives the coveted medal at the same ceremony, he fleetingly imagines he glimpses in the audience the face of the mother who believed in and inspired him.

In *Of Woman Born: Motherhood as Experience and Institution*, Adrienne Rich offers an explanation of the common tendency of literary sons to turn the mother from an instrument and indoctrinator of patriarchal values into its chief opponent. Rich terms this hostility "matrophobia," not hatred of the mother, but the fear of becoming the mother (235). A child must wrestle with the compromises and self-doubt that the mother represents, caught as she is in the misogyny of the larger social order. "Easier by far to hate and reject a mother outright," Rich observes, "than to see beyond her to the forces acting on her" (235). The mother is blamed for weakness if she is passive and accused of seizing male prerogatives if she is not. Resentment of the mother, a pawn in patriarchal society, obscures the real source of power and injustice that the child must eventually confront in a hierarchical world, the law of the father. Erica Jong's protagonist glances at the structural dimensions of this dilemma when she laments: "I couldn't rail at my Jewish mother because the problem was deeper than Jewishness or mothers" (165).

The comic son may use matrophobia to mask his similarities to the mother by ridiculing her and devaluing women in general and all traits connected with the feminine in particular. The male view of the Jewish mother is complicated by the conjunction of homophobia and matrophobia. The Jewish son's position as Other evokes fear that his difference from mainstream society will expose him to questions about his manliness. Self-conscious in a relentlessly psychological age, the Jewish humorist therefore attempts to eradicate any visible traces of attachment to the mother which could leave him open to charges of effeminacy, an insidious weapon in the arsenal of anti-Semites that derives from homophobia. This defensive strategy, intended to deflect attention away from his own shortcomings, may nonetheless unintentionally expose his latent insecurities. The master of this technique of simultaneously concealing and revealing psychic failings, of course, is film writer and director Woody Allen.

In "Oedipus Wrecks," Allen's contribution to the omnibus film *New York Stories* (1989), the Freudian pun of the title sums up the predicament of the familiar Allen persona, the Jewish son as anxiety-ridden adult. In this film, matrophobia takes the milder, more conventional form of fear of marrying the mother, a theme reinforced by the piano refrain of the soundtrack, "I Want a Girl (Just Like the Girl That Married Dear Old Dad)." In talking to his psychiatrist, the story's protagonist Sheldon Mills (Woody Allen) blames his erotic troubles on his mother (Mae Questal) and expresses the wish to be rid of her. He relates a dream of her funeral in which he drives the hearse bearing her body to the cemetery. Sam Girgus compares Allen to Philip Roth "in his self-conscious exploitation of Freud to intensify the effect of voicing the unspeakable" (*Films* 11). Allen's satire, like Oedipal parodies in post-modern literature by Thomas Pynchon and Don DeLillo, trades on the cultural currency of psychoanalytic theory, but also reveals the beginning of a decline in its cultural sway. Girgus writes that humor "subverts the absolute authority of psychoanalysis, while psychoanalysis exposes the potential of a hidden dimension of secret meaning to humor" ("Roth and Allen" 121).

In Allen's film, the humor takes a memorably visual, Felliniesque, form as the image of the Jewish mother is literally inflated beyond all bounds. The screenplay is a romance based on the son's failed desire to escape filial loyalty. Like other male comics, Allen's character enacts a double regression that lies at the heart of American-Jewish humor: a regression to childhood resentments and to ethnic origins. Sheldon Mills is a fifty-year-old lawyer whose efforts at assimilation have paid off in the ostensible rewards of worldly success: he is a partner in a "conservative" (i.e., non-Jewish) New York law firm, he has changed his family name from Millstein to Mills, and he is engaged to a blond shiksa (Mia Farrow). His adaptation to the gentile world would be complete were it not for his Jewish mother. Shortly after Mills confesses the wish that his mother would "just disappear," he takes her with his fiancée's family to a magic show. In the theater Sadie Millstein is reluctantly called up on stage to demonstrate a trick by climbing into a magic box. Once shut inside, she actually vanishes only to reappear days later as a huge talking head hovering above the skyline of Manhattan. From this supernal position, looking like a cross between the Wizard of Oz and My Yiddishe Mama, Sadie oversees her son's activities and delivers a running commentary on his childhood traits and adult lovelife to gathering crowds on the New York City sidewalks.

This carnivalesque ploy is a realization of the son's worst nightmares: his own Jewish mother as a public spectacle. Sadie's criticisms of her son and his impending marriage are broadcast from on high as public pronouncements. The personal becomes the political as even the mayor (Ed Koch in a cameo role) gets involved, responding to Sadie on the evening news. The Jewish mother personifies the return of the repressed, a voice of inner conscience that refuses to be hidden. And the mother finally triumphs. Mills's fiancée cannot bear the pressure and leaves him. Only after Sheldon has chosen a proper Jewish mate—a woman who resembles his mother in eyewear, intonation, and the desire to fatten him up—does Sadie Millstein consent to come down. Allen's visual icon shows the Jewish mother to be overpowering, omniscient, "humiliating," as Sheldon says, and, like Sophie

Portnoy, connected to magic. With the inflated vengeance of Sadie Millstein, Allen revivifies the old stereotype and proves that in comedy nothing succeeds like excess.

Jewish humor, like much ethnic humor, depends upon the burdens of dual consciousness. Allen, along with Roth and Jong, shows how the unresolved tension between ethnicity and assimilation produces mental discord that reinforces a sense of Otherness. Allen's paranoid persona reenacts the quintessential predicament of a minority member caught in the stage of both self-regard and looking over his shoulder at mainstream observers. The Jewish mother, with her repeated calls to return to the fold, serves as a keeper of the faith. Because her exaggerated features and verbal lack of inhibition transgress the bounds of social decorum, she simultaneously humiliates and saves her child from the perils of "ordinariness." Even when she most heightens the child's desire to merge into the crowd, her presence is a reminder that denial of one's origins is not honorable. Her image reactivates familiar ambivalence and frustration about passing. The Jewish mother is mocked and abused, but her refusal to release her child to the status quo of mainstream culture confers an ironic sense of postlapsarian heroism on her American offspring.

The Jewish son, then, need not light out for the territory in search of the raw material of life; for him the raw material of life resides at home. The hero's (or anti-hero's) most challenging adventure consists of negotiating the family romance. His quest for autonomy continues well past adolescence and circles back to the relationship with the mother. Insistent variations on the Oedipal theme connect the stereotype of the Jewish mother to the misogyny of psychoanalytic theories which, in versions from Freud to Lacan to recent work by Nicholas Abraham and Maria Torok, continue to blame socio-sexual maladjustment, Oedipal "wreckage," on the mother. Esther Rashkin writes that "We are all, to use [Abraham and Torok's] invented locution, *mutilés de mere* or 'mother-amputees' (rhymes with the common French expression *mutilés de guerre*: 'war-amputees' or 'war-invalids')" (17–18). This theoretical punning again reveals the gap between mythology and reality about women, for statistically the vast preponderance of domestic violence, including in Jewish families, is directed against women.

But the notion of an adult man as a "mother-amputee" fits the subject of Albert Brooks's 1996 film *Mother*. Brooks (born Albert Lawrence Einstein of a Jewish father and non-Jewish mother) universalizes the image of the Jewish mother but retains and ironically reverses key elements of the mother–son parody. He distorts the principles of both psychoanalysis and feminism by creating a protagonist who arrogantly dismisses psychoanalytic interpretations of his own plight but glibly appropriates feminist explanations for that of his mother. The film opens when California science-fiction writer John Henderson (Brooks) has just divorced for the second time. He attributes his failures with women and a bad case of writer's block to an unsupportive, flawed relationship with his mother (Debbie Reynolds). To resolve his personal and professional problems, he unilaterally decides to move back into his mother's house as an "experiment." Stereotypical Jewish mother–child role reversals are set up as the adult child intervenes in the mother's life.

He does not need a psychiatrist, John tells his brother, because a psychiatrist didn't raise him; his mother did. This rejection of psychoanalysis foreshadows the irony of a classic Oedipal triangle in which the two brothers, one overly critical of the mother and the other overly attached to her, vie for her attention. Despite John's objections to psychological explanations, the mother functions as the sexualized prize and arbiter in this fraternal rivalry when the brothers come to blows on her doorstep.

After John Henderson moves back home into his old room, he discovers a stockpile of his mother's youthful writings stored in his closet. He then confronts his mother with her own unfulfilled literary ambitions and hypothesizes that her thwarted talent caused her to resent her role as full-time mother and caregiver when he was born and resulted in the chilly relationship between them. This interpretation of the past proves cathartic for him: "I see you as a failure, Mother, and it's wonderful," he boasts. The mother acquiesces to his theory, since it appears to "help" him, she says. The therapeutic insight releases them from locked antagonism and seems to grant each a new lease on life and creativity.

The film ends with a quintessential, male, "on-the-road" scene for John, as he returns to Los Angeles, while his mother buys a computer and takes up writing again in his old room. Brooks adds a double-helix twist to matrophobia by creating a son who has unwittingly become a writer like his mother and a mother who belatedly re-emerges as a writer like her son. (Quick glimpses of work-in-progress on their respective computer screens suggest that she is the better writer.) Brooks appropriates feminist ideology by making the son a wisdom figure who raises the mother's consciousness about the personal price she has paid in sacrificing her creative aspirations for her role as mother. Yet her vocational awakening is secondary, an accidental consequence of the son's psychological quest.

As the mother figure is universalized and emptied of specific Jewish identity in the 1990s, she can devolve into a character who is merely cold and calculating. Whereas Sophie Portnoy was dangerous because of her overweening affection, some recent incarnations of the Jewish mother depict her as remote and unloving. The energy and vulgarity of the mother are toned down to mere reflexes of self-involvement in Barbra Streisand's 1997 film "The Mirror Has Two Faces," written by Richard LaGravenese (based on a French title). Lauren Bacall plays a vain and selfish Jewish mother of two daughters, whose only teaching about the Sabbath, one quips, was that Bergdorfs would be less crowded. The moral features of this mother, beautiful on the outside but cruel on the inside, mark her as an antifeminist woman, one who is willing to undermine the confidence of her daughter Rose, a Columbia professor of literature (played by Streisand) and to prevent the daughter's romantic fulfillment by schemes to keep the daughter living at home as the mother ages.

Even when the Jewish mother appears fully Americanized, she still brings to light old insecurities about appearances, and ultimately about the unacceptable risks of appearing either Jewish or old in American society. Rose is unattractive though charismatic and talented. The mother is a former beauty who is aging. The loyalty of the daughter and treachery of the mother show that the vilified Jewish mother has undergone many incarnations since her inception and returns again to haunt her child with new issues. The few women writers who have positioned the mother as a sympathetic character at the center of her own story have not gained sufficient mass to displace the grotesque stereotype, but they have managed to offer suggestive possibilities and fresh thinking on the theme.

Nora Ephron's film *This Is My Life* (1992), based on a novel by Meg Wolitzer and adapted for the screen by Nora Ephron and Delia Ephron, is a case in point. The film is not defensive or angry; it is less a response to the Jewish mother stereotype than a female-centered narrative about a mother caught in the feminist dilemma of balancing the demands of family and career. The film is narrated by both the mother, Dottie Ingels (Julie Kavner), and her oldest daughter, Erica (Samantha Mathis). Each major scene, as Sylvia Barack Fishman observes, "begins with a voiceover by the elder daughter and then continues in the voice of the mother, The overlapping voices seem to ask, 'Whose life is this anyway'"? (163). This dual voicing suggests both collaboration and traditional rivalry as the mother and daughter pursue their separate but connected struggles for independence. The ups and downs of their story depict a strong relationship of mutual respect and affection, ruffled only temporarily by competition and resentment.

The film modifies the Jewish-mother construct with brief allusions to the stereotype and innovative departures from it. Here the woman stands not as the butt of comedy but as a vital creator of comedy, the voice and performer of her own life. Dottie Ingels begins as a single mother struggling to support her two daughters in Queens after her husband has deserted the family. When she inherits some money, Dottie seizes the chance to move her family to Manhattan, where she enters the field of stand-up comedy. Wearing dotted clothing as her trademark, she fashions homespun humor from the material of her everyday life. Her jokes are gentle and humane, her themes are connection and relationships. She offers her daughters the "life lesson" that everyone in the world is only two phone calls away from everyone else.

When Dottie reaches for stardom, a heavy schedule of engagements on the West Coast keeps her away from home, and her girls resent the separation. Dottie's male agent consoles her with the advice that "Children are happy when their mother is happy." "No they're not," Dottie counters, "Everyone says that, but it's not true. Children are happy when you're *there*." Thus Dottie rejects the glibness of contemporary psycho-babble to perceive the truth underlying her daughters' feelings. When the girls run away, Dottie realizes that she is not willing to jeopardize their happiness for her shot at success in show business. This scenario reverses the usual direction of guilt: it is not a means of control employed by the mother but rather a tactic used by the daughters to bring the straying mother into line. Dottie is the Jewish mother recast as a contemporary working woman caught in a net of conflicting obligations. She perseveres by dint of down-to-earth candor, bravery, and insight. Always a devoted mother, Dottie vows to subordinate the demands of her stage role to her maternal role, although the film ends without specifying exactly how she will accomplish that.

The film explores a common dilemma for the modern woman, the tug-of-war between career and family, and it affirms the primacy of maternal responsibilities. Yet, as a variation on the Jewish-mother motif, the problem admits no satisfactory resolution: the stereotype insists that the mother is self-centered and ignorant, blind to her offsprings' suffering, but also domineering and overprotective. Any reversal of the negative stereotype carries with it the internal contradictions. Dottie, as exemplar of the positive Jewish mother, cannot surmount contemporary problems: her personal ambition for stardom propels her out into the world, but the needs and desires of her daughters draw her back home. She is appreciated by the strangers in her mainstream audience for her talent, warmth, and charisma, the same qualities that make her children yearn for her presence. In contrast to the failed artist-mother depicted by Jong or Brooks, she does not postpone her own creativity because of motherhood but takes risks to express it in the very branch of male-dominated comedy where the stereotype of the Jewish mother originated.

The acceptance and popularity of Jewish humor in the entertainment industry—stand-up comedy, film, television, recordings, and literature—have contributed to the Jewish minority's increasing sense of security and success in the United States. This position of relative comfort is reflected in changing ethnic attitudes and images. Comedy rides on the edge of discomfort. During a period of cultural transition, the stereotype of the Jewish mother was constructed to signify and mock Jews' concerns about the process of Americanization. Those concerns have since given way to other preoccupations. As traces of Jewish self-doubt about assimilation and acceptance wane, the figure of the mother has been divested of ethnic content. She has lost much of her provocative power and comic zest as a result. In the three 1990s films discussed above, the Jewish mother appears less hyperbolic, more muted, and thus flattened. Pictured as a less parochial, more universalized figure, she now negotiates contemporary issues of female identity: aging, sexuality, the competing obligations of career and family. Although the Jewish mother was portrayed as recalcitrant about change in the 1960s, in recent screen incarnations she is more progressive. She has moved with the times. But she remains a cautionary figure, who warns her child (and the audience) about the perils of complacency in a fast-paced, narcissistic society. Theories of comedy postulate that laughter can subvert, disrupt, and critique the prevailing social order, revealing pressure points in the collective consciousness. As the position of the Jewish mother has shifted from the cultural margins toward the center, she can now be used to indicate cruxes of cultural ambivalence for all Americans.

Notes

1. A standard explanation of French feminists' work is offered in Moi, Ch. 6 and 8. For a synthesis of feminist theory in relation to ethnic humor see Leveen.

2. Some critics still regard *Portnoy's Complaint* as Roth's most enduring work. See, for example, Menand, in reviewing *American Pastoral*, who concludes that the newer novel is "darker, difficult, more mature; but *Portnoy* is forever" (94).

3. A notable exception to the lack of mothers in American literature occurs in John Steinbeck's *The Grapes of Wrath*, a text often relegated to high-school reading lists. Women's sentimental fiction, which contains vivid portrayals of the mother, was disregarded by canon makers before feminist criticism. The decades of expanding the American canon since the 1960s have brought in portraits of the mother from many ethnic literatures: African American, Native American, Latino/a American, and Asian American. The mother in Toni Morrison's *Beloved* has attained canonical status and those in Amy Tan's *Joy Luck Club* and Laura Esquivel's *Like Water for Chocolate* have also crossed over into popular culture through films.

4. This aspect of the mother is comparable to the Latina daughter's perception of the all-American mother as "a girlfriend parent ... a Mom" (Alvarez 136).

5. Dinnage notes this biographical dearth of information about mothers.

Works Cited

Altman, Sig. *The Comic Image of the Jew: Explorations of a Pop Culture Phenomenon*. Cranbury, NJ: Associated UP, 1971.

Alvarez, Julia. *How the Garcia Girls Lost Their Accents*. Now York: Penguin, 1991.

Baum, Charlotte, Paula Hyman, and Sonya Michel. *The Jewish Woman in America*. New York: NAL, 1975.

Chodorow, Nancy. *The Reproduction of Motherhood: Psychoanalysis and the Sociology of Gender*. Berkeley: U of California P, 1978.

Cixous, Hélène. "The Laugh of the Medusa." Trans. Keith Cohen and Paula Cohen. *New French Feminisms*. Ed. Elaine Marks and Isabelle de Courtivron. Brighton: Harvester, 1980. 245–64.

Colwin, Laurie. *Family Happiness*. London: Hodder and Stoughton, 1982.

Dinnage, Rosemary. "The Survivor." Rev. of *Bettelheim: A Life and a Legacy*, by Nina Sutton. *New York Review of Books* 20 June 1996: 10.

Fishman, Sylvia Barack. "Our Mother and Our Sisters and Our Cousins and Our Aunts: Dialogues and Dynamics in Literature and Film." *Talking Back: Images of Jewish Women in American Popular Culture*. Ed. Joyce Antler. Hanover, NH: Brandeis UP, 1998. 153–170.

Friedman, Melvin J. "Jewish Mothers and Sons: The Expense of *Chutzpah*." *Contemporary American-Jewish Literature: Critical Essays*. Ed. Irving Malin. Bloomington: Indiana, UP, 1973. 147–58.

Girgus, Sam B. *The Films of Woody Allen*. New York: Cambridge UP, 1993.

———. "Philip Roth and Woody Allen: Freud and the Humor of the Repressed." *Semites and Stereotypes: Characteristics of Jewish Humor*. Ed. Avner Ziv and Anat Zajdman. Westport: Greenwood, 1993. 121–30.

Hemingway, Ernest. *The Sun Also Rises*. 1926. New York: Scribners, 1954.

Hyman, Paula E. *Gender and Assimilation in Modern Jewish History: The Roles and Representations of Women*. Seattle: U of Washington P, 1995.

Jong, Erica Mann. *Fear of Flying*. New York: Holt, Rinehart and Winston, 1973.

Kiernan, Robert F. *American Writing Since 1945: A Critical Survey*. New York: Ungar, 1983.

Leveen, Lois. "Only When I Laugh: Textual Dynamics of Ethnic Humor." *MELUS* 21.4 (1996): 29–55.

Margolis, Maxine L. *Mothers and Such: Views of American Women and Why They Changed*, Berkeley: U of California P, 1984.

Menand, Louis. "The Irony and the Ecstasy: Philip Roth and the Jewish Atlantis." *The New Yorker* 19 May 1997: 88–94.

Moi, Toril. *Sexual/Textual Politics: Feminist Literary Theory*, London and New York: Methuen, 1985.

Olsen, Tillie. *Silences: Classic Essays on the Art of Creating*. New York: Delacourt, 1978.

Paley, Grace. "Mom." *Esquire* Dec. 1975: 85–86.

———. "Mother." *The Collected Stories: Grace Paley*. New York: Farrar, Straus and Giroux, 1994. 325–26.

Prell, Riv-Ellen. *Fighting to Become Americans: Jews, Gender, and the Anxiety of Assimilation*. Boston: Beacon, 1999.

Rashkin, Esther. *Family Secrets and the Psychoanalysis of Narrative*. Princeton: Princeton UP, 1992.

Rich, Adrienne. *Of Woman Born: Motherhood as Experience and Institution*. New York: Norton, 1976.

Roiphe, Anne. *Lovingkindness*. New York: Simon & Schuster, 1987.

Roth, Philip. *The Facts: A Novelist's Autobiography*. New York: Farrar, Straus, and Giroux, 1988.

———. *Portnoy's Complaint*. New York: Bantam, 1969.

———. "Reading Myself." *Partisan Review* 40 (1973), 404–417. Rpt. In *Conversations with Philip Roth*. Ed. George Searles. Jackson: UP of Mississippi, 1992. 63–76.

Rothbell, Gladys. "The Jewish Mother: Social Construction of a Popular Image." *The Jewish Family: Myths and Realities*. Ed. Steven M. Cohen and Paula E. Hyman. New York: Holmes & Meier, 1986. 118–28

Sexton, Anne. "Housewife." *The Complete Poems*. Boston: Houghton Mifflin, 1981. 77.

Sowell, Thomas. *Ethnic America: A History*. New York: Basic Books, 1981.

Telushkin, Joseph. *Jewish Humor: What the Best Jewish Jokes Say About the Jews*. New York: William Morrow, 1992.

Updike, John. *Bech: A Book*. New York: Knopf, 1970.

Wylie, Philip. *Generation of Vipers*. New York, Toronto: Farrar and Rhinehart, 1942.

Yaeger, Patricia. *Honey-Mad Women*. New York: Columbia UP, 1988.

JOE MORAN

Reality Shift: Philip Roth

Philip Roth rose to celebrity in the late 1960s with the publication of *Portnoy's Complaint*, the novel with which (even after 18 further books) his name is still virtually synonymous. Dubbed 'a wild blue shocker' by *Life* magazine on its first appearance,[1] it became notorious primarily because of its comic treatment of a formerly taboo subject: adolescent masturbation. This *succès de scandale* made Roth a huge fortune (the book earned a million dollars even prior to publication through the exploitation of movie, book club and serialization rights) and turned him, albeit briefly, into one of the most famous people In America. This chapter looks at Roth's subsequent career, which has been greatly influenced by the huge gap between the kind of attention he received after the publication of this novel and his own preconceptions about the high-minded seriousness with which books and authors should be publicly discussed.

Celebrity and Scandal

Roth says that his first encounter with literature was by means of a 'priestly literary education', in which the vocation of writing itself was viewed as 'a form of ethical conduct', making him someone for whom 'the postwar onslaught of a mass electronically amplified philistine culture ... look[ed] ...

---

to be the work of the Devil's legions, and High Art in turn the only refuge of the godly'. He assumed that fame would come to him 'as it had to Mann's Aschenbach, as Honor',[2] and up to *Portnoy's Complaint* he achieved this with healthy but modest book sales and generally respectful reviews. On the publication of this novel, however, Roth was catapulted into the much more polymorphous and less manageable sphere of mediatized celebrity. Initially created by publicity overkill for the book itself, this celebrity took on a life of its own as his name began to circulate freely in all kinds of contexts: gossip columnists reported that he was dating Barbra Streisand or Jackie Onassis, or that he had been committed to a mental hospital; he was accosted in the street by fans and detractors alike; his name was used, without his permission, in television advertisements; he became an endless source of innuendo on television talk shows (one guest joked on a late-night talk show that she would like to meet Philip Roth, but wouldn't want to shake his hand).[3] In effect, Roth became fetishized for celebrity purposes as a sex maniac—he complained that

> to become a celebrity is to become a brand name. There is Ivory soap, Rice Krispies, and Philip Roth. Ivory is the soap that floats; Rice Krispies the breakfast cereal that goes snap-crackle-pop; Philip Roth the Jew who masturbates with a piece of liver. And makes a million out of it.[4]

Roth's *Portnoy* fame thus had all the ingredients of a media scandal, as outlined by James Lull and Stephen Hinerman in their book on the subject. Such scandals, they argue, are both an example of the shifting status of public and private domains in celebrity culture (the publicity surrounding *Portnoy's Complaint* centring on the most 'private' act of all), and a way of regulating transgressive behaviour and reinforcing social norms.[5] At the same time, stars are granted more moral latitude than 'ordinary' people since, as Herman Gray puts it, 'ours is a media environment where fame and celebrity, no matter how momentary, are the currency which stimulates desire and fantasy'.[6] In this sense, the *Portnoy* scandal aptly illustrated celebrity culture's simultaneous fascination with and squeamishness about sex. Unlike many celebrity scandals, however, this one was wholly fictional, a pure 'pseudo-event': Roth had almost no public profile at the time, and had retired for several months to the writer's colony at Yaddo immediately after the book's publication, so these 'revelations' were not even based on half-truths about the author. Instead, they were a combustible combination of a traditional characteristic of literary celebrity—the identification of the author with his subject matter, encouraged here by the colloquial first person and confessional tone of *Portnoy's Complaint*—and a celebrity machinery of salacious gossip and rumour more usually associated with the sphere of commercial entertainment than with 'serious' literature. As Lull and Hinerman point out, though, 'a star's moral violations ... are always recontextualized in terms of his or her "image system" ... any particular transgression is constructed and read against an image in circulation'.[7] Insofar as Roth had a public personality at this time, it was as a bookish, intellectual figure who took himself and his work seriously, and the *Portnoy* affair's appeal may have lain partly in the discovery that such a figure also had base desires and shameful secrets. This was celebrity as cheap notoriety, then, involving the almost complete collapse of Roth's cultural authority as an 'author'.

Roth's response to this was to consolidate his persona as a serious figure. Educated to believe that 'the independent reality of the fiction is all there is of importance and that writers should remain in the shadows', Roth has situated himself in 'a midway position' on 'the pendulum of self-exposure that oscillates between aggressively exhibitionistic Mailerism and sequestered Salingerism'.[8] He rarely appears in public, dividing his time between a Connecticut farmhouse and London and never appearing on American television to promote his work. It is true that he has given many interviews in every kind of publication from *Paris Review* to *House and Garden*, incorporating some of them (including ones conducted with himself) into a collection entitled *Reading Myself and Others*. However, these appearances are limited and highly controlled—he insists that print interviews confine themselves to serious, impersonal queries, maintaining that his life and work should be kept separate. Interviewers often contrast his quiet, professional manner with his fictional personae—as one writer puts it, 'Roth resembles an accountant on his day off more than the globe-trotting neurotic you'd expect from the books'.[9]

At the same time, however, Roth recognizes that his celebrity has partly been a product of his ability to shake off this high seriousness and embrace some of the profane elements of American culture in his work. He characterizes his own writing as 'redface'—combining the traits of 'redskin' and 'paleface', terms coined by Philip Rahv to denote two diametrically opposed, 'highbrow' and 'lowbrow' traditions in American writing. In particular, he suggests that *Portnoy's Complaint* and the novels which followed it grew out of his growing impatience with 'elevated notions' of fiction as 'something like a religious calling', which opposed 'high' art to mass-market 'philistinism'.[10] Alongside his European literary influences (Chekhov, Tolstoy, Flaubert, Mann and Kafka), Roth now embraced a freer verbal facility suggestive of oral performance, influenced by the comedy routines of

Abbott and Costello and the Marx Brothers and several years of psychoanalysis. His work became more 'ego-ridden ... All sorts of impulses that I might once have put down as excessive, frivolous, or exhibitionistic I allowed to surface'.[11] This mixture of low comedy and therapeutic excess was a major factor in *Portnoy's Complaint*'s success, and undoubtedly contributed to the confusion surrounding its 'autobiographical' status, the almost universally held assumption that the author was 'spilling his guts out'.[12] As *New York* magazine saw it, Roth had 'kicked the nice Jewish boy bit, the stance of the Jamesian moral intelligence, and unleashed his comic, foul-mouthed, sex-obsessed demon. His true self'.[13]

This ability to combine elements of 'high' and 'low' culture in his work has meant that Roth has had an uneasy relationship with certain New York intellectuals. These critics have accused him of borrowing a kind of stand-up patter from the world of showbusiness and nightclub comedy and dressing it up as 'serious' literature—Irving Howe, in a famous critical assault which was later fictionalized by Roth in *The Anatomy Lesson* (1983), attacked him for having a 'thin personal culture', and (in Flaubert's terms) choosing an audience over readers.[14] As a fellow Jew from a slightly older generation, Howe also took issue with Roth for trivializing serious issues about the position of Jews in postwar American society—particularly given the very recent memory of the Holocaust—in the pursuit of bestsellerdom and notoriety. Roth's arguments with his Jewish readers are usually partly to do with his mainstream fame—the Rabbis who denounced him from synagogue pulpits and community centre lecterns after the publication of his first book, *Goodbye, Columbus*, for example, did so not so much on the grounds that Roth himself was anti-Semitic but that he would, in his own words, 'fuel the fires of the anti-Semites' by presenting an unflattering view of Jews to a wider audience.[15] These arguments have been important to Roth as a counterweight to the more absurd manifestations of his celebrity. His comment that he has 'a general audience and a Jewish audience', the former of which he has 'no sense of my impact upon' but the latter of which he 'feel[s] intensely their expectations, disdain, delight, criticism, their wounded self-love, their healthy curiosity',[16] implicitly contrasts celebrity's huge constituency with this smaller Jewish readership. I want to argue that Roth brings together some of these tensions. produced by his fame in his work after *Portnoy's Complaint*.

Hypothetical Selves

Roth has described the celebrity he received after the publication of *Portnoy's Complaint* as 'one of the oddest misreadings ... that any contemporary writer has run into',[17] and says that much of his fiction since then has been an attempt to deal with this pivotal point In his career. In his subsequent books, Roth has written directly about the experience of fame but has also explored issues raised by the particular kind of celebrity he received for a novel which many readers assumed to be straightforwardly confessional. This has produced a series of progressively labyrinthine explorations of the relationship between autobiography and fiction—much of his writing after *Portnoy's Complaint* has included a recognizable surrogate of its author, in Roth's words 'a being whose experience [is] comparable to my own and yet register[s] a more powerful valence'.[18] Roth's experiments with 'autobiographical' fiction have created a kind of 'hall of mirrors' effect which has only added to the public confusion about the relationship between the author and his characters. These issues are dealt with most fully in Roth's novel series, *Zuckerman Bound* (1985), a trilogy and epilogue which follows the career of the author, Nathan Zuckerman, over a 20 year period, taking him through the youthful promise of his 20s, the celebrity of his 30s and the early burnout and creative stagnation of his 40s. There are two competing notions of literary celebrity which are played out in these books: on the one hand, fame is presented as a media invention, which vulgarizes everything it touches and entraps the author in a false and confining persona; on the other hand, it is seen as being intimately related to the author's own writing, personality and ambitions, which leads on to broader questions about the relationship between writers and their work, their readerships and their cultural identities.

The first book of the series, *The Ghost Writer* (1979), begins in December 1956, when Zuckerman spends the night at the Vermont retreat of E.I. Lonoff, a reclusive author who has rejected all the trappings of literary fame—prizes, honorary degrees, requests for interviews—and whom Nathan admires for his 'relentless winnowing out of the babyish, preening, insatiable self'.[19] As the novel progresses, however, tensions and discrepancies emerge between Nathan's motives and his behaviour, and between his idealization of Lonoff and the reality. While claiming to submit himself 'for candidacy as nothing less than E.I. Lonoff's spiritual son' (9), Zuckerman is really a young author on the make, shamelessly buttering Lonoff up in his letter of introduction and reading his own profile in the 'A Dozen to Keep Your Eye On' feature in the *Saturday Review* 50 times over. He also only mails his stories to Lonoff after being snubbed by another author, Felix Abravanel—who, with his beautiful wives and girlfriends, glitzy lecture tours and magazine profiles, is Lonoff's rival and complete antithesis.

Zuckerman's idealism about the renunciation of worldly fame has thus been bought cheaply and has a heavily self-romanticizing quality, even influencing his fantasy about one of Lonoff's students, Amy Bellette, in which he reimagines her as the Anne Frank who survives Belsen, emigrates to the United States and reads about the publication of her diary while flicking through the pages of *Time* in a dentist's waiting room. Although her greatest ambition, as announced in her diary, is to become a famous writer, she refuses to ring up *Time* to announce her survival because the diary will be less meaningful to its readers without her death and her symbolic importance as 'the incarnation of the millions of unlived years robbed from the murdered Jews' (150). In the classic adolescent daydream, though, she imagines her childhood friends and acquaintances saying to themselves: 'Who realized she was so gifted? Who realized we had such a writer in our midst?' (135). Although Roth was criticized by many reviewers for using the story of the Holocaust in this way, Zuckerman's unconscious reconfiguring of it as a cheesy and quintessentially American narrative of undiscovered star quality does show clearly the flimsiness of his claims to disinterest. Lonoff realizes this and attempts to steer Nathan away from his own life of 'reading and writing and looking at the snow', lamenting that all he has done for 30 years is 'turn sentences around' (30, 17). In turn, Zuckerman's disillusionment with Lonoff sets in when he speculates that Amy may be Lonoff's mistress. The truth is more subtle—in refusing to sleep with Amy, Lonoff has made his wife feel as though he has only done so out of a perverted sense of duty, while she has become frustrated by his endless fastidiousness and asceticism. Roth, then, refuses to idealize the life of the author-recluse, portraying it (in both Lonoff's and Zuckerman's case) as an ambiguous mixture of high ideals and *hauteur*.

In the second novel in the series, *Zuckerman Unbound* (1981), set in 1969, Nathan has left the notion of literature as a *sanctum sanctorum* firmly behind him, becoming nationally notorious with the publication of a sexually explicit novel, *Carnovsky*. Zuckerman is now the celebrity equivalent of a sideshow freak—he is stopped in the street by people who either want to insult him or touch his coat adoringly, is discussed in gossip columns and on talk shows, and receives bizarre letters and phone calls, death threats aimed at his family, and photographs of scantily-clad women offering sexual favours. Such a success is 'as baffling as a misfortune' (184), inverting all his expectations about literary success, and is made more traumatic because, for everyone else, it is wholly unimaginable—as Nathan puts it, 'being a poor misunderstood millionaire is not really a topic that intelligent people can discuss for very long' (306). Zuckerman circulates in a media maelstrom in which traditional cultural hierarchies are not respected and the distinction between 'reality' and 'fiction' is routinely ignored. His experience seems to support Rainer Maria Rilke's comment, which Roth is fond of quoting, that 'fame is no more than the quintessence of all the misunderstandings collecting around a new name'.[20]

There are similarities here with another Roth character, David Kepesh, who mutates into a six-foot high mammary gland in an earlier novella, *The Breast* (1972). Roth says that this book

> wasn't just about entrapment in the flesh and the horrors of desire, it was also inspired by some thinking I'd had to do about fame, notoriety and scandal. When the idea for the book first came to me, I had myself only recently become an object of curiosity, believed by some to be very much the sexual freak and grotesque.[21]

Interestingly, the novella does end with Kepesh contemplating an escape from the hospital where he is being treated in order to use his affliction in the pursuit of fame and fortune, claiming that 'if the Beatles can fill Shea Stadium, so can I'.[22] Kepesh's metamorphosis is a wholly absurd, meaningless event outside his control, which has no relation to his own life as the archetypal 'nice Jewish boy' with good college grades and brilliant career; similarly, at the beginning of *Zuckerman Unbound*, Nathan remains essentially bewildered, submissive and apparently blameless as events unfold inexorably around him.

Roth suggests that this debased, disposable kind of celebrity has in turn produced a dysfunctional culture of fandom, encapsulated in the figure of Alvin Pepler, a personification of 'how Johnny Carson America sees me', according to Nathan (339). Pepler introduces himself to Zuckerman in a restaurant and then, when their friendship fails to develop, proceeds to harass him with obscene phone calls and handkerchiefs soiled with semen. Pepler is himself a victim of celebrity culture, a former champion on the hugely popular 1950s TV game show, *Smart Money*, who has been forced to 'take a dive' to make way for a wealthy New England WASP contestant, Hewlett Lincoln, while his promised sweetener of a big break in television has not materialized. Roth here uses a fairly accurate rendering of the quiz-show scandals—dealt with more recently by Robert Redford in a 1994 film—as a kind of parable of the corruptions and betrayals of celebrity. Successful contestants appearing on quiz shows in the golden age of network television, the 1950s, were transformed into national celebrities (Charles Van Doren, the most famous participant, was featured on the cover of *Time* and later became a talk show star) in order to create a meritocratic narrative in which fame was conferred on 'ordinary' people through their own hard work and talent. This concealed a bureaucratized and standardized fame machine in which stars were entirely manufactured by the studios: questions and answers were provided in advance, every response and gesture scripted and the contestants instructed to play closely defined roles designed to create dramatic tension, increase ratings and perpetuate popular stereotypes. Herbert Stempel, on whom Pepler is based, for example, played the part of the poor Jewish boy from Queens, before being forced off the show to make way for the WASP golden boy, Van Doren. The quiz shows thus bought into a highly controlled myth of accessibility which surrounds many examples of mainstream celebrity: the mass-produced star represents the potential of all individuals in society to achieve success. As Stuart Ewen puts it:

> In a society where everyday life [is] increasingly defined by feelings of insignificance and institutions of standardization, the 'star' provide[s] an accessible icon to the significance of the personal and the individual ... Celebrity forms a symbolic pathway, connecting each aspiring individual to a universal image of fulfillment: to be someone, when 'being no one' is the norm.[23]

Pepler's celebrity is thus similar to Zuckerman's in being wholly artificial, and designed to perpetuate society's stereotypes about Jews. There the similarity ends: Pepler, a talentless man with a head for useless quiz-show-type facts, stalks Nathan because he has been left embittered by his brief experience of fame. He has constructed an elaborate fantasy life in which he is a brilliant writer and critic, fictional Broadway producers vie for the rights to his life story and Zuckerman steals material from him for *Carnovsky*. Nathan even begins to fear for his life at one point, speculating that Pepler may belong to a long line of assassins of celebrities: 'Bang bang, you're dead. There was all the meaning the act was ever meant to have. You're you, I'm me, and for that and that alone you die' (338). In this connection, Richard Schickel has suggested that the relationship between celebrities and their fans is based around an 'illusion of intimacy'. Celebrities are such omnipresent, apparently accessible figures in contemporary culture, he suggests, that this fosters a dangerous mixture of devotion and envy amongst their fans, epitomized by borderline personalities like John Hinckley, Jr and Mark Chapman who stalk and attempt to kill the objects of their worship.[24] This obsessional model of fandom has itself fed back into celebrity culture, being reproduced in Hollywood films like *The Fan* (1981), *King of Comedy* (1982) and *Misery* (1990). Other critics, though, have attacked this 'othering' of fans, conducted from what Joli Jenson calls a 'savannah of smug superiority'. Jenson argues that

> defining fandom as a deviant activity allows ... a reassuring, self-aggrandizing stance to be adopted. It also supports the celebration of particular values—the rational over the emotional, the educated over the uneducated, the subdued over the passionate, the elite over the popular, the mainstream over the margin, the status quo over the alternative.[25]

In *Zuckerman Unbound*, the 'Zuckermaniacs' (378) who harass Nathan are certainly an ominous sign that the distinctions between these different dualisms have disintegrated. The strength of Roth's novel, however, lies in the fact that it does not merely demonize the people who read *Carnovsky* in this way, but also begins to interrogate Zuckerman's own responsibility for his fame.

The single unifying characteristic of all Zuckerman's fans is that they assume that the author and his character are identical: he is often addressed as 'Carnovsky', and constantly complains that people have 'mistaken impersonation for confession and [a]re calling out to a character in a book' (190). During the second half of *Zuckerman Unbound*, however, when Nathan flies to Miami to be at the bedside of his dying father, the novel considers the extent to which Zuckerman has appropriated his own and other people's life stories in his fiction in such a way as to invite these comparisons. Pepler's accusation that Zuckerman is a 'heartless bastard' who has hurt his family 'in the name of Great Art' (288), now begins to be voiced by the interested parties themselves. Zuckerman's own mother fails to disguise her hurt at the portrayal of a stereotypical 'Jewish mother' in *Carnovsky*, Nathan's father, with his dying breath, apparently calls his son a 'bastard', and his brother, Henry, berates him: 'To you everything is disposable ... everything is grist for your fun-machine' (397).

Zuckerman's exasperation at his new-found notoriety is also shot through with moments of self-insight:

> Coldhearted betrayer of the most intimate confessions, cutthroat caricaturist of your own loving parents, graphic reporter of encounters with women to whom you have been deeply bound by trust, by sex, by love—no, the virtue racket ill becomes you (234).

Nathan's agent also realizes that there is a fundamental relationship between his celebrity and the book he has written, and he accuses his client of trying to 'humiliate all your dignified, high-minded gravity', and then protesting 'because nobody aside from you seems to see it as a profoundly moral and high-minded act' (305). He and his wife thus urge Zuckerman to start enjoying his success and to 'come out from behind all that disgusting highbrow disapproval of the fallen people having fun' (257).

In the third novel in the series, *The Anatomy Lesson*, these issues are increasingly played out inside Zuckerman's own head, as he simultaneously complains that the fact 'that writing is an act of imagination seems to perplex and infuriate everyone' and laments the self-centredness of his own writing, which uses his 'life as cud ... Swallow as experience, then up from the gut for a second go as art' (450, 602). His writing has always drawn on personal experience, but now he can only write about the problems of being a famous writer—so his recognition that 'the personal ingredient is what gets you going' is countered by a realization that 'if you hang on to the personal ingredient any longer you'll disappear right up your asshole' (550). Zuckerman now experiences a life crisis, as he becomes paralysed with undiagnosable and untreatable back pain and suffers from severe writer's block. Since no medical cause can be found for his back pain, there is a suggestion that his physical and creative atrophy may be interrelated, and linked ultimately to the experience of fame. Nathan's friends, as well as his analyst, argue that his pain 'is a self-inflicted wound: penance for the popularity of *Carnovsky* ... the enviable, comfortable success story wrecked by the wrathful cells' (440). Nathan, however, strongly resists this interpretation that his illness is 'expiation through suffering' (430). These two views reflect two opposing takes on Nathan's fame in the books—it is either a bizarre, anomalous event which teaches him nothing, or something for which he is, to varying degrees, answerable through his writing.

In *The Prague Orgy* (1985), the final book in the series, Zuckerman's visit to Eastern Europe allows him to contrast the misreadings of his own work with the ruthless censorship endured by his Czech counterparts. Roth himself has made this comparison between writers in totalitarian countries and in 'free' societies in the West, suggesting that 'in my situation, everything goes and nothing matters; in their situation, nothing goes and everything matters'.[26] When Zdenek Sisovsky, a young Czech writer, suggests to Zuckerman that *Carnovsky* is an unacknowledged masterpiece and that 'the weight, of stupidity you must carry is heavier than the weight of banning', Zuckerman strongly disagrees: 'It's you ... who's been denied the right to practice his profession. Whatever the scandal, I have been profusely—bizarrely—rewarded. Everything from an Upper East Side address to helping worthy murderers get out on parole' (703, 704). Nathan's involvement with the Prague literary underground also becomes an escape from the enforced narcissism of celebrity—at the height of his life crisis in *The Anatomy Lesson*, for instance, he longs for 'war, destruction, anti-

Semitism, totalitarianism ... a martyrdom more to the point ... than bearing the cocktail party chitchat as a guest on Dick Cavett' (550–1). Zuckerman finds such a cause and reverts to being the good Jewish son in *The Prague Orgy* when, attempting to recover the manuscript of an unknown Yiddish writer for publication in the West, he has the stories confiscated by the Czech Minister of Culture and is accused of being a Zionist agent (784). Zuckerman is now the famous author deigning to rescue the forgotten one, who wrote for a higher purpose than worldly renown. Recovering these manuscripts, however, also represents Zuckerman's realization that, although authors are powerless in the face of misreadings of their work, it is better to have any kind of reception than none at all: 'Think of all that his stories will be spared if instead of wrenching his fiction out of oblivion, you just turn around and go ... Yet I stay' (766).

It is clear, then, that this series of books, as an extended speculation on 'the unforeseen consequences of art' (759), is an attempt to deal with some of the issues raised by the spectacular success of *Portnoy's Complaint*. One should be careful, of course, not to reproduce the kinds of assumptions satirized by Roth in these books by claiming them as transparently autobiographical. In Roth's words, his writing is the 'transformation, through an elaborate impersonation, of a personal emergency into a public act',[27] and his fictional alter egos are 'useful fictions',[28] allowing these issues to be worked through hypothetically in his work—a form of release which is not, of course, available to Zuckerman (hence his writer's block). It may be that the novels comprising *Zuckerman Bound* thus seem more 'autobiographical' than they are because they explore the predicament of celebrity and therefore use the public facts of Roth's life most familiar to us—most obviously the fame achieved by a sexually explicit novel presumed by many of its readers to be autobiographical, and the critical controversies surrounding it. Even these elements are deliberately heightened and dramatized—while Zuckerman stays in New York to face the music after the publication of *Carnovsky*, for example, Roth retreated to Yaddo. The distance Roth achieves from his subject matter in *Zuckerman Bound*, then, allows him to interrogate his celebrity in an open and self-questioning way, presenting it as both a wholly alien presence which dislocates the author from his past, and as a more nuanced process which involves the ambition and self-promotion of the author.

'Peekaboo Narratives'

It should come as no surprise to Roth, given the nature of the celebrity culture he is part of and is examining, that his 'autobiographical' reading of reductively autobiographical readings of his work has only exacerbated the tendency of journalists and critics to make these kinds of assumptions. Although Roth has been forthcoming about this issue in his work, his response in interviews has been to resist fiercely any attempt to reference his own life through his fiction. These two approaches—openness and intransigence—are both present in Roth's autobiography, *The Facts* (1988), caught as it is between the imaginative status of fiction and the creative self-presentation of the interview and other aspects of Roth's public persona. In this book, Roth describes his disillusionment with novel-writing after suffering a breakdown in 1987, and claims that *The Facts* represents 'the bare bones, the structure of a life without a fiction', conveying 'my exhaustion with masks, disguises, distortions, and lies'.[29] Roth's decision to end the narrative just before the publication of *Portnoy's Complaint*, thus covering only just over half of his life, suggests that he is attempting to write about a former self untouched by celebrity. Much of the book works as a very conventional linear narrative, with separate chapters on Roth's childhood, college days, failed marriage and developing career. However, the book ends with a letter from 'Zuckerman' to 'Roth' which comments on the preceding chapters and problematizes this apparent transparency. Zuckerman complains that the book is too 'steeped in [Roth's] nice-guy side', suggesting that he is not the first novelist who, 'by fleeing the wearying demands of fictional invention for a little vacation in straightforward recollection, has shackled the less sociable impulses that led him or her to become a novelist in the first place'. As Nathan points out, 'with autobiography there's always another text, a countertext, if you will, to the one presented'.[30] While much of the book therefore presumes to be a candid account of the events of Roth's life, then, the coda critiques this assumption of representational innocence.

Roth's more recent fictional works point much more insistently to a notion of the self as unstable and intertextual, and to the genres of fiction and autobiography as infinitely permeable. Although this means that Roth's work is often grouped critically with that of metafictionists like John Barth and Donald Barthelme, one senses that Roth has his own agenda, working through issues which are of fundamental concern to him and which can be traced back to his first experience of celebrity. As Hillel Halkin puts it, 'the impression given by [Roth's] later books is that, had post-modernism not existed, he would have been quite capable of inventing aspects of it by himself'.[31] Roth's next novel after *Zuckerman Bound*, *The Counterlife* (1986), reiterates many of the same themes as the trilogy and epilogue, specifically the supposedly parasitic dependence of authors on their own and other people's life experiences. While Nathan's editor praises his 'gift for theatrical self-transformation', Henry continues to accuse his brother of irresponsibly reclaiming and vulgarizing his family history, and asserts that 'calling [*Carnovsky*] fiction was the biggest fiction of all'.[32] Zuckerman's trip to Israel in the novel is partly inspired by the kind of solipsistic impasse to which his celebrity has brought him, his exhaustion at living 'in the nutshell of self-scrutiny' and desire to escape from 'the writer's tedious burden of being his own cause'.[33] This dialogue takes place, however, at Zuckerman's funeral, and the entire book is made up of different sections in which Nathan and other characters die and are then brought back to life in a series of hypothetical scenarios. Each section undermines the 'truth' of its predecessor, thus reinforcing the notion of Zuckerman as only a fictionalized alter ego—indeed, Roth says that killing off Nathan was partly a way of second-guessing autobiographical readings of his work.[34]

In Roth's next novel, *Deception* (1990), a Jewish-American author named 'Philip' engages in discussions with his English mistress about his previous fictional creations, including Zuckerman, Lonoff and Portnoy, at the end of which she asks him to change his own name in the fiction we are reading to 'Nathan'. But their incessant role-playing, in which he impersonates a whole series of Roth's characters and she acts the part of Zuckerman's and Lonoff's biographer, suggests that the whole book may be an extended game of 'reality shift'. As Philip says bullishly: 'I write fiction and I'm told it's autobiography and I write autobiography and I'm told it's fiction, so since I'm so dim and they're so smart, let *them* decide what is or what isn't'.[35]

This trick of playing selves and counterselves off against each other reaches its apotheosis in Roth's 1993 novel, *Operation Shylock*. In this book, 'Philip Roth', the narrator and central character who shares many biographical details with Roth himself, discovers that a Chicago private detective who looks and sounds uncannily like him is impersonating him publicly in order to preach the gospel of 'diasporism' throughout the Middle East. The impersonator sends the 'real' Philip Roth a clumsily written critique of his reclusiveness: 'I am only spending the renown you hoard. You hide yourself/in lonely rooms/country recluse/anonymous expatriate/garreted monk. Never spent it as you should/might/wouldn't/couldn't: IN BEHALF OF THE JEWISH PEOPLE'.[36] In other words, the imposter is trying not so much to appropriate the private identity of 'Philip Roth' as to use his celebrity for his own purposes—as Jonathan Raban says, the imposter 'is a criminal, not because he steals Roth's "identity" ... but because he tries to filch the novelist's worldly prestige, an importantly different commodity'.[37]

In a bizarre twist, when the book was published Roth brought the controversy about the relationship between autobiography and fiction out of his work itself and into the extra-textual sphere by claiming, in an article published on the prime site of the *New York Times Book Review*'s front page, that all the events described in the novel actually happened.[38] Roth expanded on this in subsequent interviews: although the novel ends with a traditional disclaimer; for instance, he explained that this was inserted at the insistence of an Israeli secret service operative.[39] ('Philip Roth' ends the novel as an agent for Mossad, helping to track down Jews giving money to the PLO.) Assuming that the extraordinary events related in *Operation Shylock* are not true—and there is no evidence for them other than that presented in the novel—Roth's strategy here is puzzling, and a complete turnaround from his insistence in all his previous interviews that his writing and his life should be kept strictly separate. There might be a suspicion that this was merely a strategy aimed at publicizing his novel if Roth had not proved so fiercely dismissive of book promotion in the past, usually contriving to be out of the country as each new novel appeared.

These textual and extra-textual games have left many readers and critics impatient with Roth's insistence that his work should be treated with impersonal academic rigour. Despite achieving critical acclaim for his more recent works—including the National Book Award and the Pulitzer Prize—he is not an author to whom the media generally warms. As one *Boston Globe* reporter says: 'Roth has been the target of more venom than even Norman Mailer. He has been described as a self-hating Jewish pornographer. A malicious destroyer of women. An obsessive anti-Semite whose greatest obsession is himself'.[40] This received wisdom about the author, which is disseminated by both journalists and literary critics well-versed in the 'intentional fallacy', is implicitly based on an assumption of correspondence between the writer's life and his work. The popular view of Roth spilled over from the books pages into the news sections in 1996, when he became the subject of an unflattering portrait in a book, *Leaving A Doll's House*, written by his ex-wife, Claire Bloom, which was widely seen as 'revenge' for the fictional portrait of a marriage in *Deception*. Roth's novel *I Married a Communist* reignited the controversy in 1998, many critics and journalists assuming that Roth was 'getting his own back' for Bloom's account. (In this book, set in McCarthy-era America, the lead character, Ira Ringold, is betrayed by his scheming actress wife, Eve Frame, who publishes a confessional, untruthful book denouncing him as a Russian spy.) This desire to interpret literary works as simply a way of settling personal scores, in order to recycle them as gossip column fodder, has eerie similarities with the fame achieved by *Portnoy's Complaint* almost 30 years previously. In fact, this debasement of the public sphere, as represented by the appetite for Eve's 'true confessions', is one of the novel's principal themes. As one of its narrators says, the McCarthy era inaugurated

> the postwar triumph of gossip as the unifying credo of the world's oldest democratic republic. In Gossip We Trust. Gossip as gospel, the national faith. McCarthyism as the beginning not just of serious politics but of serious everything as entertainment to amuse the mass audience ... He took us back to our origins, back to the seventeenth century and the stocks. That's how the country began: moral disgrace as public entertainment.[41]

At the same time, it would be naive not to recognize that the unsettling combination of apparently naked self-revelation and still greater obfuscation and textual playfulness in Roth's more recent work—even if this originates in his attempt to work through and transcend autobiographical readings of his work—cannot help but make these connections between life and art easier to make. Many critics have suggested that Roth implicitly buys into the logic of celebrity, by producing what one of them calls 'peekaboo narratives' which invite speculation, gossip and rumour.[42] John Updike has referred wearily to the 'self-on-self grapple' of Roth's later work, suggesting that 'this cultivation of hypothetical selves has become an end-game'.[43] Others have accused Roth of protesting too much: Joseph Epstein has dismissed Roth's complaint about readers getting a 'voyeuristic kick' out of his later novels, suggesting that 'if a writer doesn't wish to supply such kicks, perhaps he would do better not to undress before windows opening onto thoroughfares'.[44]

Although this last comment seems harsh, dismissing Roth's experiments in autobiography as mere authorial narcissism, his post-Portnoy work does raise questions about the complex interrelationship between autobiography and fiction which are not always answered by his attempts to shut up shop in interviews. While interviewing Roth, for example, Ian Hamilton suggests to the author that it is hard not to read his works as partly confessional, and Roth replies: 'It's very easy to read it this way. This is the easiest possible way to read. It makes it just like reading the evening paper. I only get annoyed because it isn't the evening paper I've written'. Hamilton goes on: 'Surely the journalistic approach is inescapable—unless the reader forgets everything he knows or has read about you, Philip Roth'.[45] Hamilton is right: reading Roth's novels 'autobiographically' may be regrettable but is often unavoidable, even if this is accompanied by all kinds of other, more sophisticated readings. This is equally true for academic critics, generally discouraged from reading biographicist assumptions into texts since the rise of the New Criticism and its theoretical successors, but probably expunging a lot of their average readerly curiosity in more 'objective' interpretations. As Bourdieu puts it, one of the defining characteristics of the 'popular' as opposed to the 'bourgeois' or 'high-culture' aesthetic is

> the affirmation of the continuity between art and life, which implies the subordination of form to function, or, one might say, on a refusal of the refusal which is the starting point of the high aesthetic, i.e., the clearcut separation of ordinary dispositions from the specifically aesthetic disposition.[46]

In other words, human interest, and a sense of connection between the text and something concrete in the 'real' world, are what many readers look for in books. Failure to recognize this is to condemn out of hand a large number of reading practices, and to dismiss any interest in Roth's personal investment in his work as naive and prurient. It also conflates different kinds of celebrity together, equating all 'autobiographical' readings with the post-Portnoy demonization of Roth as a sex maniac. The strength of Roth's fictionalizations of celebrity—as opposed to his public comments—is that they do not do this, presenting literary celebrity instead as an awkward amalgam of authorial assertiveness and readerly misunderstanding.

It is clear that Roth's explorations into the nature of fame and his resulting experiments with conjectural autobiography, although they may have provided him with a way of writing about and coming to terms with his celebrity, have ultimately only reproduced that celebrity. It is hardly surprising, then, given the particular form of celebrity that he has received, that much of Roth's public response to fame is conducted from a level of intellectual detachment and high cultural disdain. If anything, the enormous discrepancy between these two different ways of reading—Roth's deadly earnestness and gravitas and celebrity's love of gossip and low farce—has only widened since the publication of *Portnoy's Complaint*. In his work, however, no other contemporary author has so insistently explored the competing impulses behind literary celebrity and its convoluted workings on the authorial self.

Notes

1. Albert Goldman, '*Portnoy's Complaint* by Philip Roth Looms as a Wild Blue Shocker and the American Novel of the Sixties', *Life*, 7 February 1969, pp. 58, 61–4.
2. Philip Roth, *Reading Myself and Others* (New York: Penguin, 2nd edn 1985), pp. 271–2.
3. Ibid., p. 273.
4. Ibid., p. 115.
5. James Lull and Stephen Hinerman, 'The Search for Scandal', in idem (eds), *Media Scandals* (Cambridge: Polity Press, 1997), pp. 1–33.
6. Herman Gray, 'Anxiety; Desire, and Conflict In the American Racial Imagination', in Lull and Hinerman (eds), *Media Scandals*, p. 90.
7. Lull and Hinerman, 'The Search for Scandal', p. 21.

8. Philip Roth, *The Facts: A Novelist's Autobiography* (London: Jonathan Cape, 1989), p. 4.

9. Linda Matchan, 'Philip Roth Faces "The Facts"', in George J. Searles (ed.), *Conversations with Philip Roth* (Jackson, MS: University Press of Mississippi, 1992), p. 238.

10. Roth, *Reading Myself*, pp. 83, 77.

11. Ibid., pp. 111–12.

12. Ronald Hayman, 'Philip Roth: Should Sane Women Shy Away From Him at Parties?', *Sunday Times Magazine*, 22 March 1981.

13. Howard Junker, 'Will This Finally Be Philip Roth's Year?', in Searles (ed.), *Conversations with Philip Roth*, p. 15.

14. Irving Howe, 'Philip Roth Reconsidered', *Commentary*, vol. S4, no. 6 (December 1972): 73, 77.

15. Roth quoted on *Arena: Philip Roth*, BBC2, 19 March 1993.

16. Asher Z. Milbauer and Donald G. Watson, 'An Interview with Philip Roth', in Milbauer and Watson (eds), *Reading Philip Roth* (Basingstoke: Macmillan, 1988), p. 3.

17. Quoted in Clive Sinclair, 'The Son is Father to the Man', in Milbauer and Watson (eds), *Reading Philip Roth*, p. 168.

18. Roth, *The Facts*, p. 6.

19. Philip Roth, *Zuckerman Bound: A Trilogy and Epilogue* (New York: Farrar, Straus and Giroux, 1985), p. 56. Subsequent references to this book are in parentheses next to the relevant quote in the text.

20. Roth, *Reading Myself*, pp. 79–80.

21. Sara Davidson, 'Talk with Philip Roth', *New York Times Book Review*, 18 September 1977.

22. Philip Roth, *The Breast* (London: Jonathan Cape, 1973), p. 74.

23. Ewen, *All-Consuming Images*, pp. 92–6.

24. Schickel, *Intimate Strangers*, pp. 5, 2–3, 28–9.

25. Joli Jenson, 'Fandom as Pathology', in Lisa A. Lewis (ed.), *The Adoring Audience: Fan Culture and Popular Media* (New York: Routledge, 1992), pp. 24–5.

26. Michiko Kakutani, 'Roth's Complaint', *San Francisco Chronicle*, 7 June 1981.

27. Roth, *Reading Myself*, p. 146.

28. Philip Roth, *My Life as a Man* (London: Jonathan Cape, 1974), p. 1.

29. Roth, *The Facts*, p. 6.

30. Ibid., pp. 170–2.

31. Hillel Halkin, 'How to Read Philip Roth', *Commentary*, vol. 97, no. 2 (February 1994): 45.

32. Philip Roth, *The Counterlife* (London: Jonathan Cape, 1987), pp. 214, 231.

33. Ibid., p. 288.

34. Mervyn Rothstein, 'Philip Roth and the World of "What If?"', in Searles (ed.), *Conversations with Philip Roth*, p. 199.

35. Philip Roth, *Deception: A Novel* (London: Jonathan Cape, 1990), pp. 100, 190–1.

36. Philip Roth, *Operation Shylock: A Confession* (London: Jonathan Cape, 1993), p. 87.

37. Jonathan Raban, 'A Vanity Affair', *Independent on Sunday*, 21 March 1993.

38. Philip Roth, 'A Bit of Jewish Mischief', *New York Times Book Review*, 7 March 1993.

39. Esther B. Fein, 'Philip Roth Sees Double. And Maybe Triple, Too', *New York Times*, 9 March 1993.

40. Matchan, 'Philip Roth Faces "The Facts"', p. 237.

41. Philip Roth, *I Married a Communist* (London: Vintage, 1999), p. 284.

42. Brian D. Johnson, 'Intimate Affairs', in Searles (ed.), *Conversations with Philip Roth*, p. 256.

43. Updike, *Odd Jobs*, p. 367.

44. Joseph Epstein, 'What Does Philip Roth Want?', *Commentary*, vol. 77, no. 1 (January 1984): 64.

45. Roth, *Reading Myself*, p. 129.

46. Bourdieu, *Distinction*, p. 32.

Chronology

1933	Born March 19 to Herman Roth and Bess Finkel Roth in Newark, NJ.
1951–54	After one year at Rutgers University, Newark, attends Bucknell University, from which he receives a B.A. in English, *magna cum laude*, and is elected to Phi Beta Kappa.
1955–1957	Does graduate work at the University of Chicago, from which he receives an M.A. in 1955. While there, he publishes a short story, "The Contest for Aaron Gold," which is selected to appear in *The Best American Short Stories of 1956*. Also during this time, enlists in the army, but is discharged because of a back injury.
1959	*Goodbye, Columbus*, for which he receives a National Book Award, and the Jewish Book Council's Daroff Award. Continues to publish short stories,which are well-received. Marries Margaret Martinson Williams on February 22.
1960	Taught at Iowa Writers' Workshop.
1962	*Letting Go*. Receives a Ford Foundation grant to write plays, and is writer-in-residence at Princeton University.
1963	Legal separation from Margaret Roth.
1965	Teaching position at the University of Pennsylvania.
1967	*When She Was Good*.
1968	Death of Margaret Roth in an automobile accident.
1969	*Portnoy's Complaint*. Resigns from teaching to write full time.

1970	Election to National Institute of Arts and Letters.
1971	*Our Gang.*
1972	*The Breast.*
1973	*The Great American Novel.*
1974	*My Life as a Man.*
1975	*Reading Myself and Others.*
1977	*The Professor of Desire.*
1979	*The Ghost Writer.*
1980	*A Philip Roth Reader.*
1981	*Zuckerman Unbound.*
1984	*The Anatomy Lesson.*
1985	*Zuckerman Bound: A Trilogy and Epilogue.* Compilation of *The Ghost Writer*, *Zuckerman Unbound*, and *The Anatomy Lesson*, with epilogue, *The Prague Orgy.*
1986	*The Counterlife*, which received the National Book Critics Circle Award the following year.
1988	*The Facts: A Novelist's Autobiography.*
1990	*Deception.*
1990	*Patrimony: A True Story*, which won the National Book Critics Circle Award. Married English actress Claire Bloom.
1993	*Operation Shylock*, which won the PEN/Faulkner Award.
1995	*Sabbath's Theater*, which won the National Book Award. Divorces Claire Bloom.
1997	*American Pastoral*, which won the Pulitzer Prize for Fiction.
1998	*I Married A Communist.*
2000	*The Human Stain.*
2001	*The Dying Animal.*
2001	*Shop Talk: A Writer and His Colleagues and Their Work*

Contributors

HAROLD BLOOM is Sterling Professor of the Humanities at Yale University and Henry W. and Albert A. Berg Professor of English at the New York University Graduate School. He is the author of over 20 books, including *Shelley's Mythmaking* (1959), *The Visionary Company* (1961), *Blake's Apocalypse* (1963), *Yeats* (1970), *A Map of Misreading* (1975), *Kabbalah and Criticism* (1975), *Agon: Toward a Theory of Revisionism* (1982), *The American Religion* (1992), *The Western Canon* (1994), and *Omens of Millennium: The Gnosis of Angels, Dreams, and Resurrection* (1996). *The Anxiety of Influence* (1973) sets forth Professor Bloom's provocative theory of the literary relationships between the great writers and their predecessors. His most recent books include *Shakespeare: The Invention of the Human* (1998), a 1998 National Book Award finalist, *How to Read and Why* (2000), and *Genius: A Mosaic of One Hundred Exemplary Creative Minds* (2002). In 1999, Professor Bloom received the prestigious American Academy of Arts and Letters Gold Medal for Criticism, and in 2002 he received the Catalonia International Prize.

GEORGE PLIMPTON is the editor of *The Paris Review* and the author of numerous books, including *Pet Peeves*, *Truman Capote*, and *The X Factor* .

JEFFREY BERMAN is Professor of English at SUNY Albany. He is the author of several books, including *Surviving Literary Suicide*, *Risky Writing: Self-Disclosure and Self-Transformation in the Classroom*, and *Narcissism and the Novel.*

BERNARD F. RODGERS, JR. has been a vice president of Bard College and the dean of Simon's Rock since 1987. He is the author of *Philip Roth*, *Philip Roth: A Bibliography*, and *Voices and Visions: Selected Essays*.

SAM B. GIRGUS is Professor of English at Vanderbilt University, and his recent books include *America on Film: Modernism, Documentary, and America*, *Desire and the Political Unconscious in American Literature* and *The Films of Woody Allen*, published for the Cambridge Film Classics Series.

HELGE NORMANN NILSEN is on the faculty of the Norwegian University of Science and Technology's Program in American Civilization. She is the author of *Hart Crane's Divided Vision: An Analysis of the Bridge*.

JUDITH PATERSON JONES is Associate Professor of Journalism in the University of Maryland's Philip Merrill College of Journalism. She is the author of several books, including *Sweet Mystery: A Book of Remembering*, *Sweet Mystery: A Southern Memoir*, and *Be Somebody, a Biography of Marguerite Rawalt*.

GUINEVERA A. NANCE is Chancellor of Auburn University, Montgomery. A specialist in British Romantic poetry, she has also written books on Philip Roth and Aldous Huxley.

STEVEN MILOWITZ teaches English and American literature at Ramaz School and is on the faculty of The New School in New York. He is the author of *Philip Roth Considered: The Concentrationary Universe of the American Writer*.

ALAN WARREN FRIEDMAN is Arthur J. Thaman and Wilhelmina Doré Thaman Professor of English, and Professor of Comparative Literature at the University of Texas at Austin. He is the author or editor of numerous books, including *Party Pieces: Joyce, Beckett and Performance*, *Fictional Death and The Modernist Enterprise*, and *Beckett in Black and Red: Samuel Beckett's Translations for Nancy Cunard's 'Negro' (1934)*.

ROBERT FORREY is Professor of English at Shawnee State University in Ohio where he is president of the Shawnee Education Association.

ALAN COOPER is Professor Emeritus of English at York College, City University of New York. He is author of *Philip Roth and the Jews*.

MARTHA A. RAVITS is Assistant Professor of women's and gender studies at the University of Oregon. Among her publications are "The Americanization of Anne Frank: Contradictions, Controversy, Compromise."

JOE MORAN is on the faculty in English and American Studies at Liverpool John Moores University, England. He is author of numerous articles, including "The Author as a Brand Name: American Literary Figures and the *Time* Cover Story" and "Don DeLillo and the Myth of the Author-Recluse."

Bibliography

Adair, William. "*Portnoy's Complaint*: A Camp Version of *Notes from Underground*." *Notes on Contemporary Literature* 7:3 (1977): p. 9–10.

Alexander, Edward. "Philip Roth at Century's End." *New England Review* 20:2 (1999): p. 183–90.

Appelfeld, Aron. *Beyond Despair: Three Lectures and a Conversation with Philip Roth*. New York: Fromm, 1994.

Bailey, Peter J. "'Why Not Tell The Truth?': The Autobiographies of Three Fiction Writers." *Critique* 32:4 (1991): p. 211–23.

Baumgarten, Murray and Barbara Gottfried. *Understanding Philip Roth*. Columbia: South Carolina University Press, 1990.

Bender, Eileen T. "Philip Roth: The Clown in the Garden." *Studies in Contemporary Satire* 3 (1976): p. 17–30.

Bier, Jesse. "In Defense of Roth." *Etudes Anglaises* 26 (1973): p. 49–53.

Brauner, David. "Masturbation and Its Discontents, or, Serious Relief: Freudian Comedy in *Portnoy's Complaint*." *Critical Review* 40 (2000): p. 75–90.

———. "Fiction as Self-Accusation: Philip Roth and the Jewish Other." *Studies in American Jewish Literature* 17 (1998): p. 8–16.

Chase, Jefferson. "Two sons of 'Jewish wit': Philip Roth and Rafael Seligmann." *Comparative Literature* 53:1 (2001): p. 42–57.

Cohen, Eileen Z. "Alex in Wonderland, or *Portnoy's Complaint*." *Twentieth Century Literature* 17 (1971): p. 161–8.

Cooper, Alan. *Philip Roth and the Jews*. Albany: New York State University Press, 1996.

Ezrahi, Sidra DeKoven. "The Grapes of Roth: 'Diasporism' between Portnoy and Shylock." *Studies in Contemporary Jewry* 12 (1996): p. 148–58.

Frank, Thomas H. "The Interpretation of Limits: Doctors and Novelists in the Fiction of Philip Roth." *Journal of Popular Culture* 28:4 (1995): p. 67–80.

Furman, Andrew. "Immigrant Dreams and Civic Promises: (Con) Testing Identity in Early Jewish American Literature and Gish Jen's Mona in *The Promised Land*." *MELUS* 25:1 (2000): p. 209–26.

———. "The Ineluctable Holocaust in the Fiction of Philip Roth." *Studies in American Jewish Literature* 12 (1993): p. 109–21.

Gentry, Marshall Bruce. "Ventriloquists' Conversations: The Struggle for Gender Dialogue in E. L. Doctorow and Philip Roth." *Contemporary Literature* 34:3 (1993): p. 512–37.

Gordon, Lois G. "*Portnoy's Complaint*: Coming of Age in Jersey City." *Literature and Psychology* 19:3–4 (1969): p. 57–60.

Görg, Claudia. "Portnoy, the American Jew in Israel." *International Fiction Review* 23:1/2 (1996): p. 59–66.

Grebstein, Sheldon. "The Comic Anatomy of *Portnoy's Complaint*" in Sarah Blacher Cohen (ed.) *Comic Relief: Humor in Contemporary American Literature*. Urbana: Illinois University Press, 1978, p. 152–71.

Girgus, Sam B. "Between *Goodbye, Columbus* and Portnoy: Becoming a Man and Writer in Roth's Feminist 'Family Romance'." *Studies in American Jewish Literature* 8 (1989): p. 143–53.

Gross, Barry. "Seduction of the Innocent: *Portnoy's Complaint* and Popular Culture." *MELUS* 8:4 (1981): p. 81–92.

Halio, Jay. *Philip Roth Revisited*. New York: G. K. Hall, 1992.

Hirsch, David H.. "Jewish Identity and Jewish Suffering in Bellow, Malamud and Philip Roth." *Saul Bellow Journal* 8:2 (1991): p. 47–58.

Iannone, Carol. "Jewish Fathers: And Sons and Daughters." *American Scholar* 67:1 (Winter 1998): p. 131–138.

Kliman, Bernice W. "Names in *Portnoy's Complaint*." *Critique* 14:3 (1972): p. 16–24.

Lavine, Steven David. "The Degradations of Erotic Life: *Portnoy's Complaint* Reconsidered." *Michigan Academician* 11 (1979): p. 357–62.

Lee, Soo-Hyun. "Bellow, Malamud, Roth: Jewish Consciousness of the Self and Humanism." *Journal of English Language and Literature* 36 (1990): p. 515–35.

———. "Jewish Self-Consciousness in *Portnoy's Complaint.*" *Journal of English Language and Literature* 29 (1983): p. 83–114.

Massa, Ann and Alistair Stead. *Forked Tongues? Comparing Twentieth-Century British and American Literature*. New York: Longman, 1994.

Milbauer, Asher Z. and Donald G. Watson. *Reading Philip Roth*. New York: St Martin's Press, 1988.

Nilsen, Don L. F. "Humorous Contemporary Jewish-American Authors: An Overview of the Criticism." *MELUS* 21:4 (1996): p. 71–101.

Pinsker, Sanford. "Climbing Over the Ethnic Fence: Reflections on Stanley Crouch and Philip Roth" *Virginia Quarterly Review* 78:3 (Summer 2002): p. 472–480.

———. "Art as excess: The 'voices' of Charlie Parker and Philip Roth." *Partisan Review* 69:1 (Winter 2002): p. 58.

Plimpton, George. "Como Conversazione: A Conversation on Literature and Comedy in Our Time." *Paris Review* 37:136 (Fall 1995).

Posnock, Ross. "Purity and Danger: On Philip Roth." *Raritan* 21:2 (2001): p. 85–101.

Pugh, Thomas. "Why is Everybody Laughing? Roth, Coover, and Meta-Comic Narrative." *Critique* 35:2 (1994): p. 67–80.

———. *Comic Sense: Reading Robert Coover, Stanley Elkin, Philip Roth*. Boston: Birkhäuser, 1994.

Searles, George J. *Conversations with Philip Roth*. Jackson: Mississippi University Press, 1992.

Singh, Lovelina. "The Sexual Kvetch of Philip Roth's Protagonists in *Portnoy's Complaint*, *My Life as a Man*, and *The Professor of Desire*." *Panjab University Research Bulletin* 16 (1985): p. 17–24.

Strong, Paul. "Firing into the Dark: Sexual Warfare in *Portnoy's Complaint*." *International Fiction Review* 10 (1983): p. 41–43.

Trachtenberg, Stanley. "In the Egosphere: Philip Roth's anti-Bildungsroman." *Papers on Language and Literature* 25:3 (1988): p. 326–41.

Wade, Stephen. "A Survey of Jewish-American Writing." *Contemporary Review* 276:1613 (June 2000): p. 313–316.

Walden, Daniel. "Goodbye Columbus, Hello Portnoy and Beyond: The Ordeal of Philip Roth." *Studies in American Jewish Literature* 3.2 (1977–78): p. 3–13.

Wiltshire, John. "The Patient's Story: Towards a Definition of Pathography." *Meridian* 12:2 (1993): p. 99–113.

Workman, Mark E. "The Serious Consequences of Ethnic Humor in *Portnoy's Complaint*." *Midwestern Folklore* 13:1 (1987): p. 16–26.

Ziewacz, Lawrence E. "Holden Caulfield, Alex Portnoy, and *Good Will Hunting*: Coming of Age in American Films and Novels." *Journal of Popular Culture* 35:1 (Summer 2001): p. 211–218.

Acknowledgments

"On Portnoy's Complaint," by George Plimpton and Philip Roth from *Reading Myself and Others* by Philip Roth, © 1975 by Farrar, Straus, Giroux. Reprinted by permission.

"Philip Roth's Psychoanalysts" by Jeffrey Berman from *The Talking Cure: Literary Representations of Psychoanalysts* by Jeffrey Berman, © 1985 by New York University Press. Reprinted by permission.

"The Alex Perplex" by Alan Cooper from *Philip Roth and the Jews* by Alan Cooper, © 1996 by State University of New York Press. Reprinted by permission of the State University of New York. All rights reserved.

"In the American Grain" by Bernard F. Rodgers from *Philip Roth* by Bernard F. Rodgers, © 1978 by the Twain Publishers. Reprinted by permission of the Gale Group.

"Portnoy's Prayer: Philip Roth and the American Unconscious" by Sam B. Girgus from *Reading Philip Roth*, edited by Asher Z. Milbauer and Donald G. Watson, © 1988 by MacMillan Press. Reproduced by permission of Palgrave MacMillan.

"Rebellion Against Jewishness: *Portnoy's Complaint*" by Helge Normann Nilsen from *English Studies* 65 (December 1984), © 1984 by Helge Normann Nilsen. Reprinted by permission.

"Good Girls and Boys Gone Bad" by Judith Paterson Jones and Guinevera A. Nance from *Philip Roth* by Judith Paterson Jones and Guinevera A. Nance, © 1981 by Frederick Ungar Publishing. Reprinted by permission.

"Portnovian Dilemmas" by Steven Milowitz from *Philip Roth Considered: The Concentrationary Universe of the American Writer*, © 2000 by Garland Publishing. Reproduced by permission of Routledge, Inc., part of The Taylor and Francis Group.

"Oedipal Politics in *Portnoy's Complaint*" by Robert Forrey from *Critical Essays on Philip Roth* edited by Sanford Pinsker, © 1982 by G.K. Hall & Co. Reprinted by permission of the Gale Group.

"The Jew's Complaint in Recent American Fiction: Beyond Exodus and Still in the Wilderness" by Alan Warren Friedman from *Critical Essays on Philip Roth* edited by Sanford Pinsker, © 1982 by G.K. Hall & Co. Reprinted by permission of the Gale Group.

"The Jewish Mother" Comedy and Controversy in American Popular Culture" by Martha A. Ravits from *MELUS* 25:1 (Spring 2000), © 2000 by *MELUS*. Reprinted by permission.

"Reality Shift: Philip Roth" by Joe Moran from *Star Authors: Literary Celebrity in America* by Joe Moran, © 2000 by Joe Moran. Reprinted by permission.

Index